Habermas, Kristeva, and Citizenship

Habermas,
Kristeva,
and
Citizenship

Noëlle McAfee

CORNELL UNIVERSITY PRESS

ITHACA AND LONDON

First published 2000 by Cornell University Press
First printing, Cornell Paperbacks, 2000

Printed in the United States of America

Librarians: A CIP catalog record for this book is available from the Library of Congress.

ISBN 0-8014-3706-7 (cloth)
ISBN 0-8014-8670-X (paper)

Cornell University Press strives to use environmentally responsible suppliers and materials to the fullest extent possible in the publishing of its books. Such materials include vegetable-based, low-VOC inks and acid-free papers that are recycled, totally chlorine-free, or partly composed of nonwood fibers. Books that bear the logo of the FSC (Forest Stewardship Council) use paper taken from forests that have been inspected and certified as meeting the highest standards for environmental and social responsibility. For further information, visit our website at www.cornellpress.cornell.edu.

Cloth printing   10 9 8 7 6 5 4 3 2 1
Paperback printing   10 9 8 7 6 5 4 3 2 1

Contents

Preface

For most of my adult life, I've had one foot in academe and another in politics, realms most people tend to shun. I first went from college to politics because I wanted, like many other young people, to make a difference. I tried politics of all sorts: a youthful emergence as a feminist; a brief dally with conservatism; calling on universities to divest from apartheid regimes; organizing graduate students to take a stand against U.S. intervention in Nicaragua; working for progressive legislation on Capitol Hill; building coalitions; training grassroots activists in how to use the media and lobby Congress; and labor organizing. Holding the notion that politics is war by other means, I fought against the pesticide industry, the tobacco industry, the publishing industry, and the media. I rallied for women, farm workers, writers, student workers, and Greek nationalists. I tried the politics of militance and the politics of compromise, from writing for underground newspapers to lobbying Congress. The result? The whole enterprise disheartened me. All told, I found that whether I took a radical stand or a forgiving one, the outcome was the same: nothing really changed.

This failure was understandable when "the enemy" was industry, powerful corporate interests, entrenched lobbyists, the usual powers-that-be. But it was something else altogether when "the enemy" turned out to be one's own side, that is, "the people." How many times have I, with so many other political activists, asked: Why do people do things that aren't in their own interests? Why do poor people vote for those who will make them worse off? Why do the disenfranchised buy into the "you can pull yourselves up by your own bootstraps" mentality? Marx asked the same kind of question in the 1840s: Why did the poorest Frenchmen join the Mobile Guard, the army of the reactionaries? We've come up with various answers. Marx blamed it on a "lumpenproletariat" mentality and also on "ideology." In fact, the oldest riddle for the left is this very phenomenon, also known as "false consciousness." Antonio Gramsci called it "cultural hegemony." Everyone wants a name for it that will somehow make some sense of the matter.

The masses, too often, don't know what's good for them.

Even at twenty-one, I hated this answer. It smacked of elitism and called for an elite "vanguard" to guide the people. As a result, I grew disenchanted with leftist politics and turned to more mainstream ones. But that was even worse. As a "field organizer" for Public Citizen's Congress Watch, an organization founded by Ralph Nader, I saw the same sort of thing. Most public interest groups are led by a select circle who decide what is in the public's interest and then try to get the public to believe it, so that this public will send a message to Congress and of course give money to the powerful and wise public interest group.

Such strategies are not peculiar to the left. Under the mantle of conservatism, the right proclaimed that the populace is "the moral majority," which gave Ronald Reagan a "mandate" and later condoned the "contract with America"—claims made by an elite, not the people themselves, who, as we know, don't really matter. All the people need do is consume a slate of candidates, pay their taxes, and buy into whatever Washington tries to sell.

From what I can tell, one thing common to the far left, the mainstream, and the right is a general disrespect for the public. At one point, to my dismay, something happened that tempted me to share this sentiment. It was an incident at the start of the 1984 presidential primary season when I was knocking on the doors of registered Democrats in Iowa, trying to get them to turn out for my favorite candidate. One woman standing in her front yard as I approached heard what I said and started screaming at me: "Get out of here. I don't give a damn about politics. It doesn't mean a thing to me trying to raise my kids, pay the rent, and put food on the table. Get the hell out of my yard." That shook me up. She didn't just hate Democrats; she was absolutely certain that politics was the problem, not the way out of problems. (And she harbored no hopes—some would say illusions—that politics could ever change.)

I wasn't willing to write off people like her and others who seemed perfectly intelligent yet had no will for politics. If people were to govern themselves wisely and justly, more than the political system would have to change. I felt strongly that if I were to have any hope for political change I would need to find reason to have confidence in people, myself included, and our ability to see our world and our possibilities clearly. There had to be a way to prove wrong Walter Lippmann's admonition that the public was just a phantom, hardly interested or educated enough to judge what was best politically. I knew that the last place on earth to look for such hope was in Washington, D.C., so I packed my bags and moved to a university in the hinterland. Instead of history and political science, my former fields, I turned to philosophy, the best way I saw to try to understand politics.

The discerning reader may have already detected a note of longing for the ideal citizen that modernity promised: one who understands her own interests and can act on them, a universe unto herself. It was no accident that, with my Marxist background, this was the kind of political agency I sought. (After all, Marxism is very much a product of the Enlightenment.) In fact, I found anything to the contrary quite disconcerting. I was especially put off by deconstruction and its "author," Jacques Derrida. Before leaving Washington, I covered for the Washington *City Paper* Derrida's talk at the 1988 meeting of the eastern division of the American Philosophical Association. To convey my concerns of the time, allow me to quote a rather long passage in which I describe Derrida's response to his interlocutor, Thomas McCarthy:

> Derrida rises and moves to the podium. You can see the thoroughly French mind preparing to charm the audience, to brush away the criticisms and charges, to use his lilting voice and the multiplicity of meaning to remind the audience that his antagonist is angular and dour, not the jovial, kind Frenchman.
>
> First the soft punch. "When I look for what is transcendental to effective social practice, what is so shocking?" he asks in all innocence. "I am not looking for a meta-theory of politics, but a definition. When you say culture and society, I say, what do you mean by culture and society?"
>
> This is standard deconstructo-speak. Indeed, Derrida seems to sense this and gets around to what may be his larger project, distancing him-

self from the academic cottage industry that has grown up around his work. "I friendlily but firmly protest the familiar notion of deconstruction," he says. "As its name indicates, no name indicates what it is." He's being typically Derridean, as they say, always refusing to be pinned down. "Every concept enjoys—uh, suffers—some elasticity."

This is clever, but the audience has seen this trick. What about politics, man? What about Paul de Man? McCarthy's earlier question must be ringing in Derrida's ear: "Isn't the claim for the multiplicity of meaning an excuse not to speak politically?"

So Derrida hurls forth a zinger: "I agree that I resist any straight-forward politicization because these are de-politicizing." Huh? "Using some coded schemes, even if signaled by well-known flags, is de-politicizing," Derrida continues. "So to that extent perhaps I am more political."

Hardly convincing.

The elegant French philosopher turned literary critic continues, protesting that he has been misunderstood again. Across the room, more than a few eyebrows rise. *Mais professeur,* how can you complain that you have been misunderstood when you claim that nothing can be understood? "Well," he says, "I try to avoid misunderstanding even though it is impossible to avoid."

Perhaps what is really impossible for Derrida to admit is that deconstruction is really a postmodern version of irony. And when you've got that rhythm, you can't dance politically. The social world becomes another text to decode and deconstruct. You're just playing with the multiplicity of meaning, without 'fessing up to what it ultimately means. (McAfee 1989)

In the years since I wrote this I've had quite a change of heart. I no longer think deconstruction is mere irony, but I do admit that at first blush many of the claims of deconstruction may seem devastating politically: we are not the sole authors of our works and our aims; we cannot capture truth in a phrase for there is always a remainder; we can never be completely certain of anything, even our own self-understanding. Quite likely, our sense of self is a fiction—though a needed one—we use to get along in the world. But does this all mean we "can't dance politically"? I think not. To the contrary, as I hope to show in these pages, an admission of our epistemological limitations and of our "un-centeredness" and "multiplicity" may point us in a most promising political direction: to the need for acting in the world with all these others in our midst. We cannot go solo politically. Any such notion is an illusion. The most fruitful response to our situation is to recognize how indebted we are to each other, which may allow us to forge a better future together.

In these pages I shall weave together this insight drawn from post-structuralist thought—that we are situated in a web of relationships that continuously constitute our very identity—with an understanding of politics that I have developed through my many years of work in deliberative democracy. In 1988 I became an associate of the Kettering Foundation, a research foundation that focuses on what it calls "public politics," the work that a deliberative public need do in order for democratic societies to function well. Kettering's approach has been interdisciplinary, bridging academic disciplines as well as the divide between academia and practice. In addition to my academic work on the theory of deliberative democracy, I have had the privilege of observing scores of deliberative forums, watching people practice deliberative politics. I have also had the good fortune to work with James Fishkin in the project of deliberative public opinion polling, convening representative samples of the public for the purpose of deliberating on matters of public concern and of bringing the results to bear on the policy process. I have found that the way that actual citizens deliberate together does not always, if at all, square with the way deliberative theorists say they do. Deliberating citizens rarely meet the theorists' strict standards of rationality, but these citizens do speak together productively—producing meanings, identities, community, and public will in a way that our theories have yet to capture. These deliberating citizens challenge me as a theorist to understand their communicative practice, using all the theoretical tools I can muster.

Just as my early forays into politics were concerned with the mindset of "the people," my recent theoretical work in deliberative politics is concerned with understanding the subjectivity of those who might call themselves citizens. Phenomenologically speaking, what is our situation in the world as subjects? How do we come to have a sense of self? What kind of intersubjectivity do we maintain that allows us to be and know and act in the world with others? And what does the condition of our subjectivity entail for our capacity to be agents in the public sphere? This book is an attempt to further the theoretical and practical project of deliberative democracy, using an understanding of subjectivity that comes out of the work of Julia Kristeva, Jean-Luc Nancy, and other poststructuralist thinkers who are reconceptualizing subjectivity and community. At the outset, this may seem to be an odd mix. I hope that by the end it will seem a natural and fruitful partnership.

I am indebted to many friends and colleagues for support as I wrote this book. For helping oversee the project from beginning to end, I thank Kelly Oliver, my friend and teacher. For their guidance in the early stages, I thank Bob Solomon, Doug Kellner, Louis Mackey, Katie Arens, Bob Kane, and Lester Faigley. Other colleagues provided careful readings and helpful commentary, namely, David Braybrooke, Jim Fishkin, Benjamin Gregg, Mary Beth Mader, Karen Mottola, Rick Roderick, Johanna Seibt, and Ewa Ziarek. Many thanks go to my colleagues at the Kettering Foundation for providing an innovative community of inquirers into deliberative democracy, especially David Mathews, Bob Kingston, John Dedrick, Peter Levine, and Claire Snyder. My thanks also go to other friends and colleagues, including Patricia Aufderheide, Jessica Berry, Tom Blackburn, Carolyn Bottler, Harvey Cormier, Ernesto Cortés, Jr., Katie Crosby, Jennifer Hansen, Christina Hendricks, Kathleen Higgins, Dea Larsen, Leslie Milofsky, Beth Myler, Lisa Walsh, and Roberta Westin. I also thank members of the O'Brien's group for their humor, as well as critical and constructive assessments of portions of this project. I especially thank my parents, Marika Thomas and Paul McAfee, for believing in me unwaveringly since childhood. Finally and most deeply, I am indebted to David and Guthrie Armstrong for the loving space that is the home and *chora* from which this work springs.

NOËLLE MCAFEE
Andover, Massachusetts

Habermas, Kristeva, and Citizenship

Introduction
Politics and Citizens

Ask anyone today what politics is and she or he will likely say: "It's the struggle over how to allocate resources" or "It's about who gets power." All in all, today when we think about politics we think about competition, struggle, fighting, war. There's nothing friendly or cooperative about it, unless we're "bedfellows," fellows of the sheets, frolicking and colluding to further our joint self-interest, which no doubt is at odds with someone else's. Today this notion of politics seems so commonsensical that no one apparently thinks about it. But it hasn't always been this way—which leads me to think that politics isn't *necessarily* this way. Moreover, perhaps this view of politics is the product of some larger view we hold.

Over the years I have come to see a connection between our views about politics and our views about subjectivity or, roughly speaking, about how we come to be in the world. This is most apparent when I compare the Greeks' views of subjectivity and politics with the moderns' views on these matters. (When I invoke "the Greeks" I refer specifically to Pericles and other democrats of his time in Athens, rather than to Plato and Aristotle.) In the modern era (that is, since Descartes), we tend to think that selves are substances—not just our bodies but our *psyches*, if you will, immaterial "things." The idea is that there is some "core self" that endures through time. This is what we allude to when we say things such as, "I want to get to know who I really am, to find myself," or, less prosaically, "Know thyself." These phrases point to a search for the psychic self as essential substance, something that if found will be certain and transparent to oneself. When Descartes found himself to be a "thinking thing," he thought he had hit upon this truth: the cogito, "I think therefore I am," was, he thought, indubitable. With Descartes, the moderns claimed that not only is this core self known certainly, it is rational, and thanks to its rationality it can be autonomous—and thus finally free (in the sense that it is no longer ruled by others or by its passions).

There seems to be a correlation between these two views, of the inner self as substance and of politics as a struggle. Both notions came on the scene at roughly the same time, while both were absent from Greek politics, especially Athens under Pericles, as well as absent from the views of most Sophists. During the Periclean moment in Greek history, politics was the collective arena in which people sought to judge what was the good life, and once they made such judgment they sought to attain this good life. As Christian Meier has noted,

> To the Greeks the opposite of "political" was "private," "self-interested." "Political" meant the same as "common" (*koinos, xynos*) and referred to what concerned everybody. So closely was the word—in its specific sense—connected with the polis of the free and equal that it denoted the opposite of "despotic," indeed of any form of rule by the few over the many. Thus, to broaden an oligarchy was to make it "more political." Thucydides used the term political to designate the proper form of a constitution founded on equality. (Meier 1990, 13)

That *politics* had a positive connotation for these Greeks did not mean that the polis was free from strife. The Greeks argued with each other, just as we continue many of their arguments. But their arguments were not over the allocation of resources or the meaning of politics per se but about how politics ought to be conducted. Still they all, Plato included, shared the belief that politics was the search for the collective good, a notion that arose in keeping with the idea of the polis itself. Whether the good was to be found through argument (as the Sophists thought) or through understanding (as Plato thought), it was something to be sought for the collective. Unlike the now prevalent notion that politics is a battle of friends against foes, the Greek meaning implied "the overcoming of such oppositions and the restriction of power" (Meier 1990, 4).

This brings me to the other relevant feature of the Greek democrats of Pericles' era. They did not—and there is no way of putting this mildly—think of the self as substance. For them, the self was only as solid as the polity to which it belonged. Just think of the meaning of the Greek word for someone uninterested in public life: *idiôtês*, that is, idiot—as in *idiosyncratic*, to hold only to one's own self. For the Greek democrats, if you did not belong to the city, you were less than you could be: you lacked the fullest subjectivity of citizenship. There really was no citizen-self that preceded the city. Citizen-selves were not separable from cities. As Aristotle wrote,

> The city-state is also prior in nature to the household and to each of us individually, since a whole is necessarily prior to its parts. For if the whole body is dead, there will no longer be a foot or a hand, except homonymously, as one might speak of a stone "hand" (for a dead hand will be like that); but everything is defined by its task and by its capacity; so that in such condition they should not be said to be the same things but homonymous ones. Hence that the city-state is natural and prior in nature to the individual is clear. For if an individual is not self-sufficient when separated, he will be like all other parts in relation to the whole. Anyone who cannot form a community with others, or who does not need to because he is self-sufficient, is no part of a city-state— he is either a beast or a god. (Aristotle 1998, 4–5; *Politics* I.2, 1253a19–30)

Now, I'm tempted to say that for the Greeks the city produced citizen-selves, but that already falls into the trap set up by the modern mindset, which sets up selves over and against cities. While I want to avoid this trap, I do want to indicate how *indebted* citizen-selves were to their cities. For the Greeks, at the very least, individuals and societies co-create each other. Thus, each is a coterminous *effect* of the other.[1]

Likewise, in his Funeral Oration, Pericles said, "Only among us is a man who takes no part [in political affairs] called, not a quiet citizen, but a bad citizen" (2.40.2). Being a bad citizen was no small thing, for as Christian Meier documents, apart from the household there was only the polis. Meier notes how seriously Athenians took their citizenship and asks why it is that these men (and, alas, they

---

[1] I am indebted to Karen Mottola for helping me think through this problem.

were all men) worked so fervently and gladly in their duties as citizens, why they put in so much time and effort for what seems to us to be so little in return. Meier chalks it up to social pressure, or to the extent to which life was subsumed by the polis. But he also notes that being political was seen to make you a better person—and that politics itself had such a positive connotation. Unlike the present day, when "acting politically" connotes "shrewd, cunning, crafty," for the Greeks it had the "positive sense of acting in the general interest, the converse being to act out of self-interest" (Meier 1990, 3).

Unlike the democrats, Plato held to a notion of self that is close to that of a "core self" and not an ever-changing effect. In this respect, among others, Plato marks a shift in the Greek way of thinking. For one thing, he argues that our reason can discern what is unchanging (i.e., the Forms), which can be taken to mean that the "truest" self is the reasoning one. Along these lines, Plato warned against succumbing to passions and desires, for these can never be satisfied and will only lead one astray. (Notice how much Kant continued this line of thought.) It is better, Plato said, to heed reason. Alluding to this, Charles Taylor characterizes Greek thought as believing in a core self. Describing Montaigne's thought, he writes:

> There is some evidence that when [Montaigne] embarked on his reflections, he shared the traditional view that these should serve to recover contact with the permanent, stable, unchanging core of being in each of us. This is the virtually unanimous direction of ancient thought: beneath the changing and shifting desires in the unwise soul, and over against the fluctuating fortunes of the external world, our true nature, reason, provides a foundation, unwavering and constant. (Taylor 1989, 178)

Here, however, I disagree with Taylor. Granted, this may have been the direction of Greek thought, in that eventually Plato came to hold this view—and thus turn the tide of history—but it was hardly a unanimous one. In fact, the vigor with which Plato presses his points attests to how unusual or radical this view must have been.

Reason to us may seem solid and certain, as if it were some sort of faculty that human beings had (as opposed to something they learn to do, however imperfectly), but we should note the etymology of the Greek term *logos*. It is also the root of the word for speaking, *lego*, as is shown in Homeric Greek. Richard Onians traced the Homeric use of the term for *thinking* and found that it was not a faculty or capacity for abstract reasoning but was a matter of *speaking* (Onians 1954, 13). This is surprising given the extent to which Plato and Aristotle tried to set up reason over and against rhetoric (even though Aristotle defined *man* as "the animal with speech"); they thought reason was much more than talk.[2] Moreover, in Homeric times (from which we can trace our own concepts), this "thinking" was not thoroughly coincident with one's "self." Onians writes:

> Deep reflection is conversation of one's self with one's *thymos* (mind) or of one's *thymos* with one's self. Thus Menelaos, deserted in battle, 'spake (*eipe*) to his great-hearted *thymos*: "Woe is me if I leave behind these noble arms. . . . But why did my *thymos* thus hold converse (*dielexato*)? . . . That were choicest of evils." ' (Onians 1954, 13)

In Homeric thought, to think is really to speak to one's *thymos*, that is, the seat of one's emotions. There is no thinking apart from speaking to oneself, no enduring, separable faculty of reason. Even though Plato's Socrates is found in the dialogues "talking to himself," Plato and later Aristotle argued that reason involves some sort of "seeing," not just "speaking." The Homeric conception had already been forgotten, for better or worse I will not say. If anything, our habit of isolating reason from rhetoric results from forgetting the origins of this thinking.

For the Greek democrats, it was not enough to speak to oneself. As Hannah Arendt notes, these Greeks wanted to create an arena where their speech and action would not be forgotten; thus the impetus to create the polis. One function of the polis "was to offer a remedy for the futility of action and speech; for the chances that a deed deserving fame would not be forgotten, that it actually would become 'immortal', were not very good" (Arendt 1958, 197). Only with this public "space of appearance," as Arendt puts it, can one leave one's mark; there one's subjectivity becomes inscribed, remaining for others to see.

---

[2] Even in Plato's works, there is ambiguity. He retains the speech aspect of *logos* (to give an account) while adding that it should be about something that is true. For example, in *Phaedo* 76b, Socrates asks Simmias whether those who have knowledge (*episteme*) are able to give an account of it (*logos*). Half a generation later, Aristotle seems to collapse *episteme* into *logos* while dropping the speech aspect altogether.

To be deprived of [this space] means to be deprived of reality, which, humanly and politically speaking, is the same as appearance. To men the reality of the world is guaranteed by the presence of others, by its appearing to all; "for what appears to all, this we call Being," and whatever lacks this appearance comes and passes away like a dream, intimately and exclusively our own but without reality. (Arendt 1958, 199)

Now notice that, if my reading of history is correct, the democratic Greeks' views about politics and subjectivity were diametrically opposed to the moderns' views. For the Greeks, the self is "fleshed out" by the city—that is, the polis brings about a richer subjectivity—and politics is a collective search for the good life. For the moderns of the liberal tradition, selves are substances of sorts that, if they wish, might (or might not) enter into politics, and politics is a struggle between these atomistic selves for control over resources. So far, I have not made any claims about causality; I am simply noting this correlation: a society that sees subjectivity as an effect of the polis does not see politics as a struggle *between* citizens as much as a struggle *by* citizens to attain the good life. A society that sees subjectivity as separable from the polis sees politics as an antagonistic endeavor.

Many others before me have noticed that the Greeks had a more communal understanding of politics where the moderns have a more individualistic one. And there are those who want to revive the Greek mode of politics through what they call "communitarianism."[3] Opposing them are those who prefer to improve on the individualistic, liberal, procedural forms of democracy.[4] Both camps are aware of the contrasts between the democratic Greeks' and the liberal moderns' views of politics. So I have a good deal of company in

[3] The political views of Aristotle, along with those of Rousseau and Hegel, can be seen as precursors of modern-day communitarianism, for example in the work of Alasdair MacIntyre. Under this heading one could include Benjamin Barber, Amitai Etzioni, Michael Sandel, and Charles Taylor as well. Communitarianism can also be seen as an offshoot of the civic republican tradition, which stretches from Cicero through Rousseau, Dewey, and Arendt. The salient feature of communitarianism is that it posits that there is some substantive good around which communities can form.

[4] Under liberalism I would include John Locke, John Rawls, Ronald Dworkin, and most contemporary defenders of individualism and proceduralism. Liberals, in general, advocate a value-neutral system that leaves decisions about what the good life consists in to individuals and decidedly not to communities—lest such communities impose their norms on individuals.

my observations. Yet all these theorists focus mostly on whether politics ought to be communitarian or liberal, not on what sort of selves elicit these politics.[5] I want to turn the focus to how the two understandings or paradigms of politics seem to rest upon two different understandings of subjectivity. In my view, the main problem with communitarianism is that it doesn't go far enough in rethinking subjectivity.

So now I'll make something of a causal claim: our views about whether the self *precedes* the polis or is a coextensive *effect* of the polis shape our understanding of politics. The modern view of politics is contingent upon how we moderns think of ourselves. So long as we think of ourselves as discrete, atomistic, autonomous beings, we will be saddled with a politics of antagonism and clashing interests. This is so because when we think of ourselves as discrete substances, we will tend to think of our interests and tastes as fixed and exclusive.[6] Instead of looking for ways that our interests intersect, we will focus on how they differ. Instead of seeing the polis—that is, our communities—as constitutive of our being, we will see them as separate sites of struggle. Instead of seeing our own identity and subjectivity as bound up and meshed with others, we will remain at war with our fellows.

It may seem that I want to turn back the hands of time, back to ancient Greece, where, incidentally, only men were citizens and the greatest philosophers despised democracy. Really, I do not want to do anything of the sort. In fact, I don't need to.

In many respects, modernity (of both the liberal and the humanist traditions) has not been just an era of history, it has been a project. Think of it as a long inquiry into the possibility of whether human beings can use their reason to be independent, free agents able to create just societies. Over the centuries, the project has been handed down from one generation to another, passing from Hobbes to Locke, Rousseau to Kant, Hegel to Marx and Mill; and now we find it in the

---

[5] Michael Sandel, in his critique of Rawls, comes closest to looking at the relationship between conceptions of the self and ethical-political theories. See his book *Liberalism and the Limits of Justice*.

[6] In other words we will tend to think as if these interests and tastes were attributes of a subject. Such thinking is based on a substance ontological view of subjectivity. Alternatively, one could pursue an inquiry into subjectivity using process ontological categories, an approach I explore a bit in these pages.

able hands of John Rawls and Jürgen Habermas. That after so many years this is still a project and not yet a reality (or a technology) testifies to the difficulties at hand. The problems of developing a moral and political theory have been enormous. On the whole, they seem to revolve around the conundrum of why on earth discrete individuals ought to bother being decent to each other. Or, as philosophers like to put it, "Why be moral?"[7]

Modernity has also been concerned with how reason can be used to promote freedom, justice, and equality. According to the ideals of the Enlightenment, human beings ought to be able to free themselves from servitude to traditional authority and instead use their own reason in order to ascertain what would make a society just. This is the Enlightenment ideal of autonomy.

For all that has been written on autonomy, and however much it has been taken as an unquestionable aim, few (Kant included) have actually defined it. For most theorists, it seems to have a meaning that need not be explicated. The Greek roots mean literally "self-legislating," a self making laws for itself. The opposite, it seems, is heteronomy: the inability to prevent others (whether individuals, institutions, inclinations, or forces) from making decisions for oneself. If one contrasts autonomy with heteronomy, the former seems the preferred aim, for it embodies a vision of freedom and self-determination, the opposite of being enslaved to a king or to one's passions. Yet this notion of being "enslaved" to one's desires betrays a metaphysical presupposition: that the *essential* part of oneself is not one's *desires* but something else. In the history of philosophy this *something else* is reason: that unique, nearly divine feature of human beings.

---

[7] Throughout this book I tend to treat moral and political questions in tandem. This is not just a matter of oversimplification. While both kinds of questions are normative ones, the main reason I merge them is that I doubt that we can make any nonarbitrary distinctions between the private / moral and the public / political realms. My argument revolves around what sort of subjectivity we have: if it is not discrete and individualistic, as I contend, but rather interrelated and constitutively indebted to others, then the distinction between private and public begins to disintegrate. Another reason I treat political questions as similar to moral questions is that, in discussing politics, I am focusing on civil society, in particular the public sphere, rather than governmental institutions. In my view, political questions legitimately arise from the public; they are questions about what should be: what kind of communities, practices, institutions, and arrangements we wish to have.

In order to question autonomy, Iris Marion Young has given it a strong definition:

> An agent, whether individual or collective, is autonomous to the degree that it has sole and final authority to decide on specific issues and actions, and no other agent has the right to interfere. Autonomy implies sovereignty. (Young 1990, 249)

This definition, I believe, is quite right. Autonomy is an ideal of sovereignty, as the *exclusion* of the power of other agents. Given that Kant as well as Plato takes desires and inclinations to be *threats* to reason, then these desires and inclinations seem to be agents themselves, but agents that transgress the bounds of one's true rational essence. So deep in the history of philosophy, as early as Plato, the other is already within oneself. Already (centuries before Freud's "radical" division of subjectivity) the self is split, at odds with itself, in tension, inconclusive, in process. But here this internal otherness is seen as a vulnerability, a threat, never as an opportunity for *making oneself*.

The goal of autonomy is to overcome alterity. Here what is needed is self-transparency, an ideal that modernity smuggles in: one's own intentions, desires, and motives ought to be plain to oneself. This ideal is central to classical economic theory, according to which agents act on the basis of their own preferences. The economic system reaches equilibrium when agents' respective preferences have been satisfied. Here we find an interesting mixture of acting rationally upon one's own preferences, whose roots would be, it seems, emotional. Tied to the ideal of self-transparency is the notion of self-interested *homo economicus;* this can be traced back to Adam Smith's rational choice theory, in which one acts out of self-interest, never doubting that what one understands to be in one's own interest really is. For Smith, self-interest was the basis for exchange with other human beings:

> But man has almost constant occasion for the help of his brethren, and it is in vain for him to expect it from their benevolence only. He will be more likely to prevail if he can interest their self-love in his favour, and shew them that it is for their own advantage to do for him what he requires of them. Whoever offers to another a bargain of any kind, proposes to do this. Give me that which I want, and you shall have this

which you want, is the meaning of every such offer; and it is in this manner that we obtain from one another the far greater part of those good offices which we stand in need of. It is not from the benevolence of the butcher, the brewer, or the baker, that we expect our dinner, but from their regard to their own interest. (Smith 1937, 14)

If everyone acts according to his or her own self-interests, ideally, all needs can be met. What is good for the individual can lead to good for the whole. And in this we find another value: atomistic individualism. Each person has his or her own bundle of interests and preferences, which may be at odds with those of others. Each individual is an atom, the subject of various attributes (e.g., preferences and interests). But if all seek to maximize their own, perhaps exclusive, interests, the whole system can reach equilibrium. This is a harmony of discrete individuals, a harmony brought about by individuals consulting their own preferences and then rationally seeking to achieve them by bartering with others. In this picture, our relationships with others are a form of exchange, a trading of goods. Instead of the polis we have the agora, the market.

As discrete beings, individuals have another characteristic: a self that is in its essence unchanging. While I might prefer something new tomorrow (that is, a preference or attribute of mine might change), I will be at my core the same. In this view of human nature, human beings come into the world with some essence waiting to be discovered, an essence that shapes their choices, or that, when ignored, leads to unhappiness. Given this view of human nature—that individuals are discrete selves with a core essence and a bundle of preferences—the task for human beings is epistemic, to know themselves and their world—not just to be open to the world, but to represent the world to themselves.

These ideals of subjectivity as potentially autonomous, self-transparent, and discrete do not fare well in any post-Hegelian philosophy that sees the self as a product of intersubjective, linguistic, and historical relations. Some see the contemporary understanding of the self as at odds with the Enlightenment project of overcoming tutelage. Others, though, are trying to salvage the political aims of the Enlightenment even while recognizing the Hegelian "truth" that individuals are socially and historically and intersubjectively constructed. The most prominent defender of the Enlightenment today is Jürgen Habermas. He sees in modernity the promise of a free, enlightened, just, and rational society, not the sort of rationality that Max Weber bemoaned—that of an iron cage—but a rationality that makes it possible for us to talk with each other. As Mark Warren argues, Habermas claims that people might become truly autonomous and able to make society more just (Warren 1995, 172–77) through the use of a special sort of reason, namely communicative reason, which I will discuss in subsequent pages. In making this claim, he defends modernity against its critics—those who have been quite suspicious of it, beginning with the Romantics and with Friedrich Nietzsche. Today Nietzsche's heirs are questioning most of the concepts that underlie modernity. They are asking, among other things, whether reason ought to be so revered and whether we are really as transparent to ourselves as Descartes would have us believe.

In something of a rhetorical coup, Habermas calls these critics "Young Conservatives":

> The *Young Conservatives* essentially appropriate the fundamental experience of aesthetic modernity, namely the revelation of a decentred subjectivity liberated from all the constraints of cognition and purposive action, from all the imperatives of labour and use value, and with this they break out of the modern world altogether. . . . [I]n Manichaean fashion [they] oppose instrumental reason with a principle accessible solely to evocation, whether this is the will to power or sovereignty, Being itself or the Dionysian power for the poetic. In France this tradition leads from Georges Bataille through Foucault to Derrida. Over all these figures hovers, of course, the spirit of Nietzsche, newly resurrected in the 1970s. (Passerin d'Entrèves and Benhabib 1997, 53)

Along with the "Young Conservatives," Habermas identifies two other kinds of conservatives, the neo-Aristotelian champions of premodernity (e.g., Leo Strauss) and those "neoconservatives" who want to take the technocratic achievements of modernity to promote capitalism and rational administration (e.g., Carl Schmitt "in his middle period"). Habermas seems to define *conservative* as anything that questions the tenets of modernity. By juxtaposing Foucault and Derrida alongside Strauss and Schmitt, as just another variety of conservative, Habermas is sidestepping the question of whether modernity itself is really the most progressive or liberating project. The truth is that Foucault and Derrida and other "postmoderns" are really arguing from outside of modernity's partisan positions; they're arguing that modernity was misbegotten and that we should explore a new way of thinking.

I didn't bring this up to enter the debate about "periodization," about whether or not (and, if so, when) modernity ended and post-modernity began.[8] I see the whole matter as a question of whether the project of modernity has a future—whether pursuing it would be a mistake because it could never be fulfilled. Perhaps the project arose to meet some perceived need of the time but over the centuries it has exacerbated rather than ameliorated divisiveness. Perhaps it would now be wise to leave the project of modernity behind in search of something that might better suit a world where diverse people must find a way to live together.[9] What would a "postmodern" understanding of subjectivity mean for our political practices? What kind of citizens might we be?

The project of modernity has not been just to describe what it is to be a political and moral agent in the world; it has been involved in how such agency might be possible, or, in other words, what the conditions are for effective and just political agency. We can see this tra-

[8] Anyone interested in this debate might see Fredric Jameson's "Periodizing the 60s," collected in Jameson 1988.

[9] Or we could understand modernity as holding two distinct projects, as Chantal Mouffe points out. Drawing on Richard Rorty's reading of Hans Blumenberg, Mouffe argues that the Enlightenment had two projects: (1) the political project of calling for freedom and equality, that is, self-assertion, and (2) the epistemological project of self-foundation, developing a conception of reason on which our knowledge claims can be founded. The second has fallen on hard times, especially since the modern attempt to replace the authority / foundation of God and the church with the authority / foundation of Man and Reason. (By "modern" I mean the era from Descartes until, at the least, the middle of the twentieth century.) This attempt failed because the distinctive feature of modernity, democratic revolution, cannot be supported by any foundation. Democracy is radically indeterminate. It also failed because the "abstract Enlightenment universalism of an undifferentiated human nature" could not hold up under the demands of difference: there are particular concerns, perspectives, etc., that "universal human reason" fails to encompass. Some (e.g., Habermas) think that abandoning the epistemological project of modernity means abandoning the political project. But deciding to abandon the epistemological project does not entail abandoning the political one. We can continue the political project without hanging on to the epistemological one—no need to believe in Enlightenment rationality. (Whether or not you agree with the critique of Enlightenment rationality, you ought to be able to see that the political project need not depend on it. According to Mouffe, the political project does not depend on any foundation at all.)

jectory in the development of the key term citizen. Even though the Greeks had an analogous term, the word citizen is peculiarly modern.[10] Though its coinage is Latin, it came into usage only in the fourteenth century, when it meant an inhabitant of a city. Not until the sixteenth century was it associated with the rights of membership in a city. Since the eighteenth century it has also connoted certain obligations or duties. In that century as well, the term citizen came to rest squarely on modern notions of individualism, meaning that the citizen was a being unto himself, separable from any community, the author of his own will and intentions. To paraphrase Rousseau, citizens make up a city.[11] (How different this is from the Greek notion that the city makes the citizen.) All told, the term means an individual with the ability to act—an agent—in a political community. In short, the development of the term citizen has paralleled the development of modernity's idea of what it means to belong to a political community and to be an individual subject. To this day, our notions of citizenship rest upon our notions of subjectivity. If citizen seems an odd term today, which I think it does, I believe it is because—thanks to the supposed "Young Conservatives"—our conception of subjectivity is under fire.

Just as the ancients' views of subjectivity affected their thinking on citizenship and politics, so too the moderns' views of subjectivity influenced theirs. As Charles Taylor points out, before the seventeenth

---

[10] See the *Oxford English Dictionary* for an etymological history of the term.

[11] In Book I of *The Social Contract*, Rousseau includes a footnote (no. 4) on the term *citizen* that is well worth repeating: "The true meaning of this word [*citizen*] is almost entirely lost on modern men. Most of them mistake a town for a city and a townsman for a citizen. They do not know that houses make a town but citizens make a city. Once this mistake cost the Carthaginians dearly. I have not found in my reading that the title of *citizen* has ever been given to the subjects of a prince, not even in ancient times to the Macedonians or in our own time to the English, although they are closer to liberty than all the others. Only the French adopt this name *citizen* with complete familiarity, since they have no true idea of its meaning, as can be seen from their dictionaries. If this were not the case, they would become guilty of treason for using it. For them, this name expresses a virtue and not a right. When Bodin wanted to speak about our citizens and townsmen, he committed a terrible blunder when he mistook the one group for the other. M. d'Alembert was not in error, and in his article entitled Geneva he has carefully distinguished the four orders of men (even five, counting ordinary foreigners) who are in our towns, and of whom only two make up the republic. No other French author I am aware of has grasped the true meaning of the word *citizen*."

century, the question of how community gets started never arose (Taylor 1989, 193). People were seen as parts of an organic whole, not as separable, pre-existing individuals. It was only with the advent of Hobbes's atomism and social contract theory that the thought of individuals as political atoms formed. Even though, in Locke's state of nature, these individuals interacted, the political community didn't necessarily have any intrinsic authority; authority had to be conferred by those forming the association. In this modern view, "people start off as political atoms" (Taylor 1989, 193).

> Underlying this atomist contract theory, we can see two facets of the new individualism. Disengagement from cosmic order meant that the human agent was no longer to be understood as an element in a larger, meaningful order. His paradigm purposes are to be discovered within. He is on his own. What goes for the larger cosmic order will eventually be applied also to political society. And this yields a picture of the sovereign individual, who is 'by nature' not bound to any authority. (Taylor 1989, 193–94)

Likewise, the different views of those coming out of modernism and those calling themselves postmoderns and poststructuralists elicit competing conceptions of citizenship and politics.[12] To put it starkly, there is a clash as to whether subjectivity is "by nature" fixed and atomistic or dynamic and interconnected. Hardly anyone these days would defend the notion of the self as fixed and atomistic, but this notion is manifest, however implicitly, in the works of those who defend modernism.[13] Thus, in the clash between the defenders of modernism and the messengers of postmodernism, one can in present-day philosophy discern two general theories of subjectivity,

---

[12] The terms *postmodern* and *poststructural* have distinct meanings. Following Jean-François Lyotard and Jameson, I take the term *postmodern* to designate a shift from modern understandings of history, knowledge, and culture to a new pastiche of tropes, stories, and explanations. For a detailed, critical account, see Best and Kellner, 1991. By the term *poststructural* I mean a specifically dynamic approach to the human sciences as seen in the works of Derrida, the late Foucault, Kristeva, and others who are heirs of French structuralism while departing from its static conceptions of culture, language, and other fields. Poststructuralism is not a reversal of structuralism but a dynamic outgrowth of it.

[13] In Chapter 1 I argue that even Habermas, with his careful discussion of how individuation occurs through socialization, tends toward such a view.

which entail two contrasting views of the possibility of citizenship. This clash is apparent even in contemporary continental philosophy. On the one hand there is the tradition inherited by Jürgen Habermas—modernity in general and critical theory in particular[14]—which describes the subject as a socially constructed individual who is potentially able to act autonomously and in her own interest. Habermas's modern view suggests that the subject as citizen is able to "step back" from the political community and make judgments disinterestedly. On the other hand, there is the tradition inherited by Julia Kristeva—a synthesis of semiotics, psychoanalysis, and poststructuralism—which views the subject as constituted through language, as a subject who is inherently at odds with herself, whose very identity is always provisional, a subject who is always "on trial." This poststructuralist view suggests that the citizen is always bound up with the political community, never able to completely extricate and separate her judgments from her community. This distinction is valid even though both schools of thought share an appreciation for the material conditions or structures that give rise to subjectivity.[15] The two schools of thought come closest together in the works of Pierre Bourdieu and Michel Foucault, for in these works there is an understanding that subjectivity is always being constructed out of the material and historical structures in our midst. Marx most notably made the point that history is "made behind the backs of men," thus that our agency is more a fiction or fabrication than we usually imagine. Nonetheless, I defend this distinction because in contemporary circles of critical theory and socialist feminism there is an adamant resistance to an understanding of subjectivity as a provisional, fragmentary, decentered construction. Such theorists on the left take issue with theoretical understandings of subjectivity that

[14] By *critical theory* I mean the approach adopted by the Frankfurt School (led by Theodor Adorno and Max Horkheimer) which, beginning in the 1930s, sought to develop a critical theory of society. Horkheimer coined the term. In Stephen K. White's words, "As originally conceived, critical theory would have the role of giving new life to ideals of reason and freedom by revealing their false embodiment in scientism, capitalism, the 'culture industry', and bourgeois Western political institutions" (White 1995, 4).

[15] For an account of how contemporary French poststructuralist theorists appreciate such structures, see Kristeva's essay, "My Memory's Hyperbole" (1984b), and my discussion of it in Chapter 2.

seem to deny self-conscious agency. This will be the crux of the debate examined here.

In the following pages I address the question of whether certain poststructuralist theories of subjectivity, in particular Julia Kristeva's, can contribute to the project of deliberative democracy. I take Jürgen Habermas's understanding of politics as a model for deliberative politics and hence of political agency. Habermas has made no secret of his aversion to poststructuralism, suggesting that it is anathema to progressive politics. I take on this charge, asking whether effective political agency is possible under a poststructuralist theory of the subject. For example, could Kristeva's notion of the subject as an "open system" be a model of citizenship? I answer affirmatively, concluding that by virtue of our conditions as selves always influenced by our environment and interrelations we can be effective actors in a deliberative democracy. I argue that the more we recognize our indebtedness to and relationship with the others in our midst, the more likely we are to have effective political agency, practice, and communities.

By bringing together the theories of Habermas and Kristeva, two philosophers who seem so at odds with each other, I outline an alternative outlook on political communities. Reconsidering the citizen of a public sphere as a subject-in-process, as one who *needs* others in order to know and act in the world, makes possible a more democratic politics.

In Part I, I sketch two radically different views of subjectivity—different despite their similarities. Both Habermas and Kristeva hold that subjectivity arises contingently, historically, and linguistically. Both draw on Freud and the continental tradition. Yet their differences send them in diverging directions. I show how Habermas implicitly relies on a substance ontological metaphysics, whereas Kristeva explicitly adopts a process point of view (even though she never alludes to classical process ontology, e.g., that of A. N. Whitehead). Habermas draws on a linguistic theory that takes language to be a transparent tool, while Kristeva understands language as a disruptive medium, especially as it is used by a speaking being whose energies emanate from a *chora*—a term Plato used to mean receptacle and which Kristeva uses to mean the internal wellspring of drives and energy. Though both use Freud, Habermas's interpretation of psychoanalytic theory is more akin to ego psychology (which draws on Freud's tripartite model of ego, id, and superego) whereas Kristeva comes out of a Lacanian reading, which draws on the earlier Freudian theory of the unconscious and libidinal energy. All this adds up to, for Habermas, a subject that is an autonomous agent, and, for Kristeva, a subject who is an open system, always coming to speak and to be in relation with others, including the "other" within.

In his account of how individuation arises, Habermas seems to have moved beyond an Enlightenment approach. He points to the intersubjective and communicative processes that make subjectivity come about. This would seem to put him squarely in the camp of the poststructuralists. Yet, to the contrary, his account results in a subjectivity that meets the Enlightenment ideals of transparency, universality, and reason. (He would contend that he is being *postmetaphysical*, not poststructuralist, anyway.) I argue that his theory supports these Enlightenment ideals because of certain unexamined presuppositions that allow him to bring together the contingent, contextual development of subjectivity with the universal aims of modernity. These presuppositions include the following:

- a substance ontological metaphysics;
- a psychoanalytic theory based on ego psychology, where the ego is a primordial substance;
- human nature as ideally autonomous and self-transparent; language as a tool;
- an ideal of universalizability;
- identity developed by stepping back from context.

So, though subjectivity is developed intersubjectively through communication, it ends up with the features of modern liberal individuality: it is autonomous and transparent to self and can use reason to make universal claims.

The reader will find that I favor Kristeva's view of subjectivity as a process, an open system, over Habermas's conception. Through the course of the book, I supplement Kristeva's theory of subjectivity with other views. There's an echo of Hans-Georg Gadamer's hermeneutics, references to Emmanuel Levinas's welcoming of an asymmetrical obligation to the other, and a discussion of Jean-Luc Nancy's notion of community as being-in-common. All these come together in a model of what I call "relational subjectivity," whose features include the following.

To begin with, I accept Kristeva's notion of the subject-on-trial / in-process. This understanding of subjectivity is intertwined with an understanding of language: not as an independent system, as Habermas would have it, but as a process by which the *chora* / drives create subjectivity, history, society. Here, the semiotic aspect of signification is always contesting the law, whether the "law of the Father" or the orderliness supposed by the symbolic. Another aspect of relational subjectivity is that it is an open system: alive, vulnerable, and renewable. A characteristic state of such a system is to be in love, in a dynamic relationship, perhaps in a situation of transference between analyst and analysand. To be an open system is to be in the making and in relation. A further aspect of Kristeva's theory of subjectivity that fits into my conception of relational subjectivity involves her theory of abjection, negativity, expenditure. Here we have the somewhat contradictory situation in which the other is both a threat to the borders of subjectivity and also the possibility for constitution of subjectivity.

In addition to these features drawn from Kristeva's theory, I include other characteristics under the heading of relational subjectivity. One is that, as I discuss in Chapter 5, identity is constructed in large part by virtue of the stories that others tell. Our identity is created narratively by our becoming a character in others' stories. In Chapter 6, I bring in a conception of complementary agency, which means that we are able to know the world with others better than we could alone. Alone one's perspective is always partial. With others, we can get a variety of perspectives that might add up to a more comprehensive picture of the whole. Complementary agency is a positive result of Nietzsche's perspectivalism, in that the more perspectives available to us the better we see.

To supplement my theory of relational subjectivity further, I also draw from Jean-Luc Nancy's work. In his view, the subject is not a Hegelian absolute but is in a state of *clinamen*—leaning to the other, inclining toward others, seeing others as an opportunity rather than a threat. In this view, community means being open to difference, to new self-conceptions, and to the possibility of change. This view holds that deliberative communities can have better knowledge than system experts. When they deliberate, participants in the lifeworld are able to get a better sense of the political environment and a better understanding of how various policy options would fare. Bringing together Nancy and Kristeva, we can, I argue, surmise that subjectivities as open systems allow for deliberative communities in the best sense, as open, democratic, discursive spaces in which we can thrive together.

In describing Habermas's and Kristeva's theories of politics and citizenship, I raise the central question: *Can the subject-in-process be an effective political agent?* To answer this question, I first articulate what I think it means to be an effective political agent. I find Habermas's account of this subject much more compelling than Kristeva's. Habermas's model of politics is that of deliberative democracy, an alternative to both the empty proceduralism of liberalism and the weighty and questionable substance of civic republicanism. Deliberative democracy gives the public sphere a central role in the political process, namely that of forming public opinion and will on matters of common concern. In the public sphere, the public deliberates together about what ought to be done and, it is hoped, conveys its will to the powers that be in a compelling manner. In this model of politics, one can clearly identify the critical functions that citizens must carry out in order for politics to work effectively and legitimately.

While Habermas's model of politics pushes ahead into important territory, Kristeva's political writings, oddly enough, pull us back to a cosmopolitan individualism. When she writes about politics, Kristeva seems to "forget" that the subject is an open system, vulnerable, deeply related to others, and "in process." Instead, there emerges a picture of extreme individualism, of people thrown together in polities who seem to have little relationship with each other and few duties to carry out as citizens. For Kristeva, citizenship seems to begin and end with the prerogatives of membership in a political community; it has little if anything to do with political work. The citizen is a recipient of political goods, not a creator or actor within a political system.

For such reasons, I find Habermas's model of citizenship much more promising than Kristeva's. In Habermas's theory, citizens can be understood as political actors. Still, I retain Kristeva's theory of subjectivity and ask how the subject as an open system might carry out the work of a political actor in the public sphere. Looking past what I take to be Kristeva's own limited, inadequate conception of politics, I look for the political implications of her theory of subjectivity. I argue that relational subjects can carry out the functions of citizenship that Habermas's political theory suggests.

Using Kristeva's conception of the subject as an open system and

Nancy's conception of community as *clinamen*, I describe deliberative democracy in a way that begins by seeing individuals as always in relation. Where many philosophers of deliberative democracy pay little heed to the *experience* or *inclination* of those involved in deliberation, I try to see how subjects-in-process are constituted such that deliberation—openness to what is other—is a motive force for maintaining subjectivity. Thus we avoid the peculiar question of why an individual would enter into political community; plainly we already are in political community.

Subjects in relation, in process, as open systems are always already *inclined* to deliberate. Therefore the dread that Jürgen Habermas, Nancy Fraser, and other deliberative democrats feel in the face of poststructuralist theories of subjectivity is unwarranted. To the contrary, those interested in the project of deliberative democracy should welcome this theory of subjectivity, just as subjects-in-process can come to welcome the others in their midst.

By bringing together the theories of two political thinkers who seem so at odds with each other—Jürgen Habermas and Julia Kristeva—we can see the outlines of an alternative outlook on political communities. As I hope to show, reconsidering the citizen of a public sphere as a subject-in-process, as one who needs others in order to know and act in the world, makes possible a more democratic politics. In this picture, difference is a cornerstone of community. We each have within us heterogeneous drives and instincts, and we are the storehouse of all that we have forgotten. So too our communities are heterogeneous; they abound in different orientations, backgrounds, wishes, interests. Rather than wish away these differences, we might try to embrace them. The stranger who seems so foreign may by her presence invite me to make an acquaintance with my own foreignness. That there is alterity within us and among us can lead us toward complementarity. That we are each subjects-in-process can be a new basis for democratic communities.

Part I

Subjectivity in the Making

> Desire is produced in the beyond of the demand, in that, in articulating the life of the subject according to its conditions, demand cuts off the need from that life. . . . In this embodied aporia, of which one might say that it borrows, as it were, its heavy soul from the hardy shoots of the wounded drive, and its subtle body from the death actualized in the signifying sequence, desire is affirmed as the absolute condition.
>
> —Jacques Lacan, "The Direction of the Treatment and the Principles of Its Power," *Ecrits*

> It is I who support the Other and am responsible for him. One thus sees that in the human subject, at the same time as a total subjection, my primogeniture manifests itself. My responsibility is untransferable, no one could replace me. . . . Responsibility is what is incumbent on me exclusively, and what, *humanly,* I cannot refuse. I am I in the sole measure that I am responsible, a non-interchangeable I. I can substitute myself for everyone, but no one can substitute himself for me. Such is my inalienable identity of subject. It is in this precise sense that Dostoyevsky said: *"We are all responsible for all men before all, and I more than all the others."*
>
> —Emmanuel Levinas, *Ethics and Infinity*

1 Habermas's Theory of Postconventional Identity

Jürgen Habermas came of age in the aftermath of World War II, in Germany, an ocean apart from the Frankfurt School of intellectuals who had fled fascism for the United States. Although he ultimately shared many of the aims and concerns of the members of the Institute for Social Research, his route to them had been distinctly different. As one interviewer writes:

> Habermas was 15 when the Allies defeated Germany in 1945. He had been a member of the Hitler Youth and had been sent, during the last months of the war, to "man the western defenses." His bourgeois father had been a "passive sympathizer" with Nazism. Nazi society was the only one the young Habermas had known. Then the Nuremberg war-crimes trials started, and the first documentary films on the concentration camps appeared. "All at once we saw that we had been living in a politically criminal system," Habermas has explained. His political life began with this awakening. It established what he labels the major "motif" of his politics: a vigilance against any recurrence of such "politically criminal" behavior. (Stephens 1994)

Learning of the atrocities committed by his fellow Germans, Habermas felt firsthand the dismay with modernity that had led Adorno and Horkheimer to a "negative dialectics," a pessimistic view of the progress of modernity. But where Adorno had become disenchanted with the Enlightenment, the young Habermas became all the more

determined to find its promise. "Habermas became increasingly concerned with rethinking and appropriating the tradition of German
thought that was left in shambles," writes Richard Bernstein. "Reason, freedom, and justice were not only theoretical issues to be explored, but practical tasks to be achieved—practical tasks that de-
manded passionate commitment" (Bernstein 1985, 2).

Reviving the approach of early critical theory—an attempt to use
the social sciences to develop a critical theory of society—Habermas
has sought to find reason to believe in reason. Paraphrasing Habermas's concerns, Bernstein writes:

> Can we still, in our time, provide a rational justification for universal
> normative standards? Or are we faced with relativism, decisionism, or
> emotivism which hold that ultimate norms are arbitrary and beyond
> rational warrantability? These became primary questions for Haber-
> mas. The fate—indeed, the very possibility—of the critical theory of so-
> ciety with the practical intent of furthering human emancipation de-
> pends on giving an affirmative answer to the first question and a
> negative answer to the second. (Bernstein 1985, 4)

Habermas's route in this project is a fascinating, although quite
dense, development, one that I will only briefly sketch here. Moving
away from their early work in critical theory and following Weber,
Adorno and Horkheimer had taken the "dialectic of Enlightenment"
to be a negative one. For Kant, Enlightenment was characterized by
the use of reason to question and criticize the "authorities," whether
the church or the princes, and decide for oneself what was just and
true. Reason offered a path to freedom from tutelage. But Max Weber
had shown how reason led to its own "iron cage," the iron cage of in-
strumentalism, where reason was a means for reaching predetermined ends. As Bernstein writes,

> Weber argued that the hope and expectation of the Enlightenment
> thinkers was a bitter and ironic illusion. They maintained a strong nec-
> essary linkage between the growth of science, rationality, and universal
> human freedom. But when unmasked and understood, the legacy of the
> Enlightenment was the triumph of *Zweckrationalität*—purposive-in-
> strumental rationality. This form of rationality affects and infects the
> entire range of social and cultural life encompassing economic struc-
> tures, law, bureaucratic administration, and even the arts. The growth
> of *Zweckrationalität* does not lead to the concrete realization of uni-

versal freedom but to the creation of an "iron cage" of bureaucratic rationality from which there is no escape. (Bernstein 1985, 5)

As Weber saw it, reason as *Zweckrationalität* was a tool of bureaucracies and other oppressive institutions, an instrument for gaining domination and control.

Communicative Reason

Whereas Adorno and Horkheimer all but gave in to this view of reason, Habermas sought to salvage reason, at least an aspect of it, as a still viable means for Enlightenment. To do so, Habermas noted that, in addition to instrumental reason, there are other kinds of reason. By the 1970s he had pinpointed "communicative reason" as a kind of reason that could provide a critical "ground" for freedom, a "ground" that was not, however, foundational. Communicative reason does not exist outside of human experience or as a standing edifice on which we can base our judgments. Communicative reason is immanent to our communicative action; it is the quasi-transcendental possibility of engaging in conversation, historically arising from human interests. It is typified by an *expectation*—however counterfactual—that one's interlocutor will speak sincerely, truthfully, openly, and uncoercively. If we did not have such expectations, we would never bother communicating in the first place. These expectations are how we *reason* when we talk in order to reach understanding with others; thus they are central to communicative rationality. In our everyday conversations, we expect a kind of ideal (which Habermas has called the ideal speech situation): that communication for reaching understanding should be uncoerced, egalitarian, sincere, and truthful. Habermas does not argue that the ideal speech situation actually occurs but rather that we have it as a regulative ideal by which we judge actual speech situations. Were I to find out that, in your conversation with me, you were lying to me and trying to manipulate me for your own ends, I would have *reason* to think that something was *wrong*—that you were violating the norms implicit in and constitutive of our communicative practices.[1]

---

[1] For Habermas's theories of communicative action and discourse ethics, see Habermas 1984, 1987, 1990a, and 1993, and Rehg 1997.

Habermas grants that manipulative, coercive communications regularly occur. He calls these occurrences strategic action to distinguish them from communicative action. Those myriad occurrences, which we see regularly in advertising and political propaganda, exploit our expectations that speech will be open and sincere. Strategic action is parasitic upon our usual expectations for communicative action and reason. But instead of using communicative reason, strategic action uses instrumental reason. That is, it is geared toward reaching success (i.e., attaining some given end) by whatever means necessary.

Habermas also distinguishes communicative reason from what he calls functional reason, the reason that guides systems, such as the bureaucratic, economic, and administrative systems that control various spheres of society today. Instead of being guided or "steered" by expectations of rightness and sincerity, these systems are steered by, for example, money and power. Functional reason, like instrumental reason, is in the service of meeting predetermined ends. In his major book of the early 1980s, *The Theory of Communicative Action*, Habermas draws a distinction between communicative and functional reason. He shows that participants in society see themselves from a "lifeworld" perspective, where communicative reason reigns. But, as I will discuss in Chapter 3, there is also the observer perspective of society, emphasized by Niklas Luhmann, where society is a set of systems—administrative, political, economic—that are guided by their own internal imperatives and methods. From the point of view of systems, communicative rationality is irrelevant. But even worse, the functional rationality of systems has, in the modern era, begun to encroach on the lifeworld. Traditionally, the lifeworld is the arena where norms are chosen and hold sway, where questions of the right and the good are preeminent, where actions are guided by the ends we choose and not by money or power. But as the system becomes more developed, its logic starts to seep into the lifeworld. By the end of *The Theory of Communicative Action*, Habermas has depicted a gloomy world in which the system is insidiously "colonizing" the lifeworld, where communicative reason and action are losing ground, where the possibility of Enlightenment grows ever dimmer.

Habermas's goal is to halt the encroachment of the system into the lifeworld, in part by explicating the characteristics of communicative action.[2] One thread of this project, which will be developed in these pages, has been to describe the agent who takes part in communicative action. For Habermas, the "subject" who engages in communicative action is not a Cartesian, monological subject but is rather a being who emerges intersubjectively, contingently, historically, through language. In the end, though, the subject who emerges resembles the traditional subject of modernity, a subject who, however fragile, presupposes that he or she is autonomous, self-transparent, and unified.

Beyond the Philosophy of the Subject

Habermas's work on subjectivity is an effort to overcome the Hegelian philosophy of consciousness, a quintessentially metaphysical view of self-consciousness as the ground for all knowledge, as well as to rectify the mistakes of many of his contemporaries who have taken the wrong path, as he sees it, in trying to get past this philosophy of the subject. "The modern philosophy of consciousness," he writes, "sublimates the independence of the theoretical mode of life into a theory that is absolute and self-justifying" (Habermas 1992a, 33). The philosophy of consciousness always turns consciousness back on itself, only to find itself already receding. In trying to resolve the conundrum, philosophy becomes thoroughly consciousness-centered. Moreover, the metaphysical presupposition of unity and the primacy of universals makes individuation difficult to conceive, that is, as something unique in its own right, not just as an instance of a universal.

The philosophy of consciousness never successfully accounted for individuation. Yet even as this metaphysical thinking began to wane, with the Young Hegelians and more so with the rise of the social sciences, the problematic of the philosophy of consciousness lingers on, Habermas argues, across philosophy. The problem, he thinks, is that the backlash against metaphysics has included a wholesale rejection

---

[2] In his more recent work, Habermas points to another avenue for halting the encroachment of the system upon the lifeworld: the funneling of public will, via the law, into the system. See Habermas 1996 and Chapter 3 of this volume.

of reason. In response to the procedural reason of systems, technology, and bureaucracies, Habermas maintains, some (Derrida among them) have countered that philosophy is at its heart irrational because "philosophy was supposed to [and failed to] secure its possessions and its relation to totality at the price of renouncing contestable knowledge" (Habermas 1992a, 37). Habermas contends that such philosophers as Wittgenstein, Adorno, Heidegger, and Derrida have become so skeptical of philosophy's ability to know anything that they refuse to make any positive determinations.[3] Reason has also been undermined by being contextualized, broken into domains, that is, *situated* to the extent that it becomes pretheoretical and no longer useful. Moreover, he writes, "all these attempts to detranscendentalize reason continue to get entangled in the prior conceptual decisions of transcendental philosophy" (Habermas 1992a, 43). In other words, without reason we can be taken in by the remnants of metaphysical thinking, particularly by thinking of self-consciousness as a monological venture.

The saving grace for philosophy, in Habermas's view, was the linguistic turn that took place across philosophy early in the twentieth century. Instead of consciousness being the object of study, language took center stage. Yet, according to Habermas, many fields in philosophy (e.g., analytic philosophy of language and semiotics) have missed the opportunity to use the linguistic turn to understand how individuation occurs communicatively and intersubjectively. This is because they failed to rid themselves completely of their metaphysical suppositions and failed to adopt the norms of the empirical sciences. As he writes,

> Once it renounces its claim to be a first science or an encyclopedia, philosophy can maintain its status within the scientific system neither by assimilating itself to particular exemplary sciences nor by exclusively distancing itself from science in general. Philosophy has to implicate itself in the fallibilistic self-understanding and procedural rationality of

---

[3] "Philosophy has appeared in this form as existential illumination and philosophical faith (Jaspers), as a mythology that complements science (Kolakowski), as the mystical thinking of Being (Heidegger), as the therapeutic treatment of language (Wittgenstein), as deconstructive activity (Derrida), or as negative dialectics (Adorno)" (Habermas 1992a, 37).

the empirical sciences; it may not lay claim to a privileged access to truth, or to a method, an object realm, or even just a style of intuition that is specifically its own. (Habermas 1992a, 38)

So under the mantle of empiricism, as opposed to metaphysics, he sets out to solve the puzzle that befuddled the philosophy of consciousness, by developing a theory that accounts for our actual, contingent experience of individuating ourselves.

In moving out of the philosophy of the subject, Habermas says, Wilhelm von Humboldt made a major contribution: he develops a theory of language as a synthetic, unifying fact, where the unifying force is not found in a subject but in a relation between subjects. Instead of the "'I think' of transcendental apperception, there now appears the unrelinquished difference between the perspectives from which the participants in communication reach understanding with each other about the same thing" (Habermas 1992a, 163).

Another figure Habermas turns to is Kierkegaard, who, Habermas writes, made self-positing "so much his own that he interprets self-relation as a relating-to-oneself wherein I relate myself at the same time to an antecedent Other on whom this relation depends" (Habermas 1992a, 164). But this relating occurs amid all our contingent circumstances, amid a life history not of our own making. So "in a paradoxical act, I must choose myself as the one who I am and want to be. *Life history* becomes the principle of individuation, but only if it is transposed by such an act of self-choice into an existential form for which the self is responsible" (164–65).

Thus both Humboldt and Kierkegaard reject the notion of a self coming to know itself from any transcendental standpoint; rather, the self posits itself only as one who is *situated* in the world with a particular, contingent life history. Kierkegaard sees this as an existential choice, a choice that dissolves the boundary between essential self and accidental history. By choosing to own and accept my life history, I *performatively* individuate myself. I claim myself as an individual; yet this claim requires that someone, some Other, recognize me. The traditional confession to God in the medieval era is a claim to individuate one's own unique and irreplaceable life. For Kierkegaard too the Other is God; yet before Kierkegaard, this claim to individuation had already taken a secular turn, with Rousseau, who in his *Confessions* appealed for recognition not to God but to a public, in expectation or hope of having this claim redeemed. Linguistic intersubjectivity and life-historical identity are brought together, then, "through the thought that the call, the demand, or the expectation of an Other is needed in order to awaken the consciousness of spontaneous activity in me" (Habermas 1992a, 165).

This new illocutionary mode is performative: "it is a matter of interested *presentations of self*, with which a complex claim presented to second persons is justified—a claim to recognition of the irreplaceable identity of an ego manifesting itself in a conscious way of life" (167). In a performative attitude, I can lay claim to my ego. But can I lay claim to my ego apart from others? No, Habermas asserts:

> The ego, which seems to me to be given in my self-consciousness as what is purely my own, cannot be maintained by me solely through my own power, as it were me alone—it does not "belong" to me. Rather, this ego always retains an intersubjective core because the process of individuation from which it emerges runs through the network of linguistically mediated interactions. (170)

In the performative attitude, we begin to break out of the philosophy of the subject and into a new—and for Habermas, superior—theory of communicatively constructed individuation. Yet the themes of this new philosophy are still familiar. In a 1913 essay, "The Social Self," George Herbert Mead takes up the circle of reflection that Fichte had noted. The spontaneous "I" can be known only retrospectively—but as a "me," as an object of reflection. (Note that Habermas is not questioning whether there is a "spontaneous 'I'" but only how it can be known.) Mead writes, "For the moment it is presented it has passed into the objective case, presuming . . . an 'I' that observes—but an 'I' that can disclose himself only by ceasing to be the subject for whom the object 'me' exists" (Habermas 1992a, 171).

Habermas reminds us that we should not confuse processes of individuation with processes of differentiation. To become individuated is more than just becoming different from others; it means gaining subjectivity in its own right. Here, Habermas argues, Mead has made headway. For Mead, "individuation depends upon the internalization of the agencies that monitor behavior, which migrate, as it were, from without to within. In the process of socialization, the growing person takes what the reference person expects of him and first makes it his own ... and ... there arises an internal center for the self-steering of individually accountable conduct" (Habermas 1992a, 152). When our number of roles expands and expectations conflict, we have to become detached from our roles so we can autonomously and voluntarily decide what to do. For example, any given role (wife, sister, friend, boss, student, or community leader) will include certain responsibilities, but the more roles we take on the more our responsibilities will conflict—and thus the need will arise for us to decide independently how to respond.

In abstracting ourselves from our particular roles, we become more autonomous, independent agents. "The internalizing processing of these conflicts leads to an *autonomization* of the self: to a certain extent the individual itself must first posit itself as a spontaneously acting subject" (Habermas 1992a, 152). Habermas says this is an achievement of individuality though it also sounds like a will to power of sorts, a "making" of oneself where there wasn't oneself before—though "individuation is pictured not as the self-realization of an independently acting subject carried out in isolation and freedom but as a linguistically mediated process of socialization and the simultaneous constitution of a life-history that is conscious of itself" (152–53).

The way out of this circle of reflection is through engaging with someone else through language, performatively. The epistemic self might act on instinct, but the practical relation-to-self arises from situations in which one generates normative behavioral expectations.[4] Habermas also moves away from theories of self-consciousness to a theory of self-control, as ego (self) internalizes alter's (the other's) behavioral / normative expectations of ego.

At this stage (conventional morality) in this scheme (Mead's) the "me" is "the generalized other," internalizing conventional expectations. "In the practical relation-to-self ... the acting subject ... wants to reassure ... itself" that it is a free will. It reassures itself "from the perspective of the generalized other or the community" by internalizing the community's norms so that ego can choose whether

---

[4] Notice the Kantian pattern of moving from the epistemic ego of pure reason, the empirical realm, to the (transcendental?) moral / practical ego of practical reason / freedom. Habermas argues elsewhere that these distinctions, along with the aesthetic distinction, are unavoidable today.

or not to abide by them. We are not yet at the stage that is for Habermas truly moral: the postconventional stage where the subject appeals to universalizable norms, not just the particular norms of a particular group. To be moral, for Habermas, means getting "beyond" the clan, beyond the expectations of a conventional morality (where morality is merely a matter of convention, not something that would hold true universally). Yet even in the conventional stage, the seeds of a universal morality are in place. In the conventional realm, "the 'I' in turn relates to this agency as a spontaneity that eludes consciousness." So immanent in our conventional agency, a potential, yet elusive, authentic "I" acts. When this "I" is concerned with practical matters (as opposed to purely epistemic concerns), it forms "an unconscious that makes itself noticed in *two* ways: as the onrush of impulses that are subjected to control and as the source of innovations that break up and renew conventionally rigidified controls" (Habermas 1992a, 179–80). This unconscious, then, contains both drives or instincts, in the Freudian sense, and an ego (or perhaps a superego) capable of bursting through conventional expectations.[5]

But the "me" of conventional morality still places limits on the "I." "The 'me' is the bearer of a moral consciousness that adheres to the convention and practices of a specific group" (182). Yet as society becomes more differentiated (as in a modern civil society) the "me" has an opportunity to become more individuated. As more differentiated demands are made on ego, ego must choose, must appeal to a larger universal community or posterity.[6] This pushes one out of conventional morality and into a postconventional identity where one supposes a kingdom of ends here and now "as a context of interaction and as a communication community in which everyone is capable of taking up the perspective of everyone else and is willing to do so" (185). "Progressive individuation" involves both *"differentiation of unique identities"* and *"growth of personal autonomy"* (185). Each

[5] As I note later in this chapter, Habermas seems to rely on an ego-psychological interpretation of Freud, where the ego is potentially capable of mediating between the instincts and reality—like a rider on horseback mediating between the horse's energy and the world's reality. The passage cited here supports this claim.

[6] Notice a move here similar to the Hegelian view (taken from Antigone) of the ideal being to leave the *oikos* for the polis. That is, to become truly moral, one ought—supposedly—to move beyond the private law of theology or the household to the public law of the city.

individual takes up the whole, but does so from a unique perspective (à la Leibniz's monads).

For Habermas, the practical relation-to-self—self-assurance via the perspectives of (all possible) others—is not a matter of seeking assurance or consensus regarding my thematic claim but assurance of "my claim to uniqueness and irreplaceability, . . . the claim to individuality itself" (186). This idealizing supposition allows Habermas to counter the poststructuralist critique that his universalism denies difference and particularity, for the appeal to a universal, unlimited communication community "makes it possible for individuals to exist within a community—individualism as the flip-side of universalism" (186). Yet, again, there is something hidden in Habermas's thinking: it is through a *desire* for recognition as a unique and irreplaceable being that one makes a claim to a universal community. Note the aporia: Who desires? Who is this one there in advance of the claim? Despite wanting to escape the circle of reflection of the philosophy of consciousness, Habermas has created his own circle—the circle of the spontaneous "I": created, or perhaps merely recognized, intersubjectively but still somehow there in advance.

Habermas cannot get beyond this circle. Who makes the claim of individuation to all others? The "I." As he writes, "The 'I' itself *projects* the context of interaction that first makes the reconstruction of a shattered conventional identity possible on a higher level" (187). To get out of this (unacknowledged) circle, Habermas points to societal differentiation as the agent of individuation: societal differentiation calls for a nonconventional ego identity. However, at this historical juncture, he notes, we lack an adequate level of social differentiation. So we *anticipate* that it will come and that we *will* be held accountable for the decisions we make now according to the ideal criteria (188). So prior to the ideal lifeworld conditions for individuation, becoming an "I" is still possible, thanks to the way we *perform* in using our practical reason: taking up the perspective of all possible others, becoming visible to oneself as the other's alter ego, as a unique and irreplaceable being. In communicative action, I can lay claim to my autonomy and self-realization by anticipating recognition from an unlimited communication community.

Habermas wants it both ways. He wants a subjectivity that is constituted prelinguistically through an ego interpreting the "objective meaning" of another's vocal gesture. Yet he also wants an "I" that is

internal and immanent in conventional practices. The latter conflicts
with his disavowals and renunciation of the philosophy of the subject. If in his theory some kernel of subjectivity is there in advance,
then he faces the same problems he points to in the philosophy of
consciousness, namely the problem of locating how this kernel of
subjectivity catches sight of itself. What is the source of spontaneous
action?

Even if he cannot answer this question, Habermas is right to cham-
pion Mead for breaking new ground in arguing that individuation occurs through socialization. Whether or not there is some core self preceding the community, surely subjectivity develops through
community. We come to have subjectivity with others through language and through intersubjective acknowledgment."From the structure of language comes the explanation of why the human spirit is
condemned to an odyssey—why it first finds its way to itself only on
a detour via a complete externalization in other things and in other
humans" (Habermas 1992a, 153).

Insofar as it arrives through language, subjectivity arises contingently. This view departs considerably from the Cartesian picture of
mental substance, a substance it seems that was always already
there. Mead's depiction of the development of subjectivity recognizes
that subjectivity comes about contingently, historically, and provisionally. Habermas draws on Mead's depiction of the contingent development of subjectivity, but *what develops*—that is, the effect of
this development—is not so different from the Cartesian notion of
substance. (This is due to reasons I have already suggested and others
that I will develop below.) While subjectivity arises provisionally,
when it begins to speak—or, more specifically, to engage in communicative action—subjectivity takes on the very qualities that the
modern project anticipated:

> Among the universal and unavoidable presuppositions of action ori-
> ented to reaching understanding is the presupposition that the speaker
> qua actor lays claim to recognition both as an autonomous will and as
> an individuated being. And indeed the self, which is able to assure itself
> of itself through the recognition of this identity by others, shows up in
> language as the meaning of the performatively employed personal pro-
> noun in the first person. (Habermas 1992a, 191)

In order to act, we must first call on others to recognize us as autonomous individuals. This does not mean that we are in fact au-

tonomous individuals but that we must perform as if we were in order to act in the world. It is in claiming to be autonomous individuals
that we become them. Thus, Habermas is not describing what he
takes to be an empirical fact about human nature; he is arguing that
the will to be autonomous precedes our ability to take part in communicative action—the will and the performance. By performing as if
we were Enlightenment subjects (autonomous, self-transparent, and
free to take part in an "uncluttered" communicative sphere), we
might attain the goals of modernity: freedom, justice, reason, and
progress. Though he argues that the self always necessarily has an intersubjective core, he sees subjectivity as an *achievement*, something
that can be attained and had, it seems, once and for all.

Habermas goes to great lengths to show how subjectivity is arrived
at historically and contingently—and that its "arrival" is a *performance* of sorts and requires a hermeneutic interpretation to give it
any meaning: "To be sure," he writes, "the extent to which this
meaning . . . either emerges articulated, remains implicit, or is even
neutralized in any concrete case, depends upon the action situation
and the further context. The universal pragmatic presuppositions of
communicative action constitute semantic resources from which
historical societies create and articulate, each in its own way, representations of mind and soul, concepts of the person and of action,
consciousness of morality, and so on" (Habermas 1992a, 191). Yet despite these overtures to history and context, Habermas is no fan of
the particular and the provisional. For example, the stress he places
on universalizability and autonomy belies his attempts to articulate
a truly intersubjective and ongoing constitution of subjectivity.

Still, there is much in Habermas's communicative account of subjectivity with which to agree. For one thing, Habermas claims that
individuation arises intersubjectively. We can never come to subjectivity apart from our relations with others. The self always has an
"intersubjective core." For another, we come to subjectivity by par-
ticipating in language, or more broadly, in communication. It is only
in making a normative claim to an unlimited communication community that I finally have self-coincidence as an "I." Moreover,
Habermas recognizes that subjectivity is a contingent affair, that it
arises in variable situations in which some potential subject accepts
this contingent life it is living *as its own* and claims for itself an identity. And finally, Habermas recognizes, at least implicitly, that there
is something fictitious about the autonomous subject. The self

makes a claim to an ideal unlimited community to be recognized as a unique, irreplaceable subject. This claim is never grounded on some supposed fact; it is only redeemed in communicative action. Autonomous subjectivity never exists prior to lived experience in a community of other speaking subjects.

Like those of the French Lacanian tradition, in which Kristeva is a participant, Habermas sees individuation as a result of entering into a sociolinguistic order. Our identities are constituted through language—and through a network that is interdependent. For Habermas, the process of socialization is also a process of individuation. He sees in subjectivity both a sociolinguistic dimension and a "private" dimension. In these respects, he is like his poststructuralist contemporaries. But there the similarity ends. Following G. H. Mead, Habermas maintains the notion that the private self is an autonomous one: the traditional subject of the modern tradition. He argues that we are both general and particular subjects. That is, we are simultaneously an "autonomous individual subject" and an interdependent subject, "entangled in a densely woven fabric of mutual recognition." These two self-identities have a dialectical relationship: the private, autonomous self is always constituted by its identity in an intersubjective network. Despite its debt to its relationships, the self that emerges is capable of making autonomous and universal claims about matters such as justice and morality, not a far cry from Enlightenment subjectivity.

Postmetaphysical Thinking?

Many poststructuralist and feminist philosophers have criticized Jürgen Habermas for the universalistic dimensions of his work in discourse ethics and communicative action. They claim that his universalism overlooks difference and particularity, that it posits a fixed subject immune to history, and that it is hyperrationalist. In response, Habermas has fired criticisms back, especially in his book *The Philosophic Discourse of Modernity*. But more recently, in *Postmetaphysical Thinking*, he has responded in a more novel way, by trying to identify the points of difference between his and his critics' positions. In response to charges that he favors universalism over individuality, he spells out his theory of how subjects come to individuate themselves. As I've discussed, he says that they do so by virtue of their concrete particularity, through their contingent situation, through their relations with others, and foremost through language. Individuation arises through socialization, intersubjectively and linguistically. Prior to this process, there is no subjectivity.

With this response, Habermas claims that he is not so different from his critics, for many of them also believe that subjectivity is derived through language and through relationships. But unlike his critics, especially the poststructuralists, Habermas indicates that the subjectivity that emerges from this process is fully autonomous, transparent to itself, centered, rational, and able to make valid universal claims—a picture in keeping with the Enlightenment ideal, a far remove from poststructuralism. That this view of subjectivity results from his theory and not from the others, Habermas maintains, is due to one key difference: that he holds to a theory of reason while they have rejected reason altogether.[7]

With this latter point, I disagree. But before explaining how and why, I should first note where I stand in this debate. On the one hand, I share Habermas's aim to develop a theory that furthers the goals of deliberative democracy, a discourse ethics that allows us to address our moral and political differences by talk rather than by force. The more heterogeneous our communities become, the more we need to find ways to decide together what courses of action are productive and mutually acceptable. On the other hand, I share poststructuralist and feminist concerns about the universalistic aspects of Habermas's theories of individuation and discourse. I think his understanding of subjectivity and reason is too strict; in order to engage in democratic discourse we need not act as if we are the fully transparent and autonomous selves supposed by the Enlightenment. As I suggest in subsequent chapters, we may be better off without such notions. We can deliberate effectively while being the more dynamic, relational subjects-in-process that some poststructuralist philosophers, such as Julia Kristeva, describe. So though I share Habermas's abiding concern, I object to some of his moves.

Now, I'll return to the question of why I disagree with Habermas's claim that the key difference between him and his critics is his valorization of reason. To begin with, I think he misrepresents their

---

[7] See, for example, Habermas 1992a, 210–11.

views. For example, one of his main targets is Derrida, who he claims values rhetoric more than logic and equates philosophy with literature. In a heated response to this charge, Derrida writes, "That is false. I say *false*, as opposed to *true*, and I defy Habermas to prove the presence in my work of that 'primacy of rhetoric' which he attributes to me" (Derrida 1988, 157). Derrida's point here is that Habermas himself is not following the "the elementary rules of philology and interpretation," whereas he (Derrida) is indeed concerned with logic, if not the logic to which Habermas subscribes.

While Habermas would have us believe that his own rationality leads him to produce a theory of fully autonomous and transparent subjectivity, I believe that he has another motivation. He claims, on the one hand, to have moved beyond metaphysics and adopted the "fallibilist" methods of the social sciences, yet, on the other hand, he holds patently metaphysical ideals, namely, universality and autonomy, which motivate him to pick and choose empirical research that supports his view. By saying he has adopted a "postmetaphysical" position, Habermas avoids discussing his own metaphysical presuppositions. Moreover, in appealing to the social sciences as nonmetaphysical, he overlooks the fact that social theory can never extricate itself from metaphysics—for example, that what counts as a good explanation (whether teleological, functional, etc.) can never be decided by social research alone. And, when the objects of study are human beings, we should be even more suspicious of knowledge that claims to be purely descriptive and empirical.

Now I turn to some background problems I see in Habermas's theory of individuation. First is the concept of autonomy, as it is understood in general, and in particular by Habermas. The ideal of autonomy is so deep-seated and sacred to modernity that questioning its status seems sacrilegious. Nonetheless, we should at least recognize that it is a metaphysical ideal. For example, insofar as Kant held it to be the true *nature* of human beings he was making an ontological and thus metaphysical claim. So let us be clear that when Habermas invokes autonomy, he is invoking something metaphysical, despite his claim to be doing otherwise.

The notion that human beings are, or ought to be, self-legislating permeates our thinking. Is this a thought without origin, something intrinsic to our nature as rational beings? Or is it a product of some metaphysical thinking? I think it is the latter. Habermas wants to go along with the contemporary understanding that subjectivity is brought about intersubjectively, communicatively, and through language, that is, contingently. Yet he also wants a subjectivity capable of autonomy. To achieve this, he has to integrate the provisional and situated character of subjectivity with a transcendental notion—that subjectivity entails autonomy, *that to be perfect means being unmoved by anything else.* (Hear the echo of the Aristotelian and medieval ideal of perfection: God as the unmoved mover.) That, at least, is the strict sense we get from a Kantian version of autonomy, which warns us away from heeding our attachments to others, our inclinations and emotions, everything but pure practical reason. Habermas's theory of autonomy tends in the same direction, for to make a moral claim we must detach ourselves from our particularities and affinities and appeal autonomously to a universal, abstract other.

In a discussion of Habermas's view of autonomy, Mark Warren delineates the way in which Habermas constructs the concept. First, to be autonomous is to have a reflexive relationship with oneself, a self-identity that results from being able to set goals for oneself. "The continuous core of the self resides in the reflexive traces of relations with the world that have been desired, projected, maintained, or broken" (Warren 1995, 173). Second, to be autonomous is to have "the ability to initiate projects, to bring new ideas, things, and relations into being. And agency implies some amount of control over one's life history—not apart from one's biography and context, but because these serve as resources of agency that neither impose absolute limits nor allow for arbitrary creativity" (173). So even though the self is a product of intersubjective and discursive relations, the self as agent or originator has somehow broken free of these particularities:

> A third quality of autonomy, then, is the capacity to distance self-identity from circumstances at the same time that one locates the self in terms of these circumstances. Autonomy is a kind of freedom. Internally, autonomy implies that one can adopt a reflexive attitude towards one's own internal impulses, interpreting, transforming, censoring, and providing names for needs, impulses, and desires, as well as expressing them to others as interests. Ideally, says Habermas, ego identity "makes freedom possible without demanding for it the price of unhappiness, violation of one's inner nature." With regard to the social world, autonomy implies that one can distance oneself from traditions, prevailing opinions, and pressures to conform by subjecting elements of one's social context to criticism. (173)

As we see, Habermas aims to develop a theory of the subject that is cognizant of its intersubjective origin but allows for an ability to detach, to be free, to be capable of not being moved by tradition and opinion. If successful, this would allow him to have a theory of the subject that is congruent with its contingent and historical development while also making use of the Kantian notion of critical judgment. "Universalistic action orientations" Habermas writes, "reach beyond all existing conventions and make it possible to gain some distance from the social roles that shape one's background and character" (Habermas 1987, 97).

So how does one, according to Habermas, develop the capacity to "free oneself" from one's own particularity? One develops this capacity by taking part in "intersubjective processes of reason giving and response" (Warren 1995, 174). Autonomy cannot develop monologically, it requires taking part in "a shared fabric of communicative understandings" (Warren 1995, 174). But this does not fully answer the question. There is still some vagueness about this ability to intersubjectively develop a capacity to free oneself from one's own embeddedness, to break loose from the traditions that give rise to the self in order to be able to reflexively critique those very traditions. In Habermas's texts and in the texts of those who interpret him there is a silence rather than an explanation of just how autonomy arises.

Let me venture a few hypotheses about Habermas's rationale for the development of autonomy. One is that he recognizes two moments: first, the intersubjective and discursive development of subjectivity, and second, the ability of the subject to reflexively critique its own traditions. Using Mead, as I discuss more below, he links these two movements in a developmental account. But his observation that subjects can reflexively critique their own situations may be colored by his own normative aims for the subject. The subject, he thinks, ought to be autonomous in this way, but is it ever really so? Habermas sees the *will* to autonomy as prior to, and perhaps in place of, the *fact* of autonomy. The fact that we speak, Habermas argues, attests to our will for autonomy. "Through [language's] structure autonomy and responsibility are posited for us. Our first sentence expresses unequivocally the intention of universal and unconstrained consensus" (Habermas 1979, xvii). The structure of our speaking, especially the validity claims we make when speaking (of normative rightness, sincerity, etc.), rejects any reliance on authority and hence any heteronomy. We will not be guided by any authority other than the authority that arises from ideal, democratic dialogue. In the end, then, Habermas's claims for autonomy are based upon these reasons: (1) that our speaking attests to our will to be autonomous—and thus that we at least *perform* as if we were autonomous—and (2) that the only alternative to autonomy is undemocratic authority.[8]

I want to take issue with both of these claims. We should ask what strict meaning Habermas sees in *autonomy*. If it is the ability to rule oneself without any influence from another, then we'd have to understand the self as constituted in isolation. For how can the ability to act be divorced from the ability to be? If we do grant that the self is constituted intersubjectively, socially, and historically, as Habermas says he does, then "self-legislating" can never be a solitary activity, it can never free itself from its own constitution.

This need not mean, however, that the self is doomed to act heteronomously. Here I think that Habermas's notion of *performativity* is useful. We may not be able in isolation to decide how to act, but we might need to act according to some fiction of autonomy.[9] If this is an a priori condition for the possibility of speaking, then, it seems, we are bound to a metaphysics of the autonomous subject—unless we could develop an alternative theory, perhaps of speaking beings indebted to others for the opportunity to speak at all.

Sociological Claims

Although he claimed to leave behind the metaphysical hubris of having a specialized access to truth, Habermas picks it back up again, holding up universality and autonomy as necessary or ideal features of human reality. Kant foresaw this problem when he noted that, no matter how critical we are of it, "we shall always return to metaphysics as to a beloved one with whom we have had a quarrel" (Kant 1965, 664). While the return may be inevitable, we should still inquire into its effects. As I'll now show, Habermas's metaphysical suppositions have skewed his use of the social sciences—namely, linguistics and developmental psychology—and made it possible for

---

[8] A third reason, which I discuss below, is Habermas's reliance on ego psychology rather than a libidinal model of subjectivity.

[9] Note that this brings us close to the debate between free will and determinism, with the middle ground being some sort of compatibilism: perhaps our actions are determined, but the idea of freedom can still be compatible.

him to produce a theory of autonomous subjectivity that is transparent to itself. In this section, I will not attempt to *refute* Habermas's claims (after all the burden of proving the claims should be on him). I simply want to point out those crucial junctures in his theory in which he is appealing to some questionable fact in order to realize his metaphysical ideals.

First, following Mead, Habermas adopts the view that the process of socialization includes the step of subjects' "taking the perspective of another." I take another's perspective toward me and internalize it, so that, for example, my mother's expectation that I clean my room becomes my own expectation of myself. As I develop, I come across others with their own perspectives on how I should behave. My teachers expect me to raise my hand before talking, so I internalize that expectation, and so on, until, as I discussed earlier, I have internalized sometimes conflicting roles and have a complex set of norms to follow. The sociological supposition here is that subjects absorb others' perspectives, but Habermas does not explain *who* it is that is doing this. At this stage in the development of an ego, supposedly, no "I" exists. So then *who* internalizes? Unless Habermas is smuggling in some sort of anterior subjectivity that could dialectically accomplish this feat, this developmental model of individuation through socialization does not hold up.

Along the same lines, Habermas claims that as socialization progresses we come to a point in which we detach ourselves from our social roles in order to choose autonomously. This claim rests upon the psychological research of Jean Piaget and Lawrence Kohlberg. In his six stages of moral development, Kohlberg argued that boys seem to develop their moral capacities better than girls (Kohlberg 1981). Yet, as Carol Gilligan has documented, Kohlberg's moral ideal was of the ability to act according to rules, not inclinations, again a Kantian moral ideal (Gilligan 1982, 173). Gilligan's now famous research finds that girls are better at making decisions that take into account context, relationships, and contingencies. Girls generally fail the deontological imperative of following duty for duty's sake. Habermas has written about this debate: he finds that Gilligan's research is appropriate at the conventional stage (when we're deciding about the good) but that Kohlberg's is superior for postconventional morality, when matters of justice are at stake (Habermas 1990a, 172–87). Habermas privileges the right over the good, in keeping with his postconventional ideal of universality. Accordingly, he opts for Kohlberg's account over Gilligan's. Yet Habermas's choice begs the question of whether the postconventional ideal of universality is indeed better than supposedly conventional morality—and of whether the right ought to precede the good.

Moreover, it is not clear that choosing, in the context of having conflicting imperatives, requires stepping away from our own particularities. We might instead try to find the best compromise or accommodation. As a matter of fact, many women are in this position—think of the "Supermom" or anyone who has to handle the many demands of parenthood, a household, and a career. It seems to me that, when roles conflict, such people make choices by *weighing* the relative importance and priority of the demands, not by detaching themselves from their roles. To detach oneself would be to disencumber oneself from any felt obligations and then to choose—disinterestedly, dispassionately, and "objectively"—what demand to tackle next. To weigh, however, would mean to continue feeling all the competing obligations and demands but to negotiate through these, to decide which obligations can be temporarily set aside and which cannot. Habermas's claim that people detach themselves from their particularities rests on the ideal of autonomy, making it *better* to be objective and disinterested than to have any particular interests. But as I am suggesting, this is not the only alternative. One can be interested and still make sound choices.[10]

Similarly, Habermas contends that the impetus for individuation is that a self seeks recognition from more than one's own clan—that we *desire* to move from the clan to an unlimited communication community. This desire would impel the movement toward individuation, yet Habermas (unlike psychoanalytic theorists) never offers an account of the origins of this desire.

Another juncture to attend to is his use of linguistics and the linguistic turn. Habermas claims that subjects "come with" the capacity to use language fluently and transparently. He writes: "Subjects capable of speaking and acting who . . . come to an understanding with each other about something in the world, relate to the medium of their language both autonomously and dependently: they can make use of grammatical rule-systems, which make their practices possible in the first place, for their own purposes as well. Both moments are equiprimordial" (Habermas 1992a, 43).

---

[10] Part III of this book addresses this topic in more detail. See especially Chapter 7.

That, supposedly, subjects relate to language autonomously and "can make use of grammatical rule-systems" are claims based upon Chomsky's theory of generative grammar.[11] But I should note that even Noam Chomsky recognizes that his theory is only an inference to the best explanation. There could be another equally plausible, or more plausible, explanation. Having seen children unerringly pick out ungrammatical sentences, we might infer that this means that we human beings have a "grammatical rule-system" hardwired into us. But this is only an inference, one that could be trumped by a better explanation. A good empiricist would be open to there being better explanations, but Habermas seems to accept as a given, as a fact, that subjects "make use of grammatical rule-systems." But Habermas is decidedly not interested in being a good empiricist. In his essay "Philosophy as Stand-In and Interpreter," he advocates "a type of approach that marks the beginning of new research traditions" (Habermas 1990a, 15). This would be "a blend of philosophy and science" such as we find in Marxism, psychoanalysis, as well as in the theories of "Durkheim, Mead, Max Weber, Piaget, and Chomsky" (14–15). In their respective fields, all "reconstructive sciences" (which attempt to explain "know-how"),[12] these theorists begin with their "intuitive knowledge of competent subjects" and seek to "ex-

[11] In this particular passage Habermas does not cite Chomsky, but in several other places he indicates that he takes Chomsky's theory to be correct. In a 1981 interview, he said, "It is certainly true that in the 1960s and 1970s, and this annoys the empiricist crowd, I played a large role in bringing certain theoretical methodologies into discussion, which others still had to work through—such as Wittgenstein, Piaget, Chomsky, Kohlberg, Searle, and so on. The difference is only that I still hold on to what I have learned from all of them, even when academic fashion has moved on" (Habermas 1986, 128). In a 1984 interview, he said of his work in the 1960s, "I was fascinated both by Chomsky's programme for a general theory of grammar, and by Austinian speech-act theory, as systematized by Searle. All this suggested the idea of a universal pragmatics" (Habermas 1986, 149). Also see Habermas 1986, 253–24.

[12] See Habermas's 1976 essay "What Is Universal Pragmatics?" published in Habermas 1979, especially 14–20. Habermas cites Chomsky's generative grammar as an example of a reconstructive science, that is, one interested in explicating how speakers know (know-how) and not just studying linguistic competence empirically (know-that). Even here, though, Habermas does not completely defend Chomsky's linguistic theory; in fact, he points out problems with it, namely the correlation it presumes between "the mental grammar that underlies the psychologically identifiable production of language and the corresponding processes of understanding" (20). It is striking that two decades later Habermas seems to adopt Chomsky's theory with few if any hesitations.

plain the presumably universal bases of rational experience and judgment, as well as of action and linguistic communication" (15–16). Note that, for Habermas, Chomsky and other reconstructive scientists use their *intuition* to try to locate "universal bases." (We are left to wonder why we should presume that there are any universal bases at all.) This might be a productive research approach, perhaps, but it is difficult to see how it yields anything like a defense of generative grammar, much less a reason to take as given that subjects "make use of grammatical rule-systems."

Habermas relies on this Chomskian structuralism—and it is widely recognized to be a structuralism—without citing it explicitly here. This omission may be a matter of convenience, because elsewhere in *Postmetaphysical Thinking* he denounces semiotics for being a structuralism: "Structuralism," he writes, "gets caught in the snare of abstractive fallacies." Habermas describes a semiotics that few, if anyone, would recognize. Rather, this passage could delineate a Chomskian structuralism: "By elevating anonymous forms of language to a transcendental status, [structuralism] downgrades the subjects and their speech to something merely accidental. How the subjects speak and what they do is supposed to be explained by the underlying system of rules" (Habermas 1992a, 47).

Now, I've never noticed any "rules" in semiotics, but there certainly are grammatical "rules" in generative grammar, but rules we can only infer. So the final words that Habermas says of semiotics could better apply to generative grammar: "Whoever would nonetheless like to continue to pay them their due under structuralist premises must transfer everything that is individual and innovative into a prelinguistic sphere that is accessible only through intuition" (47). If this is the case for structuralism as a whole then it would also apply to Habermas's acceptance of generative grammar. That would mean that his claims that speaking subjects "relate to the medium of their language ... autonomously" and "can [easily] make use of grammatical rule-systems" are claims accessible only through intuition.

According to the theory of generative grammar, linguistic competence is innate. This presents a conflict with Habermas's claim that there is no spontaneous ego, that the self is derived linguistically and intersubjectively. There seems to be a circularity in Habermas's reliance on both Mead and Chomsky, for who is the "self" with the innate capacity to use language prior to individuation? In a sense, I have

posed the same question to Mead: who is there in advance of the relation to take the perspective of the other? At every step, in trying to
get away from a Hegelian philosophy of consciousness, around every
corner, we come face to face with a Hegelian problematic. The linguistic turn does not dissolve the problem of how subjectivity arises.

Note that Habermas takes language to be something like a fact, a
tool we use but do not modify or transform. For Habermas, speaking
subjects "always find themselves already in a linguistically structured and disclosed world; they live off of grammatically projected interconnections of meaning. To this extent, *language sets itself off
from the speaking subjects* as something *antecedent and objective,*
as the *structure* that forges conditions of possibility" (Habermas
1992a, 43, emphasis added).

Certainly we are born into a language, so I agree that we find ourselves "already in a linguistically structured and disclosed world."
But to say that language "sets itself off" from speaking subjects overlooks and denies the way in which speaking subjects transform language as they use it. One doesn't need to be a philosopher to know
that languages are fluid and dynamic. Though we may be born into a
house of language, as soon as we begin speaking we begin to leave our
own trace. The house of language changes with every generation that
passes through it, remodeling, forming new meanings, and inverting
old ones. Habermas wants the power of language to move in one direction, but as Foucault points out, power is multidirectional, a web
in which origins elude us.[13] Language offers multiple ways of making
meaning, and, as Kristeva shows, speaking subjects use language to
signify many fields simultaneously, never univocally or transparently. As Joel Whitebook writes, "Because of the thrust of his linguistic approach, [Habermas] fails to capture the sense of an 'inner foreign
territory' which is a hallmark of Freudian thought; in principle [for
Habermas], everything is transparent" (Whitebook 1985, 157).

So, in his use of both developmental psychology and linguistics,
Habermas's background suppositions have colored his choices, allowing him to develop a theory of subjectivity that is ready and willing to
engage in communicative action. So long as his suppositions remain
in the background and not on the table, we cannot completely see
why he uses Kohlberg rather than Gilligan and generative grammar
rather than semiotics.

---

[13] See the introduction to Foucault 1972.

The Wake of Metaphysics

In *Postmetaphysical Thinking,* Habermas claims to have success-fully gotten out of metaphysical thinking and solved the riddle of subjectivity; yet in the process, perhaps unwittingly, he thinks meta-physically. In this he joins the ranks of others who have proclaimed the end of metaphysics, only to be—if Derrida is right—metaphysi-cians themselves: Nietzsche (perhaps) and Heidegger, company that Habermas would not want to keep. Were he able to acknowledge Der-rida's claim that, for all our desire to escape metaphysics, we never can, then he could see the dilemma. As Derrida notes in "The Ends of Man," "the 'logic' of every relation to the outside is very complex and surprising. It is precisely the force and the efficiency of the [meta-physical] system that regularly change transgressions into 'false ex-its'" (Derrida 1982, 135). In other words, our attempts to get out of metaphysics are stymied at every step. This does not mean that we should not try, for metaphysical thinking does tend to totalize every-thing into a system. Yet no system can or should enclose everything within it.

In trying to get out of metaphysics, Derrida notes, one has two choices, neither of which is sufficient: (1) "to attempt an exit and a deconstruction without changing terrain"—that is, to try to decon-struct a field from within—or (2) "to decide to change terrain, in a discontinuous and irruptive fashion, by brutally placing oneself out-side, and by affirming an absolute break and difference" (Derrida 1982, 135). Habermas tries to take the latter route, by "changing ter-rain" from what he calls the philosophy of consciousness to his the-ory of communicative action. But, as Derrida notes, this strategy of changing terrain still leads one to inhabit "more naively and more strictly than ever the inside one declares one has deserted" (Derrida 1982, 135). Rather than working "in the wake" of metaphysics, as he thinks he is, Habermas is still working within it, but with the blind-ers that come from having thought he'd escaped.

The "Spontaneous I": Subjectivity as Substance

Now I turn to one other point that plagues Habermas's theory of subjectivity: an implicit reliance on substance ontology. This comes through in his account of the intersubjective and communicative de-velopment of subjectivity. On the one hand he is arguing that there is no core self or individuation prior to socialization; yet on the other hand he occasionally lapses into discussing some kind of anteriority. For example, he writes, in developing subjectivity there must be some prior self-relation, prior even to: "the actor [who] comes upon himself as a social object in communication," encountering "himself as the alter ego of his alter ego" (Habermas 1992a, 172).

> As Mead explains it, the actor comes upon himself as a social object in communicative action when he orients himself to the current I-you re-lationship. . . . In the first person of his performative attitude, the actor encounters himself as a second person. In this way there arises an en-tirely different "me." Even this "me" is not, however, identical with the spontaneously acting "I," which now, as before, withdraws from every direct experience; but the "me" that is accessible in the perfor-mative attitude *does* present itself as the exact memory of a sponta-neous state of the "I." (Habermas 1992a, 172)

This self is not the same as the other person's reaction. "The self that is given for me through the mediation of the gaze of the other upon me is the 'memory image' of my ego, such as it has just acted in the sight of an alter ego and face to face with it" (172). Where or how, Habermas asks, does this originary self-consciousness arise? (Note the multiple levels of subjectivity presupposed here: the spontaneous "I," originary self-consciousness, and true individuation.)

John Dewey locates this originary self-consciousness in the mo-ment when an actor faces a problem, for then he must reconstruct a collapsed interpretation of the situation (Habermas 1992a, 174). But this does not explain how an actor "catches sight of himself," so Mead gives up on Dewey's model. Or, rather, he expands the model from that of an individual actor to that of several actors who are at-tending to a problem, whereby they might solve the problem and also influence one another's actions.

But there is still the problem of how self-relation arises in the first place, before this interaction (of several people tending to a problem). Mead and Habermas consider the prelinguistic level of self-relation as the process of one actor vocally reacting to the behavior of the other, thereby affecting both simultaneously. "The actor takes the perspective toward himself of another participant in interaction and becomes viable to himself as a social object only when he adopts as his own the objective meaning of his vocal gesture, which stimulates both sides equally" (Habermas 1992a, 177). In other words, I become related to myself by adopting the perspective of another toward me in the course of some action that misfires. Consider an example of an infant pulling her mother's hair, prompting her mother to cry out in pain, and then the infant interpreting the cry as "that hurt." According to Habermas, in such an instant the infant first sees itself through the perspective of the mother, thanks to the mother's nonlinguistic communication. The infant becomes aware of herself through the objective meaning of the other's vocal gesture.

> With this self-relation, the actor doubles himself in the instance of a "me," which follows the performative "I" as a shadow. . . . The self of self-consciousness is not the spontaneously acting "I"; the latter is given only in the refraction of the symbolically captured meaning that it took on for its interaction partner "a second ago" in the role of the alter ego. (Habermas 1992a, 177)

So, Habermas argues, even "original self-consciousness is not a phenomenon inherent in the subject but one that is communicatively generated" (177). With this move, Habermas rejects the notion of the spontaneous I or of any antecedent ego trying to posit itself. With this, he says, we get beyond the philosophy of the subject and enter a philosophy of intersubjectively and communicatively derived self-consciousness. Or so it seems.

The Self and the Ego

But as we've seen, even in Habermas's attempt to establish that it is self-control, not self-consciousness, that we are seeking, the anterior self acting spontaneously still slips in. That is, for Habermas, autonomous subjectivity is not purely a fiction—a construction; there is some independently spontaneous self there in advance. In psychoanalytic terms, this "self" is the ego. Various theorists take differing views of the development of the ego. Marcuse and Adorno subscribed to a libidinal model of ego development, where the ego was an effect of the id, of drives and energy. (Lacan would adopt a similar position.) Another approach, that of ego psychology, downplays the role of the id in favor of a model in which the ego develops of its own accord. "The controversy between id psychology and ego psychology," Joel Whitebook writes, "centers on the amount of genetic and functional independence that ought to be ascribed to the ego. The drive theorists maintain that the ego has no independent sources of its own. It is simply the byproduct of the conflict between external reality . . . and the instinctual makeup of the individual" (Whitebook 1985, 142). Whitebook describes ego psychology as follows:

> The ego psychologists . . . argued that, rather than the ego growing out of the id, both psychic institutions develop out of a prior undifferentiated phase. But, more importantly, they maintained that there is an independent source or inborn *Anlage* for ego development. Somewhere in the course of human evolution the species acquired the capacity for individual ego development so that each newborn is not faced with the task of developing an ego from scratch. (143)

In which camp is Habermas? For various reasons, Habermas has tried to overcome the dichotomy between inner and outer nature by adopting a psychological model of ego development à la Piaget and Kohlberg.[14] In this approach, the task is to see how the ego develops over a series of stages. Yet even though Habermas never embraces ego psychology per se, developmental psychology is quite compatible with it. Just because the ego *develops* does not mean that it arose *ex nihilo*. It could very well develop from some original or primary seed of sorts. Note Whitebook's discussion of two levels of autonomy of the ego in ego psychology:

> Hartmann [a founder of ego psychology] called the functions that correspond to these innate capacities [for individual ego development], such as mobility, perception etc., primary autonomous ego functions. They constitute the minimal core functions—the transcendental preconditions, if you will—that organize human experience and activity, and make higher-level achievements possible. The primary functions, that is, can become the basis for establishing secondary autonomous ego functions, such as the capacity to work. It is usually these latter, secondary capacities that we have in mind when we speak of autonomy as a life achievement. (143)

Habermas also describes autonomy as an achievement. Using the work of Kohlberg, notably his stages of the development of moral

---

[14] See "Moral Development and Ego Identity," in Habermas 1979, 69–94; and Whitebook 1985.

consciousness—of the ego's moral consciousness, that is, the super-ego—and the work of Mead on individuation through socialization, Habermas would have us believe that the ego is purely a historical and contingent development, that it arises *ex nihilo*. But insofar as developmental psychology builds upon ego psychology (and Kohlberg does pay his debts there) it also presupposes some "primary autonomous ego functions" (Kohlberg 1987, 331–32).

I have been arguing that, despite his claims to have moved beyond "the philosophy of the subject" and to adopt a "postmetaphysical" approach, Habermas is still beholden to a view of the self or the ego, however unformed, that exists prior to development. It is this supposition that helps make possible a view of subjectivity that is so in keeping with Enlightenment ideals. As I've noted, switching terrain by trying to get out of metaphysics will not rid us of this notion of anterior subjectivity. It may be an inescapable function of our thinking, if not of our "reality." Kant noted this as a paralogism of pure reason: that the soul is a substance that endures is something which we can never prove through pure reason; but we cannot but believe it in order to act. Perhaps this is the same puzzle we face now. To examine this puzzle, I move to some metaphysical themes.

The Myth of Substance

What is the nature of substance, this nature we cannot help—however wrongly—but attribute to soul or mind? According to Aristotle and later to Leibniz, the attributes of substance include independence, subjecthood, form, and independent spontaneity. This "myth of substance," as Johanna Seibt calls it, had its first modern formulation in the seventeenth century, when philosophers of science were trying to explain motion. What, they wondered, sets everything in motion? Some thought God gave an initial push to everything and thus set the universe in motion. Others, namely the Occasionalists, thought that God had a hand in every motion, being the impetus behind every movement. Leibniz took issue with both these views. He denied that the source of this dynamism could be something outside matter, not even God. No, the source of dynamism and change needed to be within substance. Borrowing from Aristotle, he attributed the dynamism of a substance to its form, that is, its entelechy or internal principle of change. This form or principle is like a script.

According to Leibniz, there are many possible worlds, each with a set of monads who each have their own internal principles of change. Some possible worlds are more harmonious than others, in that in the best possible world the principles of change of the various monads mesh most completely and toward the best end. God chose the best of all these possible worlds and released it, as one might release a toy with its spring wound. The monads then act of their own internal principle or volition, each according to its own unique perspective, so that each monad is different from the others. With this scenario, Leibniz explains how monads or substances are dynamic without having recourse to a God "pushing" every act along. Thus, monads, as substances have their own spontaneity and entelechy, which makes their actions "their own" and not the result of some other mover's action or will. I'll leave aside the question of whether or not these monads are free; it is a matter of interpretation whether their actions are determined or not, insofar as, for Leibniz, their entelechy came from God. Nonetheless, we can say that, at least in a compatibilist sense, these substances are free insofar as they act of their own (internal) accord.

This is one manifestation of the myth of substance, which, from Aristotle through Leibniz to the present, has silently supported all sorts of ontological speculations. It is a myth so deeply embedded that to think otherwise is difficult. Even though ontologists today generally avoid the term *substance*, their background suppositions are laden with it. Describing a current ontological debate, Johanna Seibt writes:

> The fact that the historical debate about existence in time has focused almost entirely on the persistence of things and persons can be traced to the historical predominance of substance metaphysics. The notion of substance shows considerable historical variation, but there is one definitional trait which figures prominently in most of the historical accounts of substance, as well as in contemporary usages of the phrase 'the traditional notion of substance'. This is the requirement that substances persist through time and change—that they are "numerically one and the same . . . [yet] able to receive contraries." (Seibt 1997, 147)

With the myth of substance as the "deep background" of much of philosophy, entire fields of inquiry arise, including the field of inquiry into subjectivity or self-identity. The question "How does self become conscious of itself?" arises precisely because of this myth:

because the self is seen, in an Aristotelian way, as a substance. Aristotle notes that "primary substances are most properly called substances in virtue of the fact that they are the entities which underlie everything else, and that everything else is either predicated of them or present in them" (1941; *Categories* 2b 15–18).

Habermas's entire manner of posing the question of individuation seems to suppose a substance ontology. Even in critiquing the philosophy of consciousness, he betrays this assumption: "using the concepts of the philosophy of the subject, Fichte can only define individuality as the restriction of oneself, as renunciation of the possibility of realizing one's own freedom—not as the productive cultivation of one's own essential powers" (Habermas 1992a, 160). Note that Habermas is critical of Fichte's goal of restricting "one's own freedom" but takes it as a given that one has "essential powers" waiting to be cultivated.

The myth of substance is also betrayed in Habermas's theory of communicative action. As Sylviane Agacinski writes:

> If Habermas's theory of the *communicative act*, for example, asserts the irreducibility of communication, it does not, for all that, break with a theory of the subject, that is, of an individual or communal thinking that coincides with itself. Thus Habermas writes in his "Preliminary Observations" to the *Theory of Communicative Action* that the discourse of argumentation allows interlocutors to "overcome their merely subjective views" and to come together in a "mutuality of rationally motivated convictions." However, this approach to communication still presumes "*initial* subjective conceptions" (my emphasis), and thus presumes an original atomization of subjects that are still isolated or capable of being isolated (this would mean every subject for itself, unshared and undivided: this would mean individuals). One would, then, have to attribute these presumed initial "subjective conceptions" to subjects that would *not yet* have communicated, and, even, that would not yet have spoken; for if this subjectivity speaks, it is divided, different from itself, and its initial plenitude or adequacy is already shared. (Agacinski 1991, 13)

So we are left to wonder how and in what form this freedom, this spontaneous "I," preexists subjectivity. The presupposition seems to be one of substance ontology, that self-consciousness or fully self-aware agency is an attribute which can be predicated of the substance

subjectivity, of that "originary self-consciousness" or "primary autonomous ego functions" which make experiential statements
possible.

Dialectical Subjectivity

In the history of philosophy we can sketch out roughly three ontological positions: (1) the rationalist and Platonic view that what is
real is unchanging; (2) the Aristotelian and Thomist view that act and
potency are central ontological matters; (3) the process ontological
view that events, processes, and states are primary (Heraclitus, the
Stoics, Hegel, Henri Bergson, Whitehead). The first view considers
change to be something that happens to substance, but believes that
substance has its own unity and continuity nonetheless. The second
view holds that change is a result of something intrinsic to substance, an internal principle of change (Aristotle's and Leibniz's entelechy). The third view holds that change is what there is, and that
unity is possible, but always secondary to change.[15]
While he tries to change terrain, away from a philosophy or metaphysics of consciousness, at times Habermas slips into describing
some anterior subjectivity as one's "own" spontaneous activity, saying, that is, that freedom is always already there. In this he falls into
the Aristotelian and Leibnizian view that substance has its own
spontaneous energy—and that the self is a substance. Yet at the same
time he wants to see the self as derived intersubjectively and communicatively. In this it would be useful to bring in a Levinasian theory, an attempt which (despite Derrida's disagreement) tries to place
the ethical relation prior to ontology. In a Levinasian understanding,
subjectivity is an effect of being called by an Other, of being indebted
to and responsible for the Other: the trade-off or payment for subjectivity. There is no subjectivity before this relationship. Subjectivity is
not something that happens to some primordial substance. It is a process, state, or event. Subjectivity results from a dynamic process. A
process ontological understanding of subjectivity accounts for the
provisional, changeable, and vulnerable quality of subjectivity.
It is in my encounters with others that my subjectivity *arises in
the first place*—not, as Habermas argues, because I address a general-

---

[15] For an overview of process philosophy, see Rescher 1996.

ized other and thus become individuated, but because an ethical obligation precedes an ontological construction of self.

We can start to see more clearly two different theories of individuation or coming-to-subjectivity. One is that there is some individuation thanks to something *intrinsic* (even if it is called forth intersubjectively through language). For Habermas, as I interpret his silence on prelinguistic inner nature,[16] the intrinsic feature is my spontaneous activity of choosing and willing, my freedom and self-agency, granted that it occurs in a contingent history (and is only *recognized* intersubjectively). Another view is that subjectivity occurs through our relations in a life history and a language. The difference between the two is whether there can be something in subjectivity apart from (or were it not for) its relations.

Can we adopt one terrain over the other, whether substance or process? We may need to take a Hegelian course, seeing these options as dialectically interacting. Substance is a myth that suffuses our thinking and ways of talking, yet without process we cannot fathom how subjectivity comes into being. It is a process of being called, as both Fichte and Levinas knew, called to respond, to account, to act. Were it not for you, there would be no me to arise. Yet even you have some soul or substance in advance of mine. Again, inescapable, but a capable dialectic. I will continue to visit these themes in the following chapters.

---

[16] See Whitebook 1985.

2 Subjects-in-Process

Now I turn to another account of subjectivity, one that is similar to Habermas's in many ways: it draws on Hegel as well as Freud; it understands the self as constituted through language and through social interaction; it is concerned with how the subject comes to be an effective agent in a social world steered by linguistic communication; and it is very much part of the continental tradition of philosophy. But beyond these similarities, Julia Kristeva's philosophy is very much *une étrangère* to Jürgen Habermas's, as strange as contemporary French philosophy is to German critical theory. The two sets of approaches, styles, and concerns are so dissimilar that the names Habermas and Kristeva are hardly ever uttered in the same breath. His Germanic concern with reason is alien to her focus on the fluidity and multiplicity of our ways of making meaning. Yet despite the divergence, the two have been working on similar projects. In the only other account I have found comparing them, Allison Weir notes the similarity of their theories: "Both Habermas and Kristeva propose models of individuation as a capacity for participation in a social world, and both presuppose that this capacity depends on a capacity for mutual understanding through the internalization of linguistic and social norms" (Weir 1995, 269). Weir's language of "social norms" and "individuation" is more suited for Habermas than Kristeva; but it is true that we can read Kristeva as concerned with coming to be a speaking subject in a world with others, using a language that helps us regulate and act in the world, even as our heterogeneous drives threaten to disrupt the symbolic order. This chapter provides such a reading.

Kristeva's Trajectory

In her autobiographical essay "My Memory's Hyperbole," Julia Kristeva provides a historical account of how her work arose. She writes her autobiography as a collective odyssey, using the first person plural.

> To write the autobiography of this "we" is surely a paradox that combines the passion for truth of the "I" with the absolute logical necessity of being able to share this truth only in part. To share it, first of all, between "us," so that this "we" survives. To share it also with you, so that an account, a report, a scheme remains (autobiography is a narration), rather than have speech fall into the fervor of dreams or poetry. Being hyperbolic, this "we" will retain from the problem ridden paths of "I"'s only the densest image, the most schematic, the one closest to a cliché. (Kristeva 1984b, 262)

Having just arrived in the "city of lights" from her home in Bulgaria, Kristeva attended the Christmas '65 midnight mass in Notre Dame. Immediately she sensed that its citizens wanted Paris to move out of its "pleasant archaicness" and become like the East European countries, which they criticized "in fascinated, hushed tones" (263). Kristeva had left Bulgaria, where she had been steeped in a francophile and francophone education, for Paris, just in time to take part in a movement that sent tremors through the Western world. Not only was Paris trying to transform itself; its students, intellectuals, and workers helped move all the West away from its postwar naiveté and formalism and toward a rupture with order, monologic meaning, and certitude. Intellectually, Kristeva and her circle (which included the *Tel Quel* group, Lucien Goldmann, Roland Barthes, and Philippe Sollers) had been trained in formalism, whether linguistic or economic, and now they were looking for new political currents. These came readily. In her autobiographical essay, she writes:

> I see the written trace of . . . change in the austere paring down of the *nouveau roman*, in its obsession with precision and details, for example, as well as the whole intellectual trend centered on the study of

forms. This formalism was the purging of that subjective or rhetorical
edema that our parents had set up to protect themselves against the
devastating suffering of wars, or that they had used to construct their
martyrdom. (262–63)

Julia Kristeva arrived in Paris just two and a half years before May
'68—when, for a moment, it seemed that students and working
people might actually change the course of history. Alluding to this
moment, Fredric Jameson writes: "The simplest yet most universal
formulation surely remains the widely shared feeling that in the 60s,
for a time, everything was possible; that this period, in other words,
was a moment of a universal liberation, a global unbinding of energies" (Jameson 1988, 207). With the demonstrations and awakening
of political consciousness taking place in the city and around the
world it seemed that "the revolution" might finally come. Students
and workers took to the streets. The '60s French radicals who called
themselves "Situationists" distributed pamphlets calling on the bu-
reaucrats in both the United States and the Soviet Union to "quake in
their boots." *We are the soviets*, they said. But in Paris in 1968—as in
the rest of the world—the revolutionary moment came and went,
without any discernible concrete effect. Modernity's promise for the
future seemed conclusively dashed. After '68, it seemed, there could
be no more faith that humankind could author its own freedom. The
literary critics were already pronouncing the death of the author, and
the philosophers were not far behind.

But that is only one way of looking at the story. Another is that this
moment in history fueled a new dynamic. As Kristeva writes,

Fundamentally, May '68, despite its romantic airs, functioned like the
fever of this process. An *analytic* process (in the etymological sense of
the term, that is, dissolving, abrasive, lucid), which leads us to a modernity that is, of course mobile, eccentric, and unpredictable, but that
breaks with the preceding years and that, or so it seems, must leave its
mark on the end of our century. (Kristeva 1984b, 263)

When she writes of "a modernity" that is "mobile, eccentric, and unpredictable," she describes what some term "postmodernity."

Fredric Jameson, among others, joins her in this assessment. He too
notes a "break" with the preceding years, a shift from modernism

with all its hopes and aspirations to postmodernism with all its disjunctures, pastiche, and unpredictability.

> . . . what emerges from the practice of theory—and this was most dramatic and visible during the high point of Althusserianism itself in 1967–68—is a violent and obsessive return to ideological critique in the new form of a perpetual guerrilla war among the material signifiers of textual formulations. With the transformation of philosophy into a material practice, however, we touch on a development that cannot fully be appreciated until it is replaced in the context of a general mutation of culture throughout this period, a context in which "theory" will come to be grasped as a specific (or semi-autonomous) form of what must be called postmodernism generally. (Jameson 1988, 194)

Kristeva writes that any "account of the intellectual path of this period should primarily be an account of change—and for some it was an explosion—of bodies, of discourses, of ways of being": "A sexuality freed from moral constraints, an image of the body no longer merely captured in a fine narcissistic surface but vaporized and sonorized with the help of drugs or rock or pop music if need be . . ." (Kristeva 1984b, 263). Jameson's and Kristeva's analyses of this historical shift differ. He claims that it is a result of the rupture between signifier and signified: "The break-up of the sign in mid-air determines a fall back into a now absolutely fragmented and anarchic social reality; the broken pieces of langues (the pure signifiers) now fall again into the world, as so many more pieces of material junk among all the other rusting and superannuated apparatuses and buildings that litter the commodity landscape and that strew the 'collage city', the 'delirious New York' of a postmodernist late capitalism in full crisis" (Jameson 1988, 201). She claims that it is a purging of the protective edema against the suffering of wars and a need to recognize the speaking subject as dynamic (no longer the author of its own intentions but its ever-evolving product). But both agree that this was a new moment (both use the term *break*) that we could interchangeably call *postmodern* or *poststructuralist*—not that the two terms had the same meaning, but that the two moments came simultaneously.[1]

---

[1] On the distinction between postmodern and poststructural, see the Introduction, note 12.

The Subject on Trial

Pulled along, or pushing along, this historic break, Kristeva, along
with many of the intellectuals of Paris, moved from formalism to
poststructuralism. During the early 1970s, she expanded her work in
structuralist semiotics to include a poststructuralist approach to psychoanalysis and the speaking subject. As she has said, she did not
abandon her concern for the situated and material aspects of life; but
she did see the need to deal with the dynamic processes through
which subjectivity is constituted. In the view of subjectivity that
Kristeva developed during this poststructuralist period, to put it
briefly, she lays bare the myth of the unitary, autonomous individual
of modernity. She argues that even though we tell ourselves we are
whole, we are in many respects strangers to ourselves (Kristeva 1991).
In effect, we are, as Freud noted, split subjects, split between our conscious and our unconscious selves.

Kristeva has been quoted as saying, "Je suis une freudienne,"
which some might take to be a rebuke against Freud's heir apparent
in France, Jacques Lacan, or as a denial that her psychoanalytic theory shares any of Lacan's permutations. But I think this would be
mistaken, for in France to be a "freudienne" is to be someone interested in psychoanalysis. And almost by definition in France to be interested in psychoanalysis is to be steeped in Lacan, even if, as in
Kristeva's case, one claims not to be a Lacanian.[2] To understand Kristeva's psychoanalytic theory, it is important to know how Lacan
adapted Freudian psychoanalytic theory.

Anyone schooled in American psychoanalytic theory would barely
recognize French psychoanalytic theory, and vice versa. This is
largely a result of Jacques Lacan's reading of Freud, which differs dra-
matically from American readings. The two "Freudianisms" can be

---

[2] In correspondence with the author (April 7, 1999), Jennifer Hansen relates a conversation she had with Kristeva in which Kristeva said that unlike Irigaray she was
not a Lacanian. Hansen takes this to mean literally that Kristeva does not subscribe
to any version of Lacan's theory. Yet, as Lisa Walsh has observed in conversations
with the author, Kristeva may have been alluding to the fact that she is not a member of the Lacanian school, "L'école de la cause freudienne," to which Irigaray had belonged (until she was thrown out for writing *Speculum*.) As Walsh notes, Lacan's influence on Kristeva and the rest of the French psychoanalytic community is
pervasive. Also, any Lacanian considers himself a Freudian. Moreover, Kristeva explicitly engages Lacan's work and terms, namely the symbolic and the mirror stage.

traced back to Freud's own work, which was of two minds, so to speak, about subjectivity. The bulk of Freud's work posited what is often called the narcissistic ego, the ego as an effect of unconscious libidinal drives. The ego is nothing more than the transitory shape of these drives' cathexes, or investments, in some desired object, whether one's own image or the image of an other. The narcissistic model, says Elizabeth Grosz, is the one to which Lacan is heir. Late in his career, Freud offered another model: the tripartite model of id, ego, and superego. Although one can argue that Freud himself never solidified this tripartite model to the extent of positing any kind of masterly ego, many of his successors have seen the goal of psychoanalysis to be to heal and strengthen the ego, to make it a master of both the id and the superego, a negotiator between inner and outer reality. Sherry Turkle writes: "In Freud's later writings, the ego emerges as that agency which is turned out toward reality, and theorists who followed him, among them and perhaps most importantly his daughter, began to focus their attention on its vicissitudes. To them, the ego seemed almost a psychic hero as it battled off id and superego at the same time that it tried to cope with the world everyday" (Turkle 1981, 52). This model produces a notion of the realist ego and gave rise to American ego psychology, which later branched off into object relations theory.

Those working in ego psychology tend to see psychoanalysis as a science and a cure. Lacan always insisted that the ego was illusory and trying to "cure" it a misbegotten adventure. For example, he argues, the notion of reality central to the theory of the realist ego is wrong. Speaking of ego psychology's understanding of reality, Lacan writes.

> One understands that to prop up so obviously precarious a conception certain individuals on the other side of the Atlantic should have felt the need to introduce into it some stable value, some standard of the measure of the real: this turns out to be the autonomous ego. This is the supposedly organized ensemble of the most disparate functions that lend their support to the subject's feeling of innateness. It is regarded as autonomous because it appears to be sheltered from the conflicts of the person. (Lacan 1977, 230–31)

For Lacan, psychoanalysis was geared not to a spurious autonomous ego but to the unconscious; psychoanalysis was not a science but rather a relationship between analyst and analysand in which the two attempt to interpret the language of the unconscious.

Unlike the ego psychologists, who adopted Freud's realist model of the ego, Lacan developed Freud's earlier, narcissistic model. Freud sketched "the bare outlines of an account of the genesis of the ego by linking it to the operations of infantile or primary narcissism," writes Grosz. "The phenomenon of narcissism, whereby the ego is able to take itself as its own libidinal object, poses a problem for the realist view; in so far as the latter relies on sharp cleavage between ego-instincts and sexual instincts, this makes it difficult to explain how the ego is able to take a part of itself as a sexual object, how it is simultaneously subject and object" (Grosz 1989, 28).

One difference between Habermas's and Kristeva's work results from their respective uses of psychoanalytic theory. As I noted in the last chapter, Habermas uses developmental psychology, which is indebted to ego psychology and a modified version of the realist ego, whereas Kristeva uses much of Lacan's model, which draws from Freud's theory of the narcissistic ego. The former operates from a substance ontological point of view while the latter suggests a process ontological framework. The theories of the realist ego and ego psychology hold that the ego is a substance of sorts. A passage from Grosz lends support to my view that each school of thought rests on a different ontological framework:

> In the narcissistic view, narcissism must be distinguished from auto-eroticism: "A unity comparable to the ego cannot exist in the individual from the start; the ego has to be developed. . . . There must be something new added to auto-eroticism—a new psychical action in order to bring about narcissism" (Freud 1914a: 76–77). The realist ego is given, a 'psychic substance', whose outlines are biologically preformed. It is structured by impingements from external reality on the subject's sensory / neuronal structure which modify the 'surface' of the id through perception. By contrast, the narcissistic ego is an entirely fluid, mobile, amorphous series of identifications, internalizations of images / perceptions invested with libidinal cathexes. Where the realist ego stands out over and above the two combatants (reality and the id), the narcissistic ego cannot be readily separated either from its own internal processes (e.g. the flow of libido) or from external objects (with which it identifies and on which it may model itself). (Grosz 1989, 28–29)

In his essay on narcissism, Freud suggests a hydraulic model of the ego, where the "shape" of the ego is simply the shape and degree of its libidinal investments, whether in itself (ego-libido) or in others (object-libido). "The more of one is employed," Freud writes, "the more the other becomes depleted (Freud 1914a, 75). On this model, the ego "is not an entity, agency, or psychical content," writes Grosz, "for the ego is constituted by relations with others. . . . If the ego is based on relations between others and its own body then its 'plasticity' of form is easy to understand: the ego is dependent on various libidinal investments for its outline and features" (Grosz 1989, 29), much as, writes Freud, "the body of an amoeba is related to the pseudopodia which it puts out" (Freud 1914a, 75).

Because the narcissistic ego can take itself as its own object, Freud suggests that the ego is "split" as a subject and an object. The notion of a split subject makes its way through the works of Freud and Lacan. But somehow, Freud suggests, something "new" must occur which allows the subject to have some sense of unity, however tenuous and illusory.

Subjectivity

Following Freud, according to Grosz, Lacan sought to explain how an infant develops a sense of self, after it loses its experience of "the Real," the entirety it experiences with its mother and the whole of the external world, which Lacan explained as "the lack of a lack" or "pure plenitude."[3] The infant leaves the Real when it realizes the (m)other's separateness, when, perhaps, the breast is absent. "From this time on, lack, gap, splitting will be its mode of being. It will attempt to fill its (impossible, unfillable) lack. Its recognition of lack signals an ontological rift with nature or the Real. This gap will propel it into seeking an identificatory image of its own stability and permanence (the imaginary), and eventually language (the symbolic) by which it hopes to fill the lack" (Grosz 1989, 35). Grosz may be wrong about the infant ever having any experience of the Real. Regardless, the key point here is that at some time in the infant's development it experiences a lack, which drives it to seek a degree of fulfillment by identifying with some other image.

Most interpreters of Lacan will agree that it is in the imaginary

---

[3] Other interpreters of Lacan, such as Kelly Oliver, argue that "the real is never directly, and rarely even indirectly, part of our experience. The real is something like the body-in-itself. The mother-infant relationship is imaginary and is broken up by the entrance into the Symbolic" (Oliver in personal correspondence with the author). See also Oliver 1993, especially 37–39.

that the child experiences what Lacan calls the mirror stage of development, the time when an infant begins to recognize its image in a
mirror. (Lacan suggests, according to Grosz, that this mirror stage is
the new psychical occurrence that provides a sense of unity.) Here it
seeks to overcome the gap it experiences by identifying with the alien
image. The infant develops a sense of "I" by recognizing its image reflected back to it in a mirror (or mirror equivalent). The child identifies with this image, even though it is alien from itself, and mistak-
enly takes it to be itself. It finds in this image a sense of self-unity
that it does not actually experience in itself. "The other is thus not
simply an external, independent other, but the internal condition of
identity" (Grosz 1989, 50). This is the way in which an ego is constituted, at least in part, through a narcissistic process of identification.
Insofar as the ego is created by identification with alien images, the
sense of unity is purely fictive.

Knowing that its identifications are based on images and specular-
ization, the child in the imaginary, by identifying with alien objects,
develops a paranoid relation with others. It knows that its recognition of itself is also a miscognition. Given this scenario, subjectivity
can hardly be the unified experience that ego psychology suggests it
can be. Moreover, Lacan's work upsets the hold that the dream of
Cartesian subjectivity has had on modernity.

Sexuality

While in the realm of the imaginary, the child is caught up in its
imaginary identifications with others, primarily its mother. It is not
until the entrance of the father that this dyad is broken. Freud intro-
duces this rupture as the oedipus complex. For the male child, the entrance of the father threatens castration, a threat that will be met if
the boy does not renounce his incestuous love for his mother in exchange for the promise of one day having his own patriarchal relationship with a woman. The threat of castration accompanies an
awareness that the mother lacks a penis and so must have been cas-
trated. By internalizing the law of the father, the boy develops a
superego. For an infant girl, the oedipus complex is much more complicated (or, at any rate, Freud's explanation is rather inadequate).
The father's entrance reminds the girl that she lacks a penis, as does
her mother, and she accepts her subordinated role in a patriarchal
system. She turns from the mother to the father as her love object,

ensuring her heterosexuality, and holds to the promise that one day she will "have" a penis by giving birth to a boy. (Because it offers little reason for the girl to turn away from her mother, this explanation for the girl's passage through the oedipus complex is inadequate.)

Lacan respects the spirit of Freud's theory while taking it in a new direction. Avoiding the biologism and near determinism in Freud's account, Lacan interprets the oedipus complex in more metaphorical, linguistic, and social terms. The entrance of "the father" may be just a symbolic or imaginary father; it might be a priest or a schoolteacher or just the image of some patriarchal figure. The father disrupts the child's imaginary relationship with the mother first with the incest taboo and then by offering the promise of language, of articulating desire symbolically. Though the child might be forbidden an erotic relationship with the mother, language offers the possibility—though always deferred—of seeking fulfillment elsewhere. The child leaves the imaginary and enters what Lacan calls the symbolic. This move occurs through the oedipal complex and into the domain of language. The incest taboo is linguistic, after all. The law of the father forbids an erotic relationship with one who has the same name, and thereafter the child's immediate gratification from (mother's) milk, physical nourishment, and total attention is deferred—for language always stands in for the desired object. Thereafter, whatever the child, and hence the adult, demands is only a stand-in for the ultimate object of desire: the desire of the other, to be the other's desire.

Language

This brings us to another central aspect of Lacan's work: his linguistic interpretation of the unconscious. Lacan brought together Freud's psychoanalytic theory and Ferdinand de Saussure's structuralist theory of language in a novel account of the unconscious as structured like a language.

Let us return to the child who has left the imaginary for the symbolic. What awaits him as he tries to fulfill his desires through language? Unfortunately, nothing but frustration and deferment, for language is only a stand-in; it always signifies the absence of what is desired. Ultimately, desire is an effect of language and the unconscious; or, rather, we never know consciously what we desire, for the object of our desire is always hidden, repressed. But in analysis, the analyst and the analysand undertake a journey of interpretation, to use the analysand's discourse as clues to the language of the unconscious. Lacan uncovered some of the ways in which the unconscious was linguistically structured, for example, in the use of metaphor and metonymy. He linked Roman Jakobson's linguistic concepts of metaphor and metonymy with, respectively, Freud's notions of condensation and displacement. These operate in a signifying chain, with desire driving us to capture a meaning with another set of terms, word for word, as it were. This is an ongoing contiguity driven by desire. On this, Lacan writes:

"The creative spark of the metaphor does not spring from the presentation of two images, that is, of two signifiers equally actualized. It flashes between two signifiers one of which has taken the place of the other in the signifying chain, the occulted signifier remaining present through its (metonymic) connexions with the rest of the chain" (Lacan 1977, 157). While both Freud and Lacan thought that the unconscious was stimulated by visual images, Lacan argues that these are expressed by the unconscious verbally, primarily through the axes of metaphor and metonymy. Where Freud noted that dreams operate through displacement and condensation, Lacan noted that these operations are linguistically expressed via, respectively, metonymy and metaphor. As Kelly Oliver explains, "Condensation is the process by which one symbol or word is substituted for another, 'word *for* word', or metaphor."

> Condensation presents consciousness with a composite image that eliminates different features and compresses similar features. Displacement, on the other hand, is when one dream image substitutes for several unconscious thoughts, "word *to* word," or metonymy. Displacement presents consciousness with what appears to be an insignificant image onto which the unconscious wish transfers its intensity. (Oliver 1995, 166)

Moreover, "the discourse of the unconscious, devious and difficult to hear, cannot be articulated in its own voice. It relies on the discourses of consciousness through which it speaks," Grosz writes. "It is thus expressed most readily as interruption, eruption, silencing, betraying, or rendering conscious discourse ambiguous." Unconscious discourse "speaks only as interference, submerged in and subverting the intentions of conscious speech" (Grosz 1989, 114).

The goal of psychoanalysis, for Lacan, is not to strengthen the ego, as ego psychology would have it, but to decipher the language of the unconscious, to discover, perhaps, what is the object of the analysand's desire. Thus, Lacan will offer little to those aiming to bolster an Enlightenment conception of subjectivity; but he does provide a language for understanding the way subjectivity, as a monological and transparent aim, is always subverted. Yet this need not spell doom for those interested in the political and social aims of the Enlightenment, for Lacan offers us a way of thinking of subjects who are always in relation with each other and with the other within.

Kristeva borrows heavily from Lacan. Primarily she borrows the idea that the unconscious is structured like a language. Kristeva agrees that the symbolic order occurs post-oedipally when a child enters into language and social relations, though she will contend that there are nonsymbolic aspects of signification as well. She also agrees with Lacan that the development of subjectivity is coterminous with becoming a speaking subject. It is a process of an as-yet-unformed self engaging in language (which is also a process). In Chapter 1 I discussed Habermas's uncritical adoption of Chomsky's linguistics. Kristeva's linguistic theory is worlds away from Chomsky's and hence from Habermas's. She explicitly takes a much more critical stance toward Chomsky. In "The Ethics of Linguistics," the first chapter of *Desire in Language*, Kristeva rebuts the notion underlying Chomsky's generative grammar—that language should be studied as a system distinct from the speaking subject. For Kristeva, language is a process by which the speaking subject constitutes history and society. She argues for considering language "as articulation of a heterogeneous process, with the speaking subject leaving its imprint on the dialectic between the articulation and its process" (Kristeva 1980, 24). Instead of studying the rules of a system, the linguist would study the ethics of a signifying process. "Linguistic ethics . . . consists in following the resurgence of an 'I' coming back to rebuild an ephemeral structure in which the constituting struggle of language and society would be spelled out" (Kristeva 1980, 34). Moreover, Kristeva maintains that focusing on language as a system rather than as a process (at least in Chomsky's generative grammar) limits the study of language unnecessarily:

> It is hard to see how notions of elision, metaphor, metonymy, and parallelism could fit into the generative apparatus, including generative semantics, except perhaps under the rubric of "additional rules," necessit.ting a cutoff point in the specific generation of language. But the dramatic notion of language as a risky practice, allowing the speaking

animal to sense the rhythm of the body as well as the upheavals of history, seems tied to a notion of signifying process that contemporary theories do not confront. (Kristeva 1980, 34)

For Kristeva, the motivations or "agents" behind the entrée into language and subjectivity are the drives and processes that psychoanalytic theory describes.

Rather than holding to Lacan's imaginary / symbolic dichotomy, Kristeva maintains that the symbolic is really juxtaposed and complicated by a semiotic realm. There is a double aspect of our use of language: the drives and "pulsions" that seep out of the unconscious express themselves in what she calls the *semiotic*; whereas our more orderly, logical use of language she calls the *symbolic*. She writes, "I distinguish the semiotic (pre-sign and pre-language) from the symbolic (signs and syntax). The semiotic and the symbolic are two modalities of the process of *significance*. I define the semiotic as prior to the mirror stage and to the phallic position" (Kristeva 1995, 229n). In an interview she cautions against translating between Lacan's theory and hers. "But it does seem to me," she notes,

> that the semiotic—if one really wants to find correspondences with Lacanian ideas—corresponds to phenomena that for Lacan are in both the real and the imaginary. For him the real is a hole, a void, but I think that in a number of experiences with which psychoanalysis is concerned—most notably, the narcissistic structure, the experience of melancholia or of catastrophic suffering, and so on—the appearance of the real is not necessarily a void. It is accompanied by a number of psychic inscriptions that are of the order of the semiotic. Thus perhaps the notion of the semiotic allows us to speak of the real without simply saying that it's an emptiness or a blank; it allows us to try to further elaborate it. (Guberman 1996, 23)

The semiotic is also part of the signifying process, in that a subject deploys the semiotic's force in order to make an utterance meaningful. As Kelly Oliver writes, "the semiotic element makes symbols matter; by discharging drives in symbols, it makes them significant" (Kristeva 1997, xv).

Kristeva argues that the roots of the semiotic are formed prelinguistically. Before the child enters language, it experiences the world "through so-called primary processes which displace and condense both energies and their inscription" (Kristeva 1984a, 25). Here she differs from Lacan, who held that signification did not occur until the child passed from the imaginary realm, with its narcissistic attachment to its mother, via the oedipal complex into the symbolic, into the "law of the father." This law includes both an injunction against incestual relations / longing for the mother and the law of orderly signification. Yet contra Lacan, as the quotation above indicates, Kristeva believes that even in the real and in the imaginary, there are "psychic inscriptions" that can manifest themselves in signification semiotically, in the child's echolalia and other intonations. And even after we pass through the oedipal complex, these inscriptions still seep into our signification. Thus the semiotic and symbolic aspects of signification are continually at work.

With these processes in mind, Kristeva coined the odd term *"le sujet en procès,"* or *"subject-in-process,"* also translated as the "subject on trial" (Kristeva 1984a) to make use of both senses of the original French. "The notion of the subject-in-process," Kristeva says in an interview,

> assumes that we recognize, on the one hand, the unity of the subject who submits to a law—the law of communication, among others; yet who, on the other hand, does not entirely submit, cannot entirely submit, does not want to submit entirely. The subject-in-process is always in a state of contesting the law, either with the force of violence, of aggressivity, of the death drive, or with the other side of this force: pleasure and jouissance. (Guberman 1996, 26)

This term *subject-in-process* is a reminder that a process of differentiation continuously constitutes our subjectivity; there is no core, fixed, unified self. We are, rather, in a human venture of "innovation, of creation, of opening, of renewal," that is, in an "open system," a term she borrows from biology. Biologists "think that a living being is not merely a structure but a structure open to its surroundings and other structures; and that interactions occur in this opening that are of the order of procreation and rejection, and that permit a living being to live, to grow, to renew itself" (Guberman 1996, 26).

To be open, for a human being, is to be alive. "The psyche is one open system connected to another, and only under those conditions is it renewable," writes Kristeva. "If it lives, your psyche is in love. If it is not in love, it is dead" (Kristeva 1987b, 15). To remain open, we need to be in love, or in psychoanalysis, where transference love can occur. The analytic situation provides an opportunity for a dynamic relationship to occur between, "on the one hand, *desires* that stem from an auto-organization based on drive echoes, and, on the other, the *memory-consciousness* of a past, set down and transmittable within language" (Kristeva 1987b, 15). In analysis, the analysand's libidinal energies are directed onto the analyst, who himself is vulnerable to experiencing counter-transference, opening up the possibility not only of interaction between systems but "of each system into its heterogeneous components" (15). Clearly the image Kristeva depicts of the human organism is radically different from the Cartesian image of human beings as fixed, discrete entities: "The image of man amenable to transference love, as an auto-regulation of connected, open systems, is basically scandalous, for it is depsychologizing and even dehumanizing. Man as a fixed, valorized entity finds himself abandoned in favor of a search, less for his truth (a point of view that conceals the fideism of a number of psychoanalysts) than for his innovative capacities" (15). The subject-in-process is always a subject in the making, thanks to its vulnerability and openness to others.

Note that in the theory that I am describing here, Kristeva is able to work through the problem of *who* precedes subjectivity. She doesn't need to make the Hegelian move of subjectivity trying to "catch sight" of itself. Nor does she need to argue that there is nothing prior to subjectivity. There is something prior, for her, but it is not a substance: "Discrete quantities of energy move through the body of the subject *who is not yet constituted as such* and, in the course of his development, they are arranged according to the various constraints imposed on this body—always already involved in a semiotic process—by family and social structures" (Kristeva 1984a, 25; emphasis added). To draw on Freud's narcissistic model of libidinal energy in cathexis, the psyche, as an open system, is the shape of its attachments. This does not mean that subjectivity arises *ex nihilo*. There is an origin, though this origin is not a substance; it is a movement. Borrowing from Plato, Kristeva calls this movement the *chora*, the Greek word for enclosed space or womb. It denotes "an essentially mobile and extremely provisional articulation constituted by movements and their ephemeral stases" (Kristeva 1984a, 25). The term *chora* represents "a *disposition* that already depends on representation. . . . Although our theoretical description of the *chora* is itself part of the discourse of representation that offers it as evidence, the *chora*, as rupture and articulations (rhythm), precedes evidence, verisimilitude, spatiality, and temporality" (26).

There is a tension between these two aspects of our signifying practices, for the semiotic aspect always threatens to disrupt the symbolic. No matter how orderly we try to be and how logically we try to speak, this order is always tenuous. "Our discourse—all discourse—moves with and against the *chora* in the sense that it simultaneously depends upon and refuses it" (26). Thus our very identity, Kristeva writes, is "on trial." And our subjectivity, being heterogeneous, is constantly being reformed and remade. So there are at least two sources of heterogeneity and openness: the *chora* as the wellspring of desires and energy movements, which is manifest in the semiotic elements of signification, and the vulnerability of the subject as a system open to other systems. The subject-in-process is always a subject-in-relation, internally and externally. He or she is never constituted once and for all, but is always a provisional, tenuous, open system, hence *alive* in the fullest sense.

Being a literary critic as well as a philosopher and psychoanalyst, Kristeva uses the distinction between the semiotic and the symbolic to describe texts as well, namely to distinguish between what she calls the *genotext* and the *phenotext*. These will coexist in any given literary work, but especially in works by avant-garde authors. The genotext "will include semiotic processes but also the advent of the symbolic" (Kristeva 1984a, 86), while the phenotext is a structure that "obeys rules of communications and presupposes a subject of enunciation and an addressee" (87). Whereas the genotext is a process—set in play by drives, dispositions, and environment—the phenotext signifies "the emergence of object and subject" and categories of meaning (86). Notice that by highlighting that the genotext is a process and not a structure, Kristeva is claiming that written texts signify, at least in part, thanks to their dynamic (i.e., process) aspects. She writes:

> even though it can be seen in language, the genotext is not linguistic (in the sense understood by structural or generative linguistics). It is, rather, a *process*, which tends to articulate structures that are ephemeral (unstable, threatened by drive charges, "quanta" rather than "marks") and nonsignifying (devices that do not have a double articulation). It forms these structures out of: a) instinctual dyads, b) the corporeal and ecological continuum, c) the social organism and family structures, which convey the constraints imposed by the mode of production, and d) matrices of enunciation, which give rise to discursive "genres" (according to literary history), "psychic structures" (according to psychiatry and psychoanalysis), or various arrangements of

"the participants in the speech event" (in Jakobson's notion of the linguistics of discourse). We may posit that the matrices of enunciation
are the result of the repetition of drive charges (a) within biological,
ecological, and socio-familial constraints (b and c), and the stabilization
of their facilitation into stases whose surrounding structure accommo-
dates and leaves its mark on symbolization. (86–87)

At its richest, the genotext draws from the semiotic *chora*. In the
modern era, according to Kristeva, only the literary avant-garde (e.g.,
Mallarmé, Joyce) have been able to achieve this. Thus she explores
the works of the literary avant-garde, all in keeping with her project
of understanding the process of subjectivity.

Even as one enters and remains in the realm of symbolic language,
for Kristeva the predifferentiated realm of the *chora* never entirely re-
cedes. Hearing the *chora*'s call threatens the subject's identity, an
identity as a self differentiated from others. We could draw an analogy between Kristeva's notion of the *chora* and Levinas's hither side
of metaphysics. Through the semiotic, a trace of the *chora* enters the
symbolic and threatens the polarities (e.g., self and other) that make
up the subject's self-identity, just as the hither side of being disrupts
metaphysical logic. While Kristeva never to my knowledge uses Levinas directly, we can find his trace in her writings, most notably in
chapter 6 of her first book, *Revolution in Poetic Language*. There she
uses Derrida's "grammatology" (a.k.a. deconstruction) to explain
how the subject's unity is always "on trial" or threatened by the
chora. Grammatology, she argues, helps explain how *something
other* than being leaves its trace. "Negativity is inscribed in arche-
writing as a constitutive absence: the 'absence of the other,' 'irre-
ducible absence within the presence of the trace'": "*différance* is
therefore the formation of form" (Kristeva 1984a, 141). To explain
this further, she turns to a line from Derrida's essay "Violence and
Metaphysics," written about Levinas—still, no mention from her of
Levinas. The line she quotes refers obliquely to Levinas: we recognize
in negativity, she writes, a "strange dialogue between the Jew and the
Greek, peace itself." From her manner of quotation, one would think
Derrida was referring to Hegel, but in fact Derrida is referring to Lev-
inas's position between two philosophic traditions. Let me quote
Derrida's passage more fully:

Are we Greeks? Are we Jews? But who, we? Are we (not a chronologi-
cal, but a pre-logical question) *first* Jews or *first* Greeks? And does the

strange dialogue between the Jew and the Greek, peace itself, have the form of the absolute speculative logic of Hegel, the living logic which *reconciles* formal tautology and empirical heterology after having *thought* prophetic discourse in the preface to the *Phenomenology of the Mind*? Or, on the contrary, does this peace have the form of infinite separation and of the unthinkable, unsayable transcendence of the other? To what horizon of peace does the language which asks this question belong? (Derrida 1978, 153)

In this passage, Derrida is pointing to Levinas's peculiar position between two traditions and urging him not to try to move by Hegelian negation but to respect the alterity of what cannot be captured by language, even though we're destined to try.

It is interesting that Kristeva quotes this passage about Levinas without mentioning him and then goes on to use Levinas's term, the trace, to explain the alternative to Hegelian negation: "Through this *ingathering*, the trace absorbs and, in this sense, reduces . . . the 'terms', 'dichotomies', and 'oppositions' that Hegelian negativity concatenates, reactivates, and generates." The trace "unfolds only within the stases of the semiotic *chora*." Issuing from the *chora*, the trace expresses what the subject has had to repress in order to enter into language. By way of grammatology, the trace "disturbs logic and its subject" (Kristeva 1984a, 141–42). Still, Kristeva suggests, Derrida's grammatology does not go far enough in describing the heterogeneity of the signifying process, the extent to which "the nondeferred and impatient drive charge" irrupts semiotically:

This unleashing of the heterogeneous element as nonsymbolized and nonsymbolizable operates neither on the path of becoming-sign-subject-beings, nor in their neutralization, but in precipitating—as in a chemical reaction—the deferring stage in the expenditure of the process of the subject and signifiance. A heterogeneous energy discharge, whose very principle is that of scission and division, enters into contradiction with what has been traced, but produces only flashes, ruptures, and sudden displacements, which constitute preconditions for *new* symbolic productions in which the economy of *différance* will be able to find its place as well. (145)

Again, we see that the *chora*'s energies seep into signifying practices, opening up the subject to heterogeneity, keeping her alive and open to otherness. Note how the subject is constituted as a speaking being:

her signifying practices are central to her subjectivity, actually making subjectivity possible.

A Subject-in-Process

For Kristeva, *significance* and subjectivity are matters of process, not substance. Throughout her work, we find allusions to process, movement, dynamics, positioning, and stages; never hints of substance, attribute, essence, or any notions of "catching up to" any "originary consciousness." If anything is originary it is movement, like the movement and "ceaseless heterogeneity" of the *chora*. Although Kristeva does value a development of some stable subjectivity, one that is fluent in the ways of the symbolic, this subjectivity is nonetheless always in process and on trial. Being an open system, subjectivity is never achieved once and for all. For one thing, there are always aspects of experience that must be expelled to constitute subjectivity—aspects that always haunt subjectivity. In *Revolution in Poetic Language*, Kristeva describes this as scission, separation, and rejection: a movement that precedes desire. "We must designate an event that occurs before and within the trajectory of Hegelian negativity, an event that lies between and beneath the psychoanalytic distinction between 'desire' and 'need', one that moves through and is inherent in biological and signifying development but links them together" (1984a, 146). In a chapter on Freud's notion of expulsion, Kristeva identifies rejection or expenditure as this key moment. It is a separation that occurs prior to any positing within language, but is always manifested in any poetic language, that is, any language richer than pure logical notations. Negativity, as rejection and expenditure, *produces* meaning and subjectivity.

This notion of expelling something in order to create subjectivity is the main thread of Kristeva's book *Powers of Horror*. In it she describes the familiar feeling of being drawn to something even as one is repulsed by it:

> There looms, within abjection, one of those violent, dark revolts of being, directed against a threat that seems to emanate from an exorbitant outside or inside, ejected beyond the scope of the possible, the tolerable, the thinkable. It lies there, quite close, but it cannot be assimilated. It beseeches, worries, and fascinates desire, which, nevertheless,

does not let itself be seduced. Apprehensive, desire turns aside; sickened, it rejects. A certainty protects it from the shameful—a certainty of which it is proud holds on to it. But simultaneously, just the same, that impetus, that spasm, that leap is drawn toward an elsewhere as tempting as it is condemned. Unflaggingly, like an inescapable boomerang, a vortex of summons and repulsion places the one haunted by it literally beside himself. (Kristeva 1982, 1)

Those things that are so difficult to face are not objects per se, for they are not some correlate of subject; rather they are things that threaten my constitution as an "I," as having subjectivity. These things are abject, they are "jettisoned" things, which we radically exclude and yet which draw "me toward the place where meaning collapses" (2). The repulsion I feel in facing the abject protects me from losing my subjectivity:

A massive and sudden emergence of uncanniness, which, familiar as it might have been in an opaque and forgotten life, now harries me as radically separate, loathsome. Not me. Not that. But not nothing, either. A "something" that I do not recognize as a thing. A weight of meaninglessness, about which there is nothing insignificant, and which crushes me. On the edge of nonexistence and hallucination, of a reality that, if I acknowledge it, annihilates me. There, abject and abjection are my safeguards. The primers of my culture. (2)

The abject both threatens subjectivity and protects it. It is both the vandal and the policeman of the self. Yet, again, the abject is not a substance but a movement at the edge or boundary of subjectivity, of the process of *signifiance* that creates subjectivity. Hovering at the edge, at the border between meaning (the symbolic) and meaninglessness, abjection is an event that returns whenever one pushes the borders of subjectivity. No wonder then that we call some psychiatric patients "borderline," for they are in fact vulnerable to falling out of the symbolic and into asymbolia.

The one by whom the abject exists is thus a *deject* who places (himself), *separates* (himself), and therefore *strays* instead of getting his bearings, desiring, belonging, or refusing. . . . Necessarily dichotomous, somewhat Manichaean, he divides, excludes, and without, properly

speaking, wishing to know his abjections is not at all unaware of
them. . . . Instead of sounding himself as to his "being," he does so concerning his place: "*Where* am I?" instead of "*Who* am I?" For the space
that engrosses the deject, the excluded, is never *one*, nor *homogeneous*,
nor *totalizable*, but essentially divisible, foldable, and catastrophic. (8)

To find and maintain security within the borders of subjectivity,
one feels an increasing compunction about being clean and proper.
Those "things" we find most abject, excrement and death, threaten
our "proper" boundaries the most: the boundaries that maintain subjectivity, ultimately, for Kristeva, the boundaries that prevent one
from falling back into the maternal body. All abject experiences come
back to the maternal. "There, I am at the border of my condition as a
living being. My body extricates itself, as being alive, from that border" (3). The "utmost of abjection" is the corpse. "It is death infecting
life." We can reject it but we can never part from it; "it beckons to us
and ends up engulfing us"—perhaps just as the womb beckons, the
womb that Freud linked to the fear of death. The issue is not cleanli-
ness per se, but "what disturbs identity, system, order" (3).

In *Powers of Horror* there is still a choice, a possibility, of maintaining borders in the face of the abject maternal body, at least by
staying clean and proper. But in a later work, *Black Sun*, in which
Kristeva discusses melancholia, the only way for the subject to
achieve autonomy is to kill—at least psychically—the mother. "Mat-
ricide is our vital necessity, the sine-qua-non condition of our individuation" (Kristeva 1989b, 27–28). As Ewa Ziarek notes, "The ethos
of this position only confirms the primacy of identity and its violence
in Western metaphysics" (Ziarek 1993, 75). Were we to follow Kristeva's lead in *Black Sun*, it seems that our response to alterity would
always be somehow to attempt to master or, conversely, annihilate
it. But this would overlook the promise of the subject's relation with
the other that is at the heart of so many of Kristeva's other texts, especially *Strangers to Ourselves*, which I will discuss in Chapter 4. I
think that here it would be appropriate to follow Ziarek's redefinition
of melancholia, incorporating Levinas's work on alterity, as an
"ethics of otherness." This would require, Ziarek writes: "a displacement from the concern with the subject—its individuation, its an-
guish, its wounds, its crisis—to alterity ontologically and ethically
prior to the subject. In a certain way, melancholia already registers

this reversal; the crisis reveals that the subject and its means of representation are always already overwhelmed by the other" (Ziarek 1993, 74). Here Ziarek quotes Kristeva's description of melancholics: "In the tension of their affects, muscles, mucous membranes, and skin, they experience both their belonging to and distance from an archaic other that still eludes representation and naming, but of whose corporeal emissions, along with their automatism, they still bear the imprint" (from Kristeva 1989b, 14). Ziarek points out that this imprint could hardly have been initiated by the subject. "Rather, the mark of alterity points to the subject's indebtedness to the other, to a forgotten maternal gift, which enables our ethical orientation to the world" (Ziarek 1993, 74).

Although Ziarek says she is doing "violence" to Kristeva's texts, by halting the violence that the subject might aim at its mother, by pointing it toward acceptance of alterity rather than annihilation of it, she is really emphasizing one aspect of Kristeva's ambivalence about the *sujet en procès*, a subject always on trial and precariously poised between subjecthood and disintegration. Alterity always promises and beckons but threatens the borders of the self. Ziarek is pointing to the part of Kristeva's work that sees the other as a promise, especially the originary (m)other. If we can see this originary (m)other as the very possibility for our own subjectivity, then we might embrace an ethics of alterity that welcomes heterogeneity and so makes possible a politics conducive to heterogeneous contemporary polities.

Throughout Kristeva's work on semiotics, psychoanalysis, and the speaking subject, we can identify tensions between movement and stasis, or what ontologists would describe as process and substance. Process or movement always threatens to undermine stasis or substance. We see this in the tension between the semiotic and the symbolic, between the genotext and the phenotext, and between the *chora* and subjectivity. Abjection is just one manifestation of this friction, a friction that in many respects is constitutive of identity. We are able to come into subjectivity, however tenuous it remains, thanks to a dialectical interaction between movement and stasis. We may need a fiction of an autonomous and stable identity in order to act in the world (as Kant has noted in his paralogisms and antinomies), but this fiction is forever called to account: to the *chora*, to the movement and process that precede all identity.

From Subjectivity to Citizenship

In this chapter and the previous one, I've sketched two radically different views of subjectivity—so different despite the similarities they share: Both Habermas and Kristeva argue that subjectivity arises contingently, historically, and linguistically. Both draw on Freud and the continental tradition. Yet as we've seen, their differences send them in opposite directions. Habermas implicitly relies on a substance ontological metaphysics, whereas Kristeva explicitly adopts a process point of view. Habermas draws on a linguistic theory that takes language to be a transparent tool, while Kristeva understands language as a disruptive medium, especially as it is used by a speaking being whose energies emanate from a *chora*. Though both use Freud, Habermas's version is closer to ego psychology (which draws on Freud's tripartite model of ego, id, and superego) whereas Kristeva comes out of a Lacanian reading, which draws on the earlier Freudian theory of the unconscious and libidinal energy. All this adds up to, for Habermas, a subject that is an autonomous agent, and, for Kristeva, a subject that is an open system, always coming to speak and to be in relation with others, including the "other" within.

Now that I've sketched these theories of subjectivity, I turn, in the next part of this book, to the heart of the question I am raising: Need we have a Habermasian notion of the self in order to conceive of the self as an agent in a political community, that is, as a citizen? Or might we also be able to consider subjects-in-process as candidates for citizenship? Is it possible to be an open system and an effective political agent?

PART II

POLITICS AND THE PUBLIC SPHERE

The time is coming when we shall have to rethink our views on politics.
—Nietzsche, "Nachlass," *Werke in Drei Banden* III

3 Habermas on Citizens and Politics

Over the course of thirty-five years, Habermas's writings have maintained a striking unity of focus and concern, looking into the capacities that people have to create a more just society, which, with some qualification, may mean a more rational society. As I've noted, by "rational" Habermas does not mean only the instrumental rationality of bureaucratic systems but also the kind of rationality that the Enlightenment promised: a rationality that would enable human beings to become more free and equal. The bulk of Habermas's writings has focused on the development of such rationality, specifically communicative rationality, and its applications epistemologically, socially, and morally. It has been in part an attempt to develop a nonfoundational yet transcendental basis for making judgments. That is, in a "postmetaphysical" world we can no longer appeal to metaphysical foundations on which to ground our judgments—yet there is a foundation, internal to our communicative practices, that allows us to ground our claims. In any situation in which we try to come to understanding with others, Habermas argues, we must hold certain validity claims (that as speakers we are being sincere, appropriate, and truthful), or else we would not bother to talk together at all. The necessity for holding these validity claims transcends cultures, histories, and other particularities. It is a universal feature of our communicative practices.

Understandably, this project of developing a theory of communicative action (and, from it, discourse ethics) has occupied Habermas for most of his career. Yet another prong is evident in two of his books, interestingly one of the earliest and one of the most recent. The first is *Strukturwandel der Öffentlichkeit* (1962; translated as *The Structural Transformation of the Public Sphere*) and the second is *Faktizität und Geltung: Beiträge zur Diskurstheorie des Rechts und des demokratischen Rechtsstaats* (1992; translated as *Between Facts and Norms*). Both these books (as well as a portion of volume 2 of *The Theory of Communicative Action*) focus on the social world, politics, and the formation of public opinion. Thus, his works center on two interrelated themes: (1) the capacities of social agents in their communicative actions and (2) the political realm in which they interact. These themes, it should be stressed, are strongly connected. Habermas's understanding of communicative reasoning, of how speakers in a linguistic community must implicitly reason, led to his work on how speakers come to agreement on both empirical and moral concerns. The latter became known as discourse ethics, which has implications for political reasoning as well.[1]

The Public Sphere

In order to situate the focus of this chapter—Habermas's views about agency in the public sphere—I turn to the theme of the political realm. The first thing to note is his development of the concept of the public sphere, which was the focus of *The Structural Transformation of the Public Sphere*. The public sphere is, he wrote in a separate essay ("Offentlichkeit"),

> a domain of our social life in which such a thing as public opinion can be formed. Access to the public sphere is open in principle to all citizens. A portion of the public sphere is constituted in every conversation in which private persons come together to form a public. . . . Citizens act as a public when they deal with matters of general interest without being subject to coercion; thus with the guarantee that they may assemble and unite freely, and express and publicize their opinions freely. . . . We speak of a political public sphere (as distinguished from a literary one, for instance) when the public discussions concern objects connected with the practice of the state. (Habermas 1989, 231)

[1] For an excellent discussion of Habermas's discourse ethics, see Rehg 1987.

The political public sphere, which is my concern here, is not so much a physical place as it is an occurrence: any time two or more individuals come together to discuss matters of politics the public sphere takes place. Otherwise "private" individuals create a public sphere when they talk together about public concerns. In this respect, the public sphere is neither part of the private realm of the household and of individuals, nor is it part of the official structures of governance. It occurs in a third, intermediate space.

Interestingly, Habermas's book on the public sphere was translated into English, and thus gained a much broader audience, in 1989 when another, related area of political thought was being reopened: investigations into the nature of civil society. Through most of the twentieth century, most people had thought of politics as the domain of governments as distinct from the private realm of individuals. In a democracy, individuals took on a political role when they intervened in the functioning of governments, whether by voting, demonstrating, or writing letters to Congress; but there remained a neat division between public and private along the lines of government and private individuals. Events of the late 1980s—the fall of the Berlin Wall, the rise of civic associations in Poland, East Germany, and Czechoslovakia, the break up of the Soviet Union—brought new attention to an old concept: civil society, a "third" realm between private individuals and the state (or government). "The words 'civil society'," writes Michael Walzer, "name the space of uncoerced human association and also the set of relational networks—formed for the sake of family, faith, interest, and ideology—that fill this space" (Walzer 1991, 293). Civil society thus is the space between the private sphere of individuals and the governmental sphere of the state; it is the space of public associations in which people enter into common life by joining with others—whether to form a softball league or to protect the environment.

Civil society is the network of all those nongovernmental associations, both formal and informal, that bring people together: from garden clubs to neighborhood associations, churches, labor unions, interest groups, coffee klatches, bowling clubs. Their objects do not matter; they may be aimed at hobbies or at discussing public concerns. What they share is a way of bringing people out of their homes and workplaces and into a network of other associations. People do not necessarily act politically in these associational groups but,

through the interrelated associations of civil society, people can develop the capacity to create and articulate public will and direction,
to address immediate concerns, and to decide the legitimacy of their
governments.

At best, civil societies foster an open, democratic culture that helps
set their political communities' direction and hold their governments accountable. There is nothing hallowed about civil society in
itself: it can be racist, exclusionary, backward and recalcitrant. (Just
think of the "civil society" of the U.S. South during the era of Jim
Crow.) Many of the democratic "elite" (well-educated voters, philan-
thropists, policymakers, and officials) worry about relying on civil society for just this reason, for after all the public is often, it seems, re-
actionary and ignorant; but this is no reason to shun civil society. To
the contrary, it is all the more reason to tend to its health and openness. Civil society can provide a bulwark against illegitimate use of
state power. In fact, one of the first things a totalitarian state will do
is ban public associations—in effect banning opportunities for the
people to come together and voice their displeasure with the state. In
the absence of such a voice, the state can masquerade as legitimate.
To the extent that civil society provides opportunities for deliberation about public matters, public opinion can form and provide
means by which to judge the state's legitimacy. Public opinion can
also form about what direction policy ought to take. This is, to be
sure, the idea behind democracy—that the will of the people should
guide public policy. The introduction of political representation does
not obviate this democratic imperative. According to a Jeffersonian
model of democratic politics (in contrast with a Madisonian one),
representatives should heed the public will—and there ought to be
opportunities for public will to form. (Note that in the late 1980s the
rise of civil associations in some East European countries preceded,
by a matter of weeks, the fall of totalitarian governments. Likewise,
note that China all but bans civil associations—a policy designed to
silence any public opposition. In South America, some corporatist
states have allowed civil associations but have tried to prevent them
from associating with each other.)

It is in this context that the translation of Habermas's book on the
public sphere appeared: in a world where real political attention was
being turned to civil society, where both theorists and activists were
wondering what was needed to make democracy work, where there
was a general suspicion that "good government" is insufficient, that

there must also be a vibrant civil society.[2] Now, as noted, civil society is comprised of a wide assortment of associations, not all aimed at addressing matters of public concern. Still, civil society can be considered as the space or realm in which the political public sphere arises. One could conceive of the public sphere as a segment or aspect of civil society; whenever and wherever two or more people discuss matters of the state, then the public sphere occurs: it is the occurrence of public dialogue on matters of public policy. In this sense, the public sphere is always a discursive space. (We could consider Habermas's subsequent work on communicative action as an attempt to understand the ways in which discourse can occur in keeping with democratic ideals. The regulative ideal of the ideal speech situation promotes free and equal participation in the discourse of the public sphere. It also offers a way to spot and criticize speech aimed at manipulation, coercion, and distortion.)

Society as System and Lifeworld

In Habermas's work on the political realm, he makes a distinction between "system" and "lifeworld." In his sociological analyses of society, the lifeworld is identified as the "context-forming horizon" of social action (Habermas 1984, xxv); it consists of the background assumptions, cultural norms, expectations, and meanings that we use to interpret and make sense of our experience and to coordinate our actions with others. The system, on the other hand, is society conceptualized in terms of the division of labor and functions into separate spheres of actions and goals (e.g., the banking system, the political system, the educational system), each with its own predetermined ends and selected means for achieving them. The difference between system and lifeworld is really a difference of perspective, two different points of view from which to try to understand society. The system perspective is external to society, taking it as an object of understanding, while the lifeworld perspective is that of a participant, making sense of society while being internal to it.

[2.] For a sampling of some of the literature that has proliferated in this area, see Cohen and Arato 1992, Putnam 1993, Seligman 1992, Walzer 1992, Keane 1988, and Perez-Diaz 1993.

(Granted, no one can get "outside" his or her own culture to develop a truly objective point of view, but in our hermeneutic practice of taking something as an object of understanding we may conceptualize it as a system.) Habermas develops the distinction between system and lifeworld in volume 2 of *The Theory of Communicative Action*, in the context of distinguishing between communicative and functionalist or instrumental reason. From a lifeworld perspective, the key form of reason is communicative; it is through communicative action that the complex lifeworld is produced and reproduced (Habermas 1984, xxv), that ends are chosen and purposes decided. From an external, systems-theoretic perspective, the operative form of reason is functional or instrumental, selecting means to predetermined ends.

Different theorists tend to approach society from one perspective or the other. Someone like John Rawls would, implicitly at least, consider society from a lifeworld perspective, looking for the overlapping consensus that participants in a political community might share and communicatively reproduce. Conversely, theorists such as Emile Durkheim and Niklas Luhmann adopt, indeed develop, the systems-theoretic approach, "realistically" looking at the constraints and imperatives that various subsystems impose upon social actors. In the words of Thomas McCarthy: "From one point of view, society is conceptualized as the lifeworld of a social group in which actions are coordinated through harmonizing action orientations. From another point of view, society is conceptualized as a self-regulating system in which actions are coordinated through functional interconnections of action consequences" (Habermas 1984, xxviii). Habermas argues that adopting either perspective to the exclusion of the other is one-sided. The facticity of systems needs to be understood hermeneutically—we have to understand what systems mean to people and how these meanings prompt them to act within their boundaries. Conversely, even the background horizon of the lifeworld has its own ends and means and potential for internal differentiation, so the lifeworld should be an "object" of analysis along with other "systems." Habermas integrates both the lifeworld and the systems-theoretic perspectives into a two-level analysis of society, seeing society as both a "system that has to satisfy the conditions of maintenance of sociocultural lifeworlds" and a "systematically stabilized nexus of action of socially integrated groups" (Habermas 1984, xxix).

Yet even as he integrates both the lifeworld and the system perspective into his analysis, Habermas notices that there has been an increasing differentiation or decoupling between the system and life-world aspects of society. In traditional societies, most if not all aspects of life were regulated by tradition, kinship, and culture. In some traditional societies, the institution of marriage might have regulated a number of different arenas: property relations, intertribal disputes, systems of authority, material production and reproduction, and so on. But as society became less traditional it also became more differentiated, with different aspects of life splitting off and developing a degree of autonomy from traditions and kinship networks. In ancient Greece, for example, we see the splitting off of the public realm of the polis from the private realm of the oikos, each maintaining or developing its own norms and procedures—and, as in the story of Antigone, sometimes coming into conflict. In modern societies, the most notable example is the splitting off of the economic system, especially with the introduction of money as an impersonal, exchangeable medium. Differentiation has also affected most other aspects of life, with separate systems for separate functions such as banking, administration, politics, education, and the law. Each system develops its own means for achieving ends, the more so as it increases in complexity. Think of the various checks and balances, accountability structures, departments, and the like, built into large, complex systems. Each system carries out specific functions, developing its own "functional" reason to do so. In this way, each grows "increasingly independent of the normative structures of the lifeworld," writes Thomas McCarthy, becoming "quasi-autonomous" (Habermas 1984, xxxi). Instead of being guided by the communicatively developed norms of the lifeworld, these systems are "steered," as Habermas puts it (borrowing from Talcott Parsons), by other media: namely money and power.

This whole process of differentiation, of the decoupling of system and lifeworld, is part and parcel of modernity. In large measure it is promising, for it allows for a degree of independence from often authoritarian traditions and conventions. In traditional societies there was little differentiation between spheres of life, but this was at the price of rigid, conventional norms and structures, not amenable to the "public use of reason." As Kant noted in his essay "What Is Enlightenment?", freedom from tutelage was concomitant with using one's own reason as a public justification for a norm, rather than deferring to authorities (whether tradition, the church, or the king) to justify norms. This public use of reason rather than deference to authority and convention is what Habermas calls "postconventional" morality. So, as this public—that is communicative—reason begins to be the means for justifying norms, the lifeworld becomes less traditional and more rational.

But there is a paradox at the heart of modernity, for the rationalization of the lifeworld also poses problems: the "rationalized lifeworld makes possible the rise and growth of subsystems whose independent imperatives strike back at it in a destructive fashion" (Habermas 1984, xxxiii). The lifeworld is vulnerable in the domains of social integration and symbolic reproduction, that is, in the domains where participants in the lifeworld should use communicative reason to decide on meaning, purpose, identity, goals, and directions. But as subsystems develop, their methods and reasoning tend to encroach upon these lifeworld domains, giving rise to what Habermas calls the "colonization of the lifeworld." This occurs when reasoning appropriate to systems is applied to social life—when, for example, children use the courts to settle a dispute with their parents; when parents give their children money instead of gifts for birthdays; or when people are treated as clients of the state and consumers of public services rather than as citizens with the ability to develop a public will on matters of policy:

> This media-induced shift to purposive-rational action orientations calls forth the reaction of a hedonism freed from the pressures of rationality. As the private sphere is undermined and eroded by the economic system, so is the public sphere by the administrative system. The bureaucratic disempowering and desiccation of spontaneous processes of opinion- and will-formation expand the scope for mobilizing mass loyalty and make it easier to decouple political decisions from concrete, identity-forming contexts of life. (xxxiv)

Modernity has not made society more just. While the prerogatives of citizenship have been expanded to more and more people, the tasks of citizenship have been distorted into the role of consumer. Likewise, capitalism has not made the labor-for-wage relationship better in any real way, instead it has transformed the identity of worker into that of consumer. The colonization of the lifeworld turns citizens into clients and workers into consumers, thereby minimizing opportunities for overcoming capitalism's and modernity's injustices.

Still, Habermas would be the last one to give up on modernity. Despite its failings, he thinks it still holds promise—a promise afforded by the development of communicative rationality as well as by the rise of "new social movements," such as the environmental movement, the women's movement, movements for communal living, and other movements for alternative lifestyles. Instead of beseeching government for more services or a better distribution of wealth (which would only exacerbate the tendency to commodify and colonize the lifeworld with systemic means), these movements are asking us to rethink and change the way the system encroaches upon domains of life that ought to be regulated communicatively, through norms that people arrive at democratically, discursively, and publicly.

Despite this promise, *The Theory of Communicative Action* ends on a bleak note, with the threat of "formally organized domains of action" taking over the functions that properly belong to communicative action (Habermas 1987, 403). Habermas calls for a critical theory that can take on this threat and seek out ways not only to protect the lifeworld but to allow the public will generated in the lifeworld to have some guiding effect upon bureaucratic and administrative systems. Habermas's call, really, is for rekindling the promise of democracy—that the will of the people should guide public policy. His analysis of modernity shows just where this promise is dashed: in the decoupling of systems from the lifeworld, in the colonization of the lifeworld by functional and instrumental reason, and in the increasing autonomy and lack of accountability of the system to the lifeworld. The solution for Habermas is to find a way for the public sphere to develop its communicative rationality and to set limits to, indeed influence, the systems that have become so autonomous. An articulation of this project did not arrive until 1992, with the publication of *Faktizität und Geltung* (in English in 1996 as *Between Facts and Norms*).

Translating Will into Law

One difficulty with changing the relationship between the system and the lifeworld, however, is that, by their natures, systems each have their own "language" that develops around their specific functions. Something that occurs in the environment, say the transfer of property, will make sense in the legal system only if it is accompanied by deeds or other legal documents; and it will make sense in the economic system only if it is exchanged via money or some equivalent means. Each system has its own *semantics* or *"grammar for interpreting the world"* (Habermas 1996, 346):

Unlike individuals in the state of nature, autopoietic systems no longer share a common world. To this extent, the problem of successful communication among independent and self-referentially operating units, each with its own perspective on the world, corresponds almost exactly to the familiar phenomenological problem of constructing an intersubjectively shared world from the egological achievements of transcendental monads. No more than Husserl (or later, Sartre) solved this problem of intersubjectivity, has systems theory managed to explain how autopoietically closed systems could, inside the circuit of self-referential steering, be induced to go beyond pure self-reference and autopoiesis. (346)

The problem with a purely systems-theoretic approach is that, according to it, each system has its own "language game" and lacks the means to communicate with other systems. What is lacking is a way to transfer or translate one language into another.

This problem is particularly acute in trying to transfer or communicate between systems and the political public sphere. From a systems-theoretic point of view, even the political public sphere is itself part of a system, the political system, which like other systems is self-enclosed. From a lifeworld perspective, the political public sphere is steered by communicatively derived norms. From either perspective, it is difficult to see how the political public sphere could communicate its norms, aims, and choices to the very systems that ought to heed it, namely the bureaucratic and administrative systems—the arenas that in a democracy should be guided by the will of the people. The difficulty with having systems heed the opinion, will, and norms that emerge from communicative action in the lifeworld stems from the inability of systems to fathom this communicative discourse or any foreign media, especially when they come in the form of *norms*.

Systems theory wants to deny the importance of norms as a motivation for action—leaving it instead to functional imperatives or matters of pure self-interest (e.g., in the rational choice model of politics). To the contrary, Habermas insists that normative considerations are never avoidable. "As soon as specialized knowledge is brought to politically relevant problems," he writes, "its unavoidably normative character becomes apparent, setting off controversies that polarize the experts themselves" (Habermas 1996, 351). Political matters can never be treated purely empirically, as matters of people acting only out of self-interest or in the service of some predetermined end. On matters of social integration—that is, politics—there is always the question of what ought to be done, a question that, for the sake of democratic legitimacy, requires input from the public.

> It is against the life-historical background of violated interests and threatened identities that the effects of deficient system integration are first experienced as pressing problems. Therefore, it is counterproductive, not only from the viewpoint of legitimacy but also from a cognitive viewpoint, for attunement processes between governmental and societal actors to become independent vis-à-vis the political public sphere and parliamentary will-formation. . . . [I]t is advisable that the enlarged knowledge base of a planning and supervising administration be shaped by deliberative politics, that is, shaped by the publicly organized contest of opinions between experts and counterexperts and monitored by public opinion. (351)

In Habermas's view, systems neither can nor do avoid the normative aspects of political problems. They are not as self-enclosed as pure systems theory would have it; there is another language that systems can understand: the language of the law. In *Between Facts and Norms*, Habermas argues that the "language of law brings ordinary communication from the public and private spheres and puts it into a form in which these messages can also be received by the special codes of autopoietic systems—and vice versa" (354). Law functions as a "transformer" between the ordinary language of the lifeworld and the specialized language of various systems.

How does this work? Ideally, potential political problems get the attention of the public and are discussed in the public sphere. In this discursive space, through deliberation, public will is formed. This public will puts pressure on more formal deliberative bodies, namely legislatures, who in some measure turn this will into law—and into a language that administrative, economic, and other systems can understand. In this way, law binds together the public sphere and the supposedly semi-autonomous systems. From the standpoint of modernity or democracy, the only way for these systems to be considered legitimate is for them to be accountable in such a way to the public sphere. It is not enough that systems produce outputs that are "good for the public," as a guardian model of politics would have it (e.g., as in Plato's *Republic*); to be democratic they must respond to inputs that the public generates.

As to whether this ideal occurs in fact, Habermas takes a middle position. On the one hand, there are real limitations on the ability of civil society and the political public sphere to affect governmental systems and thus public policy. First (and this is not so much a limitation as a condition), "civil society can develop only in the context of a liberal political culture . . . in an already rationalized lifeworld" (Habermas 1996, 371). Second, the political public sphere can, at best, only *influence* governmental institutions; it has no political *power* on its own. To acquire power, public opinion must pass through more formal, institutionalized deliberations: "public influence is transformed into communicative power only after it passes through the filters of the institutionalized procedures of democratic opinion- and will-formation and enters through parliamentary debates into legitimate lawmaking" (371). Third, even once it is translated into law, public will can have only modest effects in modern, complex, functionally differentiated societies.

> Politics indeed continues to be the addressee for all unmanaged integration problems. But political steering can often take only an indirect approach and must, as we have seen, leave intact the modes of operation internal to functional systems and other highly organized spheres of action. As a result, democratic movements emerging from civil society must give up holistic aspirations to a self-organizing society, aspirations that also undergirded Marxist ideas of social revolution. Civil society can directly transform only itself, and it can have at most an indirect effect on the self-transformation of the political system generally, it has an influence only on the personnel and programming of this system. But in no way does it occupy *the position* of a macrosubject supposed to bring society as a whole under control and simultaneously act for it. (372)

With these caveats, Habermas recognizes the real limitations to the public sphere's ability to effect public policy.

Yet, on the other hand, Habermas maintains that, under certain conditions, civil society can work through the public sphere to make a difference in how politics is conducted and problems are addressed. Despite the general conception that politics is the domain of governments and elites and not the public, Habermas contends that it is possible for the public to generate political change. In fact, since the early 1970s (and before) movements arising from civil society have brought new concerns to political agendas. Habermas points to ecological concerns, feminist issues, the antinuclear movement, third-world movements, and others as examples of new concerns brought to the agenda by the political periphery—the public of citizens. Citizens can act as sensors, experiencing new crises and, via the public sphere, raising awareness of these crises as political problems.

> In a perceived crisis situation, *the actors in civil society* ... *can* assume a surprisingly active and momentous role. In spite of a lesser organizational complexity and a weaker capacity for action [than governmental systems have], and despite the structural disadvantages mentioned earlier, at the critical moments of an accelerated history, these actors get the chance to *reverse* the normal circuits of communication in the political system and the public sphere. In this way they can shift the entire system's mode of problem solving. (380–81)

So, despite his realism about the power that large systems can exert over the lifeworld, Habermas remains an optimist about the public's capacity to develop public will that can affect public policy.

Citizenship

My brief sketch of Habermas's political theory brings me to the question of citizenship, that is, agency in the public sphere. As I have discussed, Habermas thinks it is possible for the political public sphere to exert an influence upon public policy—but only when the conditions are right. These conditions are not externally imposed; they must be generated from within civil society and within the public sphere. That is, they must be created by a public of citizens.[3] And once the conditions are in place, then there are certain functions that must be carried out in order for public opinion to have a public influence.

Habermas notes all these things, yet he doesn't tie these conditions and functions to citizenship per se but to the tasks of a civil society and a political public sphere. When he writes on citizenship, his discussions revolve around the competing views of it in the liberal and the civic republican models. In the liberal tradition individualism

---

3. Additionally, however, the lifeworld must be sufficiently rationalized for a political public sphere to emerge. See Habermas 1996, 358–59.

and negative rights are emphasized, while in the republican tradition identity with the state is emphasized. Under liberalism,

> citizenship is conceived along the lines of an organizational member-
> ship that grounds a legal status. . . . [I]ndividuals remain outside the
> state. In exchange for organizational services and benefits, they make
> specific contributions, such as voting inputs and tax payments, to the
> reproduction of the state. In the second [republican] interpretation, cit-
> izens are integrated into the political community like the parts of a
> whole, in such a way that they can develop their personal and social
> identity only within the horizon of shared traditions and recognized po-
> litical institutions. (Habermas 1996, 498)

Although Habermas is not satisfied with either view, he does argue that the republican, "holistic" approach has an advantage over the liberal model: "the holistic model makes it clear that political auton-omy is an end in itself that can be realized not by the single individ-ual privately pursuing his own interests but only by all together in an intersubjectively shared practice" (498). Moreover, the republican model anticipates that citizens will be "oriented toward the common good" (499), that not only will they enjoy membership in the state but they will be inclined to use their rights of participation; they will feel obligated to have a hand in self-governance. So the difference be-tween liberal and republican conceptions of citizenship comes down to this: the rights of membership (private autonomy) versus the incli-nation to participate (public autonomy). Certainly both are impor-tant, and the republican view does offer an advance over the liberal one. Yet neither analysis alone addresses what I see as central issues: the *capacity* of citizens to participate in a meaningful way as well as an explication of what *functions* such citizens should carry out.

Given that so little political theory takes seriously the role that cit-izens should have in a democracy, it is no wonder that little attention has focused on the capacities and functions of citizenship. In general terms, Habermas does specify what a deliberative public should do:

> The public sphere is a warning system with sensors that, though un-
> specialized, are sensitive throughout society. From the perspective of
> democratic theory, the public sphere must, in addition, amplify the

> ms, that is, not only detect and identify problems but
> and *influentially* thematize them, furnish them with
> s, and dramatize them in such a way that they are
> lt with by parliamentary complexes. Besides the "sig-
> ere must be an effective problematization. The capac-
> sphere to solve problems on its own is limited. But this
> e utilized to oversee the further treatment of problems
> inside the political system. (359)

uch as this one, and from the overall outline of his
we can determine what, implicitly at least, a Haber-
of citizenship would take to be the capacities and
functions of citizenship. This would include the following:

- citizenship should be seen as an intersubjective enterprise; it cannot be carried out by isolated individuals;
- citizens have to create the space in which citizenship can occur;
  that is, they have to move beyond their purely private networks and
  into more public ones, in the process creating and maintaining civil
  society;
- from within this civil society, citizens need to create discursive
  spaces in which they address matters of common concern—that is,
  they need to create the political public sphere;
- effective citizenship calls for the ability to "ferret out, identify, and
  effectively thematize latent problems of social integration" (Habermas 1996, 358);
- citizens will need to engage in this opinion- and will-formation process spontaneously, without the prompting of formal systems; otherwise the channels of communication would flow from center to
  periphery rather than the deliberative-democrat way, from periphery to center;
- citizens should be able to bring these issues to the attention of formal legislative bodies "in a way that disrupts the latter's routines"
  (Habermas 1996, 358).

While spontaneous and informal, the work that a public of citizens
does makes social integration possible among otherwise semi-autonomous systems. It provides new knowledge for more formal bodies to use in their deliberations; it makes political legitimacy possible—as well as providing means for identifying illegitimate

political actions and institutions. All in all, it is crucial to developing a more deliberative democracy.

Deliberative Democracy

Since the mid-1980s, there has been a resurgence of an old idea: that the people ought to be the authors of their own government and laws. Today this idea goes by the name "deliberative democracy"; it is an alternative to both the empty proceduralism of liberalism and the weighty and questionable substance of civic republicanism. Deliberative democracy gives the public sphere a central role in the political process, namely that of forming public opinion and will on matters of common concern. In the public sphere, the public deliberates together about what ought to be done and, it is hoped, conveys its will to the powers that be in a compelling manner. This idea now animates work being done from a range of philosophical orientations: analytic political and legal philosophy, continental critical theory, pragmatism, American feminist social and political theory, and even some rational choice theory. Some political theorists (such as Robert Dahl) are relinquishing their allegiance to interest-based models of politics and coming to emphasize the democratic notion that governments and policies derive their legitimacy from deliberatively generated public will. Many socialist theorists are using deliberative theory to turn their focus from the welfare state to civil society, discourse theory, and the public sphere. Some feminist philosophers see deliberative theory as a means by which different voices and perspectives can be used in democratic decision making and in creating new public political forums for previously marginalized groups. Deliberative democratic theory is bridging these orientations and creating new philosophical terrain.

Two contemporary philosophers are primarily responsible for current interest in deliberative theory: John Rawls and, as I have discussed, Jürgen Habermas. With the publication of Rawls's *Theory of Justice* in 1971, the market, utilitarian-inspired theory of politics, known as the interest-based model, lost ground in favor of a neo-Kantian model of democratic legitimacy. In short, Rawls's theory of justice renewed the Kantian injunction found in "Perpetual Peace" that, to quote, "I am not under any obligation even to divine laws (which I can recognize by reason alone), except in so far as I have been able to give my own consent to them" (Kant 1970, 99). In other words, we should be the author not only of our own morality but of our government. Working out of a quite different tradition, the critical theory of the Frankfurt School, Habermas contributed to deliberative theory with his work on discourse ethics and the public sphere, showing how a nonspecialized public sphere could reach agreement about issues that affect the public in common and develop public will that might guide public policy. Both Rawls and Habermas draw on Kant's rational ideal of democratic political legitimacy. But where Kant saw the rational agent deliberating alone, Rawls and Habermas describe dialogical models of democratic legitimacy. Habermas especially sees democratic legitimacy as springing from a communicative public sphere.

In the past few years, several books and articles have come out on deliberative theory, with authors staking out different positions. Still, I think most would generally agree with the definition of deliberative legitimacy stated by Seyla Benhabib:

> Only those norms (i.e., general rules of action and institutional arrangements) can be said to be valid (i.e., morally binding), which would be agreed to by all those affected by their consequences, if such agreement were reached as a consequence of a process of deliberation that had the following features: 1) participation in such deliberation is governed by the norms of equality and symmetry; all have the same chances to initiate speech acts, to question, to interrogate, and to open debate; 2) all have the right to question the assigned topics of conversation; and 3) all have the right to initiate reflexive arguments about the very rules of the discourse procedure and the way in which they are applied or carried out. (Benhabib 1996, 70)

Others would supplement this definition by stressing that the participants should be free and equal. Their consensus should be freely reached, not coerced. They should have equal standing and opportunity to shape the deliberations. (Deciding what the ideal of equality involves has been a central line of inquiry.)

The exciting aspect of deliberative theory is that it offers a practical, democratic model to replace the interest-based model of politics that has been so influential during the twentieth century. In brief, the interest-based model sees politics as a struggle over finite resources, as a plurality of competing interests, in which citizenship is reduced to voting on the basis of self-interest. The real pessimists, such as Joseph Schumpeter and Walter Lippmann, doubted that citizens had any real grasp of what would be in their own interest, much less the public interest. In a way reminiscent of Plato's criticism of "democratic man," they noted that people were uninformed and easily manipulated. Thus, the best kind of government would be one ruled by a cadre of experts. For Schumpeter, the point of voting was to elect those who might best judge what was in the public interest. To support this view of politics, these theorists only needed to look around, for there was ample empirical evidence that people in fact behaved this way.

But political philosophers have never let empirical data stop them from making normative claims about what an ideal political arrangement would be. As counterpoint to Schumpeter and Lippmann, the early part of this century had John Dewey and Hannah Arendt arguing for an alternative understanding of democratic politics. And soon after mid-century, the New Left was calling for a more participatory model of politics, drawing on the civic republican tradition still intact in our political heritage. Several feminist theorists continued this effort, including Carole Pateman and Jane Mansbridge.

Deliberative theory offers a way of approaching participation at its most fundamental level: at the level of authoring policy and legitimating government. While based on a Kantian ideal, it has found support in the actual events of the post–Cold War era, with the fall of governments in Eastern Europe, regimes that fell nearly as soon as public associations arose and decried their illegitimacy. These associations had the hallmarks of deliberative democracy: they emanated from the nongovernmental public sphere; they were open, public associations that citizens joined in order to develop and voice a public will on matters of common concern. Effectively they told their governments this: "You who say you are the 'people's government' are not legitimate agents of the public sphere." And within a matter of days these governments stepped down. Apparently, deliberative democracy—insofar as these events were examples—was not only good in theory, it was also good in practice.

Challenges to Deliberative Theory: Pluralism, Difference, and the Private Sphere

The political transformation of Eastern Europe was one chapter in our recent history: it showed that a political, deliberative public sphere might be able to bring down governments. But now we are in another chapter whose leitmotifs seem to be culture wars and civil wars, where the various parties take to their corners and entrench themselves in their own positions. Though we may be glad to have left behind the myth of America as a melting pot, many the world over are wondering how today's multicultural communities can survive. In the Americas, Eurasia, and Africa, countries are riven by ethnic and cultural divisions. Developing any kind of social unity is difficult, let alone the kind of consensus that Habermas and other deliberative theorists consider necessary. The question we now face is whether a political public sphere can both be heterogeneous and come to any *positive* agreement about matters of public concern.

Liberal theory offers a familiar answer to the problem of difference and pluralism. It makes a neat dichotomy between the public and the private, such that our differences and particularities are relegated to the private realm or the "background culture" whereas in public we have equal citizenship and an interest in the public good. According to liberal theory, in publicly discussing matters of common concern, citizens should speak in terms that all others would accept. They should use a language shorn of particular biases and idiosyncrasies, a language with common currency. In public deliberations, according to a Rawlsian liberal view, participants should limit the reasons they use to ones that others could accept. In a pluralist society, participants will have a wide variety of "comprehensive doctrines" about what the good is, but these are to remain in the private domain. When we deliberate with others, we should offer reasons that the public at large would find compelling. In this way, it does not matter how many ethnicities, creeds, and religions a society has, for these particularities will remain outside the public conversation. Our public selves will speak in terms that are widely shared. In a liberal model of pluralism, our private selves may differ considerably, yet our public selves are really alike—having equal dignity, respect, opportunity, and freedom.

Many feminists have criticized this distinction between public and private on a variety of grounds. To name a few: that the distinction devalues the work that is done in the private sphere, including care and nurturing; that it valorizes a universalist, male conception of the human self; that it calls for sameness and denies the merits of difference; that it privileges reason over emotion and traditionally male ways of acting over traditionally female ways; and that it sees the self as unencumbered and discrete rather than as situated in a web of relationships.

These are important criticisms, but they do not get to the central problem with the public / private distinction, at least as it is played out in the rough and tumble of politics. The central question in political communities where difference seems to make any kind of agreement impossible is this: participants have little reason to leave their comprehensive doctrines behind and limit themselves to public reasons, for the heart of their debates is usually over some aspect of their comprehensive doctrines. For example, someone who thinks that abortion is murder, that a fetus is a person, wants to make *public* this view that Rawls argues is part of a comprehensive doctrine. It is the fact that this view is not widely shared that drives the opponent of abortion in an attempt to make abortion a public issue. Likewise, a religious fundamentalist who wants to reform the state along the lines of his religion is also seeking to make the private public. Liberal theory says that such arguments are not publicly acceptable—they do not abide by the idea of public reason. But liberalism doesn't say *why* anyone should care to respect this public / private distinction, especially given the strong motives people have to make their *particular* concerns public ones.

Many may have little sympathy for the examples I've used, religious fundamentalists and pro-lifers who want to undermine the public / private distinction. But certainly we can recall other cases in which what was at issue was a narrow public view: Consider a once "widely shared" view that women need not vote because their husbands did so for both of them. Using the criteria of public reason, the women's suffrage movement might have been stymied by the fact that many would have thought it unreasonable that women should vote. Without making an extended argument for it here, let me venture to say that many, if not all, difficult political issues are about what should become a publicly acceptable view. The content of what should count as a public reason is always politically contested. Liberal theory may help formulate the problem, but it doesn't help solve it.

Deliberative democracy theory, with its roots in Habermas's discourse ethics, does offer a way for people with radically different views to try to reach an understanding on matters of common concern. It doesn't rule out any topics a priori. Unlike liberal theory, which would dismiss some issues as nonpublic, deliberative theory calls on participants to try to reach some kind of accord on any matter that affects others. As William Rehg writes, "The actual interests of the participants make up precisely the matter under discursive examination, and the institutional shape of justice is left to the real results of such examination." This point is important, Rehg notes, because "it moves practical discourse beyond liberal models of 'neutral dialogue,' which typically strike more controversial topics from discussion" (Rehg 1997, 80).

Deliberative democracy theory begins with real, flesh-and-blood participants, who bring with them all their histories, particularities, and idiosyncrasies to the table of public deliberation. There they join to reach by rational argumentation a consensus about what should be done on matters of common concern. Habermas does not expect a consensus to be definitive and final, for the participants should continue to reassess and decide again. The outcomes of a deliberative procedure are always provisional, as they should be in a democracy (otherwise current generations would be undemocratically bound by others' decisions).

Yet many of the constraints built into rational argumentation aimed at reaching consensus may themselves be undemocratic. For one, as some feminists argue, the emphasis on consensus and universality seems to close off many of the differences and much of the heterogeneity of public life (Meehan 1995). For another, as Iris Young (1997b) argues, the concern with "rational argumentation" seems to deny the validity of other forms of communication. As I shall suggest, the presumption that the participants are autonomous, self-transparent users of a more-or-less fixed language steers us away from seeing citizens as subjects-in-process. And this leads us to overlook other forms of community that might arise from subjects who see themselves as always already in relation together.

4 The Split Subject in the Public Sphere

What alternative politics does a theory of the subject-in-process suggest? What concerns should we have about the agency of those whose subjectivity is always a tenuous, fragile, and deeply intersubjective affair? Were we to reject the model of subjectivity that Habermas holds in favor of a model of subjectivity that Kristeva proposes, would deliberative democracy be possible? Would this theory be useful for feminist politics? As I argue in this chapter, Kristeva herself does not provide an answer to these questions, for her model of politics trails far behind her theory of subjectivity. I show how other strategies, including radical democratic and socialist feminist ones, also fall short. In closing I point to some interpretations of Kristeva's work that can send us in promising directions.

Kristeva's Politics

When Kristeva arrived in Paris in the 1960s, she immediately joined the cultural and intellectual movements sweeping the city, movements that were intrinsically political. Her political activism led to a trip to China, an interest in Maoism, and an investment in the revolutionary potential of events of 1968. But as the promise of the late '60s dissipated, so too did her involvement in politics on the large scale. Some might say that she abandoned politics altogether, but Kristeva would disagree.

In several interviews, Kristeva has discussed her move away from trying to address politics on the macro scale to her work at the psychoanalytic, small scale. "I don't think we can approach political questions with a general discourse," she told interviewers in 1985 (Guberman 1996, 24). Five years earlier she said that from Emile Benveniste she learned, "It would be better to take up again the basic presuppositions, start from the small things, the small notions" (15). Rather than take up the grand problems of history, she prefers to look at "the minimal components that constitute the speaking being" (15). The "concrete problems" that she has concerned herself with, since her refusal of Maoism, are love, melancholia, and abjection. She sees these as political as well as personal problems: "Finding a subject for reflection that involves individuals in their daily anxiety is a political concern," she said in 1985, "and seen as such, political concerns should, I think, be both more modest and more effective" (25). In a 1989 interview she makes the same point: "We must try to be as concrete—I would even say microscopic—as we can be. . . . [W]e must not try to propose global models. I think that we risk, then, making politics into a sort of religion, while it seems to me that concrete interventions are more important. For example, I consider that my work as an analyst is political work, to take it in a microscopic and individual sense" (42).

In Chapter 2 I discussed Kristeva's theory of subjectivity, which has in large part emerged from her work as an analyst, from her focus on the "micro" level of politics. Some of the ideas that have developed from her psychoanalytic work have applications at the macro level as well, particularly those that are the focus of her book *Étrangers à nous mêmes* (translated as *Strangers to Ourselves* in 1991) and the essays collected in *Nations without Nationalism* (1993).

In *Strangers to Ourselves*, Kristeva draws on her own experience as a foreigner and her work in psychoanalytic theory to explore a political question: why the foreigner seems so radically strange, why he has such difficulty becoming part of an adopted community. She points to the Freudian notion of the unconscious, saying that the ultimate foreigner is the foreigner within each of us, our own internal strangeness, our unconscious. "Strangely, the foreigner lives within us: he is the hidden face of our identity, the space that wrecks our abode, the time in which understanding and affinity founder" (Kristeva 1991, 1). It is because we have not come to terms with this internal strangeness that we project strangeness onto others. That is

why the foreigner is so compelling and still so threatening: he reminds us of our own internal not-at-homeness. The only way to
come to terms with the foreigners in our midst is to come to terms
with the foreigner within. "The foreigner comes in when the consciousness of my difference arises, and he disappears when we all acknowledge ourselves as foreigners, unamenable to bonds and communities" (1).

This experience of radical strangeness becomes a political problem
when it is used to deny rights to foreigners and when it places political communities in antagonistic relationships with immigrants and
others. To address this, Kristeva proposes some political remedies,
such as international agreements that would grant reciprocal rights
to immigrants. Still, she sees such steps as only a partial solution, for
the problem is as much psychological and metaphysical as it is political (Kristeva 1991, 195). To deal with the problem at this level, Kristeva proposes psychoanalysis, though one wonders how feasible such
a solution is at a societal level.[1] Still, her analysis of the situation is,
I think, pertinent. If "the personal" is left untended, it becomes political. In other words, if we do not find ways to deal with internal foreignness—if we do not come to be at home with ourselves—we will
not be at home with those others in our midst, those with whom we
are struggling to share political community. Community itself will
be difficult to achieve. It may well be that problems that affect modern political societies, such as problems of racism, nationalism, and
xenophobia, are at least in part a result of the psychic maladies affecting subjectivities today.

Kristeva's experience and identity as a foreigner imbues her more
explicit political theory as well, found in the essays collected in *Nations without Nationalism*. The central issue in her writing on politics is how *l'étranger* can come to be at home in a new nation. How
can someone who is so *other* become a part, a member, of another political community? Perhaps as a consequence of her concern with
membership in a political order, Kristeva's views resonate with liberal and Enlightenment themes. For one, she draws heavily on Montesquieu's writings, especially his notion of cosmopolitanism. For another, much like liberal theorists, Kristeva comes close to equating
citizenship with nationality; that is, she conceives of citizenship as
the state of having the rights and privileges of membership in a na-

---

[1] For a more detailed assessment, see McAfee 1993.

tion (Kristeva 1993a, 11). But for her, the term *nation* stands for something heterogeneous and dynamic (Kristeva 1993a, 57), rather than unified and static.

Kristeva shares with Habermas a dislike for the tendencies of the republican tradition, including Hegel's conception of *Volksgeist*, "spirit of the people." For Kristeva, the problem with this notion is that it flattens out differences within a nation, subsuming heterogeneity under a monolithic people and making those who are *other* into enemies: "A libertarian mainspring at the beginning, that sort of nationalism, more or less consciously dependent on the *Volksgeist*, changes—only too rapidly as one can see—into a repressive force aimed at other peoples and extolling one's own" (Kristeva 1993a, 54). When we conceive of our political community as a unity, Kristeva warns, we risk becoming exclusionary. Thus, she poses the question:

> Is there a way of thinking politically about the "national" that does not degenerate into an exclusory, murderous racism, without at the same time dissolving into an all-encompassing feeling of "S.O.S.–Absolute Brotherhood" and providing, for the span of an evening, all who represent groups (historical identities that have been respectively persecuted and persecuting) with the delight of being on a boundless ocean? (51)

Instead of the notion of *Volksgeist*, Kristeva prefers Montesquieu's notion of the *esprit général*, which she argues preserves heterogeneity and multiplicity within civil society, including the private sphere that allows individuals to flourish. Montesquieu's conception of the *esprit général*, she writes, reformulates the national whole as (1) a "*historical* identity," (2) a "*layering* of very concrete and very diverse causalities (climate, religions, past, laws, customs, manners, and so forth)," and (3) a possibility of developing an even higher "spirit of concord and economic development" with other groups (55). She quotes Montesquieu: "Europe is no more than a nation made up of several others, France and England need the richness of Poland and Muscovy as one of their provinces needs the others." Thus, the notion of *esprit général* makes possible a conception of the nation that is a contingent and variable entity (as a historical identity), kept together through tradition but always vulnerable to instability and change, as well as an entity "endowed with a logical multiplicity whose diversity is to be maintained without the possibility of having one social (logical) stratum dominate the others" (56).

So, instead of being a "weighty and determinist" entity, the nation, in Kristeva's view, is an open and dynamic system. Likewise, her conception of citizenship opens up. She quotes Montesquieu: "Men, in such a nation, would be confederates rather than citizens," meaning that instead of being an abstract conception, citizenship is a heterogeneous and dynamic process—a way of forming constellations with others.[2] Kristeva writes:

> As the liberal empiricist Robert Aron foresaw . . . the *esprit général* could be realized by means of a clever alternation between the *political* and the *national, dynamics* and *inertia* (might one say today, between "citizenship" and "nationality"?). Such an administrative interpretation of Montesquieu is not without cleverness. It seems, nevertheless, that the philosopher of the Enlightenment had elaborated a higher perception of the national presence, one that avoided isolating, on the one hand, abstract and evolutive politics (citizenship) and, on the other, the weighty, deterministic national (nationality); but he suggested a concept . . . involving the integration, without a leveling process, of the different layers of social reality into the political and / or national unity. (Kristeva 1993a, 57)

Thus, in her reading of Montesquieu, Kristeva articulates a conception of nation that allows for a commonality without eradicating difference. One can be a citizen of such a nation, a member of such a whole, without melting away any of one's own specificity or difference.

In keeping with this notion, Kristeva considers herself a cosmopolitan, one who can choose her national identity and transgress the orthodoxy of origins: "Thus when I say that I have chosen cosmopolitanism, this means that I have, against origins and starting

---

[2] Some might protest that I am setting up a homology between subjectivity and community, insofar as I describe them both as open and dynamic systems. Yet I am not isolating these two things from all other things and equating them with each other. I would, following process philosophers, say that the quiddity or "whatness" of anything is not a substance but a continuously unfolding process that is always reverberating in interactions with other processes, events, and relations. The symbolic mode of signification attempts to still this movement, to put bounds around entities, to exclude what is other. The metaphysics of the symbolic is substance ontology; whereas process philosophy can be seen as an attempt to understand "what there is" in a way that respects the movement of the *chora*. Still, following Derrida, we should be wary of any attempt, whether by substance or process ontology, to enclose everything within a system.

from them, chosen a transnational or international position situated at the crossing of boundaries" (Kristeva 1993a, 16).

How transgressive, though, is this cosmopolitanism? Not very, I would argue. It does not seem to follow very well from her theory of subjectivity as an open system. In her writings on subjectivity, we find a subject who is always open and in relation with others, whose attempts to achieve some stability through the symbolic process are often in vain, for the semiotic, the *chora*, the unconscious always threatens order and stability. Even in *Strangers to Ourselves* we find a subject-at-odds with herself and so with others. In these depictions, it would be odd to consider the subject-in-process as a discrete individual. To the contrary, as an open system, the subject is always in relation with others and otherness. Yet, when Kristeva begins to talk about politics at the macro level, the individual suddenly appears. Granted she is an individual heterogeneous in regard to others—but lost is her internal heterogeneity as well as her constitutive relationality with others. No, here we have a cosmopolitan ideal of a "paradoxical society." Even at the end of *Strangers to Ourselves*, Kristeva writes: "The multinational society would thus be the consequence of an extreme individualism, but conscious of its discontents and limits, knowing only indomitable people ready-to-help-themselves in their weakness, a weakness whose other name is our radical strangeness" (Kristeva 1991, 195). From this description, it does not seem that Kristeva thinks these subjects help each other; rather, in their *extreme individualism* each attends to herself.

When she writes about politics, Kristeva "forgets" that the subject is an open system, vulnerable, deeply related to others, and "in process."[3] She moves to an Enlightenment model of cosmopolitan individualism. Granted, it is an ideal that preserves difference and multiplicity, but not necessarily any more than liberal pluralism would. To

---

[3] Norma Claire Moruzzi makes a similar claim in her essay "National Abjects: Julia Kristeva on the Process of Political Self-Identification" (Oliver 1993a). Moruzzi argues that Kristeva avoids putting the logic of abjection into her work in *Strangers to Ourselves*. If she had, she might have seen that "degeneration of the fixed identity of the nation-state . . . need not mean the end of political identity or participation. Yet Kristeva hesitates before this political implication of her own earlier work. Instead, it seems, when confronted with the very insistent emergence into public view of the formerly hidden bodies of familiar, abject strangers . . . Kristeva retreats to an understandably personal, if personally contradictory (to her own previous theorizations), assertion of humanistic quietude. If abjection, to achieve the generative transformation Kristeva has mentioned, demands the death of the ego, her latest work seems to

somebody steeped in an Enlightenment model of politics, Kristeva's politics would seem safe and harmless. But not everyone is so quick to "forget" Kristeva's radical model of subjectivity. Some will take her notion of the subject as heterogeneous and in process and see how it fares in the political realm. In what follows I examine two such analyses, one that takes on Kristeva's views explicitly and another that looks at the political consequences of a more general poststructuralist theory. As I show, neither analysis is adequate. Still, they do pose the question more directly: what kind of political agent can a subject-in-process be? First I turn to a position taken by Nancy Fraser, who, as a theorist sympathetic to Habermas and to deliberative politics in general, offers a good starting point for evaluating the political implications of Kristeva's theory of subjectivity. While I disagree with her argument that Kristeva's theory of subjectivity is politically counterproductive, it is instructive in showing the political implications that a theory of subjectivity can have.

Nancy Fraser's Pessimism

Since about 1980, there has been a tension between certain approaches to feminist theory on this continent and those in Europe, especially of late between socialist feminism here and poststructuralist feminism in France. A major point of disagreement is the possibility of constructive social change under a poststructuralist theory of subjectivity. I take this question very seriously, for I believe that our theories of subjectivity do shape our conception of political agency. For this reason, I am interested in the essay written by Nancy Fraser, "The Uses and Abuses of French Discourse Theories for Feminist Politics," in which the author considers the wisdom of using Julia Kristeva's theories of discourse and subjectivity.

Fraser takes issue with Kristeva's work on two main points. The first has to do with the intellectual tradition to which Kristeva belongs, which Fraser describes as "structuralist" rather than "pragmatic." Along with some other socialist and materialist philosophers, Fraser argues that structuralism is incompatible with

---

be asserting, perhaps in spite of herself, that here is one ego that is not yet dead" (Oliver 1993a, 146–47). I share Moruzzi's concerns about Kristeva's avoidance of the deep heterogeneity in national identities as well as Moruzzi's interest in bringing together abjection and nationality.

developing a materialist-historical understanding of society—that the two approaches are mutually exclusive.[4] Fraser identifies

> two distinct models of discourse that have been developed in recent French thought: 1) a structuralist model that treats language as a symbolic system or code and that is derived from Saussure, presupposed in Lacan, and abstractly negated in deconstruction; and 2) a pragmatic model that treats languages as sets of multiple and historically specific institutionalized social practices and that is associated with Mikhail Bakhtin, Michel Foucault, and Pierre Bourdieu. (Fraser 1992b, 177)

Fraser contends that structuralism is ahistorical and rigid: "Saussure insisted that the study of langue be synchronic rather than diachronic; he thereby posited his object of study as static and atemporal, abstracting it from historical change" (181). She contrasts this with what she terms pragmatic, material-historical analyses that look at real, evolving conditions of human life and make room for change, that is, they see history as contingent. Now, this criticism of structuralism rests upon an assumption that those who examine structures see them as fixed. However, many, perhaps most, structuralist theorists see structures as contingent, historical features. A structuralist account can offer a *series* of synchronic views of a given society or system. It doesn't necessarily claim that any particular synchronic picture is unchangeable or ahistorical. To the contrary, the most compelling structuralist views—Lévi-Strauss's approach to kinship relations, Saussure's approach to language, and, I might add, Foucault's early work—take structures to be the *result* of material, historical conditions. Given that these and other "structuralists" see structures as consequences of material-historical processes, Fraser's distinction between the two schools is tenuous at best.

Fraser's argument is interesting for its attempt to delineate schools of thought and their relationships. As I read between the lines, I see her attempting to draw a genealogy of "pragmatic," materialist thought from Marx through Bourdieu and Foucault: all those theorists who concern themselves with people's real, lived experience.

---

[4] This may well be the case with a structuralist theory such as Althusser's, which some have called a structuralism without any people in it. In a conversation with the author, Rick Roderick described Althusser's theory as having "no history, no people, no drama, no Marx." See also E. P. Thompson's polemic against Althusser, *The Poverty of Theory*.

She seems to want to contrast this with another "family" of structuralists, those who seem, according to her, to be oblivious to lived experience and to opt instead for empty abstractions, useless for feminist politics. I want to suggest a different genealogy, drawing from an autobiographical essay Kristeva wrote in 1984. Describing the development and focus of her intellectual circle of the 1960s and '70s, Kristeva writes:

> For us, structuralism . . . was already accepted knowledge. To simplify, this meant that one should no longer lose sight of the real constraints, "material," as we used to say, of what had previously and trivially been viewed as "form." For us, the logic of this formal reality constituted the very meaning of phenomena or events that then became structures (from kinship to literary texts) and thus achieved intelligibility without necessarily relying on "external factors." From the outset, however, our task was to take this acquired knowledge and immediately do something else. (Kristeva 1984b, 266)

In this genealogy, contra Fraser's, the movement from structuralism to poststructuralism is not a reversal but an expansion. These transitional figures saw in structuralism a way of finding the meaning of a system, which they used in their further explorations. For Kristeva the move was to an understanding of *dynamic* subjectivity through psychoanalytic theory. Structuralism provided a way to understand meaning through synchronic understandings of real constraints; through poststructuralism, these intellectuals recognized that these structures are manifestations of volatile, complex, unpredictable, and often subterranean processes.

Fredric Jameson offers a way of making sense of these two contrary genealogies. First he points to a particular moment of structuralism: "The moment of high structuralism—whose most influential monuments are seemingly not philosophical at all, but can be characterized, alongside the new linguistics itself, as linguistic transformations of anthropology and psychoanalysis by Claude Lévi-Strauss and Jacques Lacan respectively—is, however, inherently unstable and has the vocation of becoming a new type of universal mathesis, under pain of vanishing as one more intellectual fad" (Jameson 1988, 186). Jameson points out the two possible trajectories for this high structuralism. First, "the breakdown products of that moment of high structuralism [which] can then be seen, on the one hand, as the reduction to a kind of scientism, to sheer method and analytic technique (in *semiotics*)"; and second "on the other hand . . . the transformation of structuralist approaches into active ideologies in which ethical, political, and historical consequences are drawn from the hitherto more epistemological 'structuralist' positions'" (186–87). The first trajectory, which leads to a static scientism, is the one Fraser points to. The other is its antithesis or outgrowth: "this last is of course the moment of what is now generally known as *poststructuralism*, associated with familiar names like those of Foucault, Deleuze, Derrida, and so forth" (187).

All this is to say that Fraser's dismissal of "French theories" as rigidly structuralist is off the mark. At this turn in history (beginning in May 1968), structuralism transformed itself into a dynamic theory of change. The structuralism that was static withered away, a dead relic of an old formalism.

Still, Fraser's second and main disagreement with Kristeva remains to be addressed. Fraser maintains that Kristeva's theory splits the subject in two and does not allow for effective political agency. Fraser argues on pragmatic grounds that such theory should be avoided. Fraser's rejection of Kristeva's theory rests in large part on a modernist understanding of what political agency requires: namely, autonomous, unified subjectivity, which allows one to know one's own interests and have the power to further them. Fraser's modernism, on this score, is shared by many other theorists of emancipation, many American feminists included. They all seem to have in common the supposition that only unified, autonomous subjectivity can lead to political agency. On this ground, they reject poststructuralist theories, because these suggest a heterogeneous subjectivity that is always in flux, never unified and centered. Now, with Fraser and other modernists I share the goal of political agency. As a feminist, I am particularly interested in political agency for women and other heretofore marginalized people. I differ, however, with the supposition that only the unified, autonomous subjectivity promised by modernism can lead to such political agency. In fact, I think that modern theories of subjectivity will always fall short of this goal. Moreover, I see in poststructuralist theory a promise of a rich and powerful form of political agency.

The way Fraser divides the field between structuralist and pragmatic models of language warrants a moment's attention. Fraser's grouping of these "distinct" models of discourse is unusual, for, as

the essay attests, the first group, structuralism, includes deconstruction, since deconstruction only abstractly negates the model, leaving
all the structures in place. The second, pragmatic model, which
"treats languages as sets of multiple . . . practices" and is associated
with Foucault, sounds quite a bit like poststructuralism, at least in
its attention to the variability of language games and the social construction of individuals. But as a "pragmatic" model, this second
group, which she ultimately supports, is geared toward maintaining a
very modern (as opposed to postmodern) understanding of political
agency. Even though she invokes Bakhtin, Foucault, and Bourdieu at
the outset she does not make use of their approaches in the body of
the essay. Instead, she employs a particular criterion: that a theory is
useful for feminist politics only if it allows for a subjectivity that is
unified and autonomous.

As I see it, the real pair that Fraser sets up is (1) any poststructuralism that has its roots in linguistic models of the unconscious (which
includes Kristeva as well as Derrida) as opposed to (2) socially specific
models of identity formation that subscribe to a modernist theory of
subjectivity.

At the essay's outset, Fraser says she wants to explain why "feminists should have no truck with Lacan and . . . only the most minimal truck with Julia Kristeva." In the process, she says, she wants "to
identify some places where . . . we can find more satisfactory alternatives" (177). It is telling that she uses the word *satisfactory* here, for
clearly she has something in mind that a theory ought to *satisfy*.
That something is a particular understanding of feminist politics, the
substance of which is indicated by the four things she says a discourse theory ought to do.

> First, it can help us understand how people's social identities are fash-
> ioned and altered over time. Second, it can help us understand how, un-
> der conditions of inequality, social groups in the sense of collective
> agents are formed and unformed. Third, a theory of discourse can illu-
> minate how the cultural hegemony of dominant groups in society is se-
> cured and contested. Fourth and finally, it can shed light on the
> prospects for emancipatory social change and political practice. (178)

The first and second points are about how social identity is formed
and maintained; the third is about power, how some groups gain and

maintain "hegemony" over others—the hope being that marginalized groups can one day gain hegemony; and the fourth is about how these groups become effective agents for change. These points indicate that for Fraser feminist politics is about how individuals form social identities and gain political agency in a model that views politics as an antagonistic endeavor.

In spelling out what she thinks a discourse theory ought to do she implies certain metaphysical and ethical views about identity and politics. Her concern about identity is about how an individual (substance) identifies with others socially. The *subject* of this relation is unexamined: "To have a social identity, to be a woman or a man, for example, just *is* to live and to act under a set of descriptions" (178). One's social identity is a matter of answering to a description, as if one hears "lesbian" or "chicana" and responds "here!" The "one" responding is a given, already constructed individual. Though individual identity is presupposed, social identity is constructed discursively. The latter proposition, that social identity is discursively constructed, is compatible with both modern and poststructuralist theories. But the former, that individual identity is given, is bound to a substance ontology of self. In other words, it is in keeping with a modern view that there is some core self that endures through time, even if certain attributes of the self change.

Fraser believes that to think of one's own identity as tentative, provisional, and fictional destroys the possibility of one's acting as a social agent. To make her case, she traces the roots of Kristeva's position to Lacan. She focuses on a select few features of Lacan's thought in order to tie him to what she describes as Saussure's a-historical, closed structuralism. She admits that her reading of Lacan is oversimplified: "let me illustrate these problems by reconstructing, and criticizing, an ideal-typical reading of Lacan that I believe is widespread among English-speaking feminists" (181).

> I shall bracket the question of the fidelity of this reading, which could be faulted for exaggerating the centrality of phallo-centrism to Lacan's view of the symbolic order and for overemphasizing the influence of Saussure at the expense of other, countervailing influences, such as Hegel. *For my purposes*, this ideal-typical Saussurean reading of Lacan is *useful* precisely because it *evinces with unusual clarity* difficulties which beset many "poststructuralist" theorists whose abstract at-

tempts to break free of structuralism only render them all the more bound to it. (181; emphasis added)

I find this approach to Lacan problematic, for it leads Fraser to distort Lacan's and ultimately Kristeva's views. Briefly, she argues that Lacan treats language ahistorically; without giving any textual support, she claims that Lacan thinks that the symbolic order is monolithic rather than heterogeneous; she maintains that his model is deterministic; and she contends that such models ignore the social context of communication (as if the family and our relations with others weren't crucial contextual domains). Unfortunately, she cites Lacan only once, and then on a minor tangent.[5]

Having made these characterizations, she writes Lacan off:

> With the way blocked to a political understanding of identities, groups, and cultural hegemony, the way is also blocked to an understanding of political practice. For one thing, there is no conceivable agent of such practice. None of the three moments that comprise the Lacanian view of the person can qualify as a political agent. The speaking subject is simply a grammatical "I" wholly subjected to the symbolic order; it can only and forever reproduce that order. The Lacanian ego is an imaginary projection, deluded about its own stability and self-possession, hooked on an impossible desire for unity and self-completion; it therefore can only and forever tilt at windmills. Finally, there is the ambiguous Lacanian unconscious, sometimes an ensemble of repressed libidinal drives, sometime the face of language as Other, *but never anything that could count as a social agent.* (184; emphasis added)

Despite the errors and simplifications in her reading of Lacan, Fraser's characterization of Lacan's position is not entirely off the mark: for Lacan, subjectivity is incomplete and self-unity is fictional. Now notice that she rejects such a notion of subjectivity because she cannot fathom how such a subject could be a social agent. On this ba-

---

[5] Fraser writes that "to the extent that Lacan has succeeded in eliminating biologism—and that is dubious for reasons I cannot take up here—he has replaced it with psychologism" (Fraser 1992b, 182). She footnotes the phrase "for reasons I cannot take up here" by noting that "many feminist critics have shown that he fails to prevent the collapse of the symbolic signifier into the organ. The clearest indication of this failure is his claim, in 'The Meaning of the Phallus', that the phallus becomes the master signifier because of its 'turgidity'." Note that Fraser cites Lacan on a point she is willing, with qualification, to grant him. This is the only text by Lacan that she lists in her notes or bibliography.

sis alone, she rejects Lacan's theory, admitting that she is not concerned with the validity of the theory: "I have focused here on conceptual as opposed to empirical issues," she writes, "and I have not directly addressed the question, is Lacan's theory true?" (184–85). This pragmatism upholds an unexamined view: that subjectivity has to be complete and unified for political agency to be possible. Since Lacan's view does not accept this supposition, it fails the test.[6]

Having brought down Lacan, she turns to Kristeva. Here she is more attentive to the complexity in Kristeva's theory. In the end she praises Kristeva for the extent to which she is concerned with contextual, historical matters, and condemns her for the areas of her work in which she succumbs to a "quasi-Lacanian neostructuralism" (188). Recall that, using a Lacanian approach to psychoanalysis, Kristeva argues that one's own identity is never unified and formed; it is not really "constructed" but always under construction. And just as any construction site is a dangerous place, one's own place of subjectivity, always under construction, or as Kristeva says, always "in process," is perilous. One can never be sure of one's self, one's desires, one's psychic borders. For example, in describing how identity is constructed by abjection, by the infant abjecting the mother's body to form its own boundaries, Kristeva writes about how abject things continue to haunt and taunt. Her language bears witness to the inherent instability of subjectivity in Kristeva's theory: "A weight of meaninglessness, about which there is nothing insignificant, and which crushes me. On the edge of non-existence and hallucination, of a reality that, if I acknowledge it, annihilates me. There, abject and abjection are my safeguards. The primers of my culture" (Kristeva 1982, 2).

As I've said, Kristeva does use and revise many of Lacan's notions. The main one with which Fraser takes issue is Kristeva's revision of his notion of the symbolic order—the order of language and taboo that the infant enters into through the mirror stage and the oedipal complex. Kristeva argues that when an infant enters the symbolic realm of language it cannot completely leave behind its primal desires, "pulsions," and rhythms. This anarchical realm remains with the infant in what she calls "the semiotic." So from infancy onward a subject has two registers for signifying: the orderly symbolic and the

---

[6] One might wonder: If subjectivity were complete and unified in itself, why would it need politics—or, for that matter, society?

anarchic semiotic. Kristeva finds something promising, even revolutionary, in semiotic signification. It can help break through the Law
of the Father and offer other modes of subjectivity. But Fraser will
have no truck with this. She accuses Kristeva of adopting an "addi-
tive approach," through which she adds something good to an otherwise bad theory. "Simply adding the two together, then, cannot and
does not lead to pragmatics. Rather, it yields an amalgam of structure
and antistructure. Moreover, this amalgam is, in Hegel's phrase, a
'bad infinity,' since it leaves us oscillating ceaselessly between a
structuralist moment and an antistructuralist moment without getting to anything else" (188).

Fraser also maintains that Kristeva's theory focuses on *intra*subjective tensions rather than *inter*subjective—political—tensions since it
focuses on individuals and not communities (189). In stating this,
Fraser does not discuss the portions of Kristeva's work in which she
has turned to the political questions of how subjects-in-process, foreign to themselves and each other, can come to live together
peaceably.

Fraser criticizes Kristeva's theory of split subjectivity, again, because "neither half of Kristeva's split subject can be a feminist political agent" (189). In the end, Fraser gives three reasons that the "semiotic 'subject'" as she calls it cannot be a feminist political agent: (1)
"First, it is located beneath, rather than within, culture and society;
so it is unclear how its practice could be *political* practice." Already,
I can identify two mistakes. First off, Kristeva does not suggest that
there could be a "semiotic subject," for subjectivity is always a *relation* between the other within and the others in our midst; there is no
separable semiotic self. Second, this subject is constituted socially—
both in the family and in the public world of language and law—so it
is not "beneath culture." (2) The second reason Fraser dismisses Kristeva's theory of subjectivity as a viable candidate for political agency
is that it is involved in transgressing social norms, not creating new
ones. (3) And the third reason is that this sort of subjectivity "is defined in terms of the shattering of social identity" and so cannot "figure in the reconstruction of the new, politically constituted, collective identities and solidarities that are essential to feminist politics"
(189). On points two and three, we should note that the first step in
any kind of political change and creation of new political formations
is to criticize and question the received norms, forms of identity and
social formations. There is nothing counterproductive to politics in

the transgressing of social norms and the shattering of any particular social identity. To be a subject-in-process is to be a subject open to change, to other visions of politics and other political formations.

Let us return to the aims that Fraser asked of a discourse theory: (1) that it help us understand how individual identity is formed; (2) that it help explain the formation of collective identities; (3) that it help show how cultural hegemony is formed and contested; and (4) that it shed light on the possibility of constructive social change. Despite Fraser's attempts to argue otherwise, Kristeva's theory of subjectivity can contribute to the aims of points one, two, and four. I discuss how this is so later in this chapter and in the next chapter. As for point three, I question the aim itself—or at least the terms in which it is posed. The language of cultural hegemony, developed by Antonio Gramsci, tends to reduce politics to a necessarily antagonistic endeavor and to elevate hegemony as the end of politics. On this point, I think I am closer to Habermas's view than is Fraser. Moreover, Fraser's views on subjectivity and hegemony are not necessarily tied together. As I show in the next portion of this chapter, someone can hold quite the opposite view on subjectivity and, unfortunately, also construe politics as a matter of gaining hegemony. We should devote as much attention to how we think of politics as to how we think of subjectivity.

Chantal Mouffe's Politics of Hegemony

I turn now to an argument about feminist politics made by Chantal Mouffe, the co-author with Ernesto Laclau of *Hegemony and Socialist Strategy* as well as the author and editor of numerous books and articles on feminism, postmodernism, and political theory. While she does not address Kristeva's theory of subjectivity per se, she does adopt a poststructuralist theory of subjectivity, one in keeping with Kristeva's theory. As a feminist, Mouffe is committed to improving the situation of women and other marginalized groups through an approach she and Laclau call "radical and plural democracy," which brings together the postmodern critique of universal, unified subjectivity with the political aims of a postmarxian, Gramscian project. Though I share many of her political and philosophical presuppositions, her work goes in a direction that I find problematic and potentially damaging for feminist political theory.

In her essay "Feminism, Citizenship, and Radical Democratic Politics," Mouffe seeks to apply the theory of radical democracy to feminist politics. To do so, she argues that feminists need not postulate an essentialist notion of women's subjectivity in order to develop an effective conception of democratic, feminist politics. By *essentialist* she means any claim that certain qualities or functions associated with women are central to women's identity as women. In fact, she contends, there is no need to hold to any essentialist notion of identity to support the possibility of feminist political action or, for that matter, any form of democratic politics. Mouffe believes that the notion of sexual difference—that is, the idea that there are specific and pertinent differences between the sexes—should be politically irrelevant. Instead of looking for essential identities, feminists should look for ways to find common cause with others who have been denied the democratic ideals of free and equal citizenship in a society that purports to be democratic. The goal, for Mouffe, is for such oppressed people to join together as a "we" to gain hegemony over "them," all those oppressors. (Hegemony is the process by which a collectivity forms contingently and rules by consent rather than force.)

I take issue with Chantal Mouffe's argument at several levels. First, her claim that certain kinds of feminist theories are essentialist is mistaken, primarily because she uses the term "essentialist" much too broadly. Second, Mouffe's attempt to deny the salience of the notion of sexual difference fails for a number of reasons, mainly because the political issue *at stake* for feminist politics is how our culture can learn to deal with the fact of sexual difference. Finally, Mouffe's view of feminist, democratic politics is off track. Politics should not be approached as a struggle for hegemony. The questions that feminists raise do not concern just women; they concern all those whose subjectivities are mired in the struggle to attain identity and agency, both women and men.

The Question of Essentialism

Mouffe disagrees with those feminists who argue that, "without seeing women as a coherent identity, we cannot ground the possibility of a feminist political movement in which women could unite as women in order to formulate and pursue specific feminist aims" (Mouffe 1992, 371). The problem with this approach, she says, is that it unnecessarily holds to an essentialist view of women. Although she never defines just what she means by "essentialist," from her criticisms I gather that for her it is any attempt to delineate a "coherent identity"—to designate criteria that would apply universally to a set of people.[7]

In feminist discussions, usually, to say that someone is making an essentialist claim about women is to say that she is making a claim about women's biology. Colloquially, "biology is destiny" whereas cultural norms are constructed and so can be changed. Now, there are very good reasons to doubt whether such attempts to delineate biology from culture work;[8] but at the least someone using the term "essentialism" to castigate certain views ought to acknowledge these distinctions. Yet Mouffe does not do so.[9] She labels "essentialist" any theory that takes the category of "woman" seriously. But many of the theorists she calls essentialist would say that they are talking about the way women have been socially, historically, and culturally *constructed*, not about any kind of supposed female *essence*.[10]

[7] Mouffe does not address the distinctions that are commonly made in distinguishing essentialism from, say, nominalism: Are we talking about women *de re* or women *de dicto*? Is it a matter of what woman is in herself or of what she is called? Of how she is "naturally" versus how she's been constructed socially? Many feminists are careful to make distinctions between, for example, what a woman is biologically and what she is taken to be culturally.

[8] See, for example, Luce Irigaray's work on sexual difference which calls into question whether the sex / gender distinction is viable. Another important book on this topic is Judith Butler's *Bodies That Matter*, which offers a very nuanced and sophisticated deconstruction of these concepts. See also Diana Fuss's book *Essentially Speaking* and Tina Chanter's essay "Kristeva's Politics of Change: Tracking Essentialism with the Help of a Sex / Gender Map" (Oliver 1993a).

[9] Instead she argues that whole schools of feminist theory are essentialist. Here she includes the ethics-of-care work being done in Anglo American theory, as well as certain communitarian approaches and even some liberal theory.

[10] Cultural feminists take advantage of the contingent fact that women have been historically relegated to the private sphere and denied the benefits that have come with membership in the public realm of politics. Women have been seen as mired in the particular rather than capable of universal perspectives, as tied to nature rather than to "civilization," as emotional rather than rational, more concerned with maintaining relationships than with instituting justice. Many cultural feminists want to revalue the qualities associated with women's position in the private sphere, to say that there is something valuable about being sensitive to particularities and contexts, to being caring and nurturing, and to many of the other qualities that have coalesced in women's supposedly subordinate position. Now, one might question the merits of this "transvaluation of values" for not interrogating the overall system that led to women's positioning in the private sphere—one might also want to undo the insidious binary between public and private—but one should recognize that cultural feminism's attempt to value what has been denigrated is not necessarily based upon any

My guess is that when Mouffe charges certain theories with essentialism she is not being completely ingenuous: her primary concern
seems to be not with essentialism per se but with those who make
any identity claims, or rather, with those who take any particular aspect of one's identity as being more politically pertinent than others.

The Salience of Sexual Difference

Mouffe wants to develop a conception of citizenship where sexual
difference should become "effectively nonpertinent." She argues that
the goal of politics should be to become free and equal citizens in a
democratic order. This requires, she writes,

> a conception of the social agent . . . as the articulation of an ensemble
> of subject positions, corresponding to the multiplicity of social rela-
> tions in which it is inscribed. . . . There is no reason why sexual differ-
> ence should be pertinent in all social relations. . . . [W]e can perfectly
> imagine sexual difference becoming irrelevant in many social relations
> where it is currently found. This is indeed the objective of many femi-
> nist struggles. (Mouffe 1992, 376–77)

While I agree with Mouffe's point that as social agents we have "an
ensemble of subject positions," I disagree with her view that "the objective of many feminist struggles" is or ought to be to make sexual
difference irrelevant, especially with regard to issues central to feminist politics. Let me address my disagreements one by one.

(1) For all my criticisms, I agree with Mouffe's overall point that
an anti-essentialist approach to feminist politics can be very fruitful,
that we need not rely on an a priori, fixed identity of woman in order
to be feminist political agents, and that we all have multiple subject
positions.[11] For example, I am a white, southern, middle-class
woman, a mother, who has been both a boss and a labor organizer, a
first-generation Greek immigrant and a sixth-generation Texan. I

---

essentialist claims. It is very much based upon the contingent, historical, and muta-
ble situation in which women have been thrown.

[11] For an excellent discussion along these lines, see Iris Young's chapter "Gender
as Seriality: Thinking about Women as a Social Collective," in Young 1997a.

hold a number of multiple, often clashing subject positions, none *necessarily* any more salient than any other. Yet for political and other purposes I may find one aspect of my identity to be particularly relevant. Moreover, the political situation I find myself in, at any given time, will render some aspects of my identity more pertinent than others. Many feminists would argue, myself included, that the political and cultural situation we are still in today makes sexual difference significant. And it is significant in some very deep ways, ways that affect the very construction of subjectivity and agency. Unlike many other subject positions, sexual difference draws our attention to the way subjectivity is constituted in the first place.

(2) Mouffe's goal of attaining free and equal citizenship does not address the social and psychological mechanisms that may be present that institute marginalization in the first place. For example, the binary opposition, which Mouffe briefly discusses, between the public and the private, can be seen in Derridean terms as a means for creating a positive sense of "public" that would not exist without a negative place holder, "private." Our sense of "public" is constructed at the expense of what falls under the heading of "private." Hélène Cixous has identified a range of binary pairs that, in the end, denigrate women (Marks and de Courtivron 1980, 90–98). These include form over matter, activity over passivity, logos over pathos, culture over nature, and masculine over feminine. Cixous asks, Where is she? Woman has been identified with the lower parts of these binaries. Cixous's goal is not to invert the binaries, as some ethics-of-care feminists might have us do, but to dissolve the kind of metaphysical thinking that leads to these couplings. It is not enough to say that nature is as good as culture; we must find a way to undo the system that sets these terms in opposition. Along these lines, we could say that the liberal political system has been built upon this same operation. This is, in fact, what Carole Pateman alludes to when she says that the category of citizen has been conceived of as male: as part of the public rather than the private realm.[12] If the concept of citizenship is

---

[12] Mouffe cites Carole Pateman's critique of liberal feminism, which is that liberal feminists adopt the category of "citizen" without critiquing how the category is patriarchal, constructed in the masculine image. Pateman argues for a "sexually differentiated" conception of citizenship that would recognize women *as* women and value motherhood. She sees the subjection of women as concomitant with the private / public distinction, where the public realm of conventional relations is dominant over the natural realm of "emotion, love and ties of blood." Mouffe cites Pate-

based upon a masculine ideal, then the liberal political system to which Mouffe wants admittance as "free and equal" is constructed on the basis of denying her and all "others" admittance.

(3) Mouffe herself brings in the notion of a "constitutive outside," which suggests that for her identity is developed on the basis of difference, on recognizing separateness from an other. If this is the case, then sexual difference would also have a hand in developing personal and political identity. In her discussion of politics she assumes that "there cannot be a 'we' without a 'them' and that all forms of consensus are by necessity based on acts of exclusion" (Mouffe 1992, 379). She writes, "There will always be a 'constitutive outside', an exterior to the community that is the very condition of its existence." Returning to the public / private distinction, we could say that women's position outside the public realm is part of what constitutes this realm in the first place. This is hardly a new thought: Hegel wrote that women are the eternal irony of the community. Julia Kristeva picks up on this with the insight that women have always been the "irrecuperable foreigners," always on the margins (Guberman 1996, 45).

Mouffe makes these claims about the construction of a community's political identity, but they could as easily be said about the construction of personal identity. Some might argue that just as the community is constructed on the basis of there being a constitutive outside, personal identity is based upon realizing one's own separateness from others: from, for example, the mother's body. Mouffe sees difference—in the form of the "constitutive outside"—as central to the formation of a community's political identity, but she disregards the role of difference in the construction of personal identity. Some of the very figures she cites to support her own position, namely Freud and Lacan, claim that sexual difference is central to ontogenetic development. Given the overall scheme of Mouffe's argument about subjectivity and politics, she cannot so easily dismiss the political relevance of sexual difference.

(4) Often the political issue *at stake* for feminist politics is about how our culture can learn to deal with the fact of sexual difference. As Mouffe herself points out in her essay, if the law were to treat everyone just the same, then many of the specificities of women's real situation would go unheeded. This problem comes to the fore on

man's paper presented to the meeting of the American Philosophical Association, St. Louis, Mo., May 1986, "Feminism and Participatory Democracy."

matters from pregnancy leave to physical requirements for jobs. It also arises in less obvious ways: in the degrees to which women's voices are heeded, their concerns acknowledged, and their specificity recognized. On this point, I'm thinking of Luce Irigaray's work on the ethics of sexual difference where she argues that male subjectivity has been possible because man has denied any content to female subjectivity. Woman is his other, his reversed mirror image. If women were to be seen as genuinely having their own subjectivity, the metaphysical thinking of one term's being built upon the negation of its other would be shattered. The challenge is for both sexes to develop the possibility of attaining subjectivity without the operation of negation—to open ourselves up to difference, to welcome the other in all his or her specificity, not to look for some kind of equivalence or homogenization.

The Aims of Politics

Politics for Chantal Mouffe is the struggle to attain hegemony—for all those subjects who have been denied membership as free and equal citizens in a supposedly democratic order to attain this membership by exerting a collective force over the other. For her, *politics* is about *polemos*: war, struggle, not just an agon but an antagonistic endeavor. Given her construction of political subjectivity, in which all agents are reduced to one of two camps, *we* or *they*, this is not surprising. But whether it is justified, whether it is fruitful, is what I am now asking.

Mouffe's ideas about citizenship are not unlike the liberal's view: her notion of a "chain of equivalence" allows her to locate a commonality, nearly a universality, among political agents: they all share the ideals of liberty and equality. No matter their differences in affiliations, orientations, and various subject positions, this *public* affirmation draws them together, into one, into a collective agent, a "we." This construction is based on what Irigaray has called, disparagingly, "love of the same," a love incapable of recognizing and appreciating difference. By "love of the same," anything that threatens to be different is negated, denied subjectivity and agency. Mouffe's we / they dichotomy assimilates all who are "like me" (by her chain of equivalence) to the same and negates the humanity or legitimacy of the other. The other becomes "they," an enemy to be overcome.

To an extent, this is understandable, for the ultimate political struggle throughout the ages has been to attain subjectivity, to be recognized as having dignity, humanity, freedom, will, agency, to have the capacity to shape what one or what we as a community might become. But this struggle is always thwarted, a wrong turn always presents itself, in our limited imaginations—where the only way we can imagine ourselves as agents is at the expense of others, by denying them their freedom and subjectivity. If we can locate a root to what is commonly called *patriarchy*, I would say it is this: a misadventure on the part of male subjects to attain subjectivity by denying women subjectivity, by holding woman as the place, the site, the home / womb that nourishes and replenishes, that allows men their entrance into the public sphere. Fortunately, I think we are coming into a time where we can develop a new imaginary, one that I believe both Luce Irigaray and Julia Kristeva are helping create. This could be an imaginary in which the other need not be seen as a threat or as a stepping stone. For Irigaray, this means imagining "a possible place for each sex, body, and flesh to inhabit. Which presupposes a memory of the past, a hope for the future, memory bridging the present and disconcerting the mirror symmetry that annihilates the difference of identity" (Irigaray 1984, 19). Instead of there being one sex and its mirror image, we need to develop the capacity to recognize (at least) two sexes, so that women as well as men might finally have the space to develop subjectivity and agency.

Kristeva has a different, though not incompatible, analysis and diagnosis of our political situation. As I have suggested, even though her explicit political theory is lacking, her theory of subjectivity provides a key to a more robust political theory. Recall that for Kristeva the root of our estrangement from others—of our antipathy to foreigners, strangers—and our tendency to turn strangers into enemies is our own internal strangeness. "With the Freudian notion of the unconscious," Kristeva writes, " . . . the foreigner is neither a race nor a nation. The foreigner is neither glorified as a secret *Volksgeist* nor banished as disruptive of rationalist urbanity. Uncanny, foreignness is within us: we are our own foreigners, we are divided." That is, we take what we find so strange within and project it onto the other, "making of it an alien double, uncanny and demoniacal" (Kristeva 1991, 181). Uncanny, *unheimliche*, at home but not at home: this sensation is strongest, Freud noted, in our dread of death, of returning to whence we came, the mother's womb. "The *death* and the *femi-*

nine, the end and the beginning that engross and compose us only to frighten us when they break through" (Kristeva 1991, 185), this is the dreaded foreigner, a projection of the self ill-at-ease, not quite "at home" with his or her own internal territory. Before we can ever be at ease with the others in our midst we must come to terms with the other within. This is the challenge not only for the development of a stable subjectivity but for the development of a democratic political order, for the possibility of a community in which people can come to be at ease with those who seem so different. Thanks to the insights of psychoanalytic theory, Kristeva suggests, we can develop a new imaginary in which a cosmopolitan political community becomes possible:

> It is perhaps on the basis of that contemporary individualism's subversion, beginning with the moment when the citizen-individual ceases to consider himself as unitary and glorious but discovers his incoherences and abysses, in short his "strangeness"—that the question arises again: no longer that of welcoming the foreigner within a system that obliterates him but of promoting the togetherness of those foreigners that we all recognize ourselves to be. (Kristeva 1991, 2–3)

Kristeva argues that we need to find a way to welcome difference, not to try to overcome it, much less overcome an other or a "they." The foreigner is not just the literal immigrant; we are all foreigners to ourselves, even we with full citizenship within a nation. As I see it, a theory of citizenship needs to take account of our interrelatedness, not by a mere prescription for tolerance but by a new complementarity that makes use of our interrelatedness.

Drawing on both Kristeva and Irigaray, I think we can develop an alternative to the politics of hegemony, a new account of subjectivity and feminist politics: instead of a politics of triumphing over the other, we need a politics of inclining toward and welcoming the other. We can conceive of politics not as a struggle for hegemony but as a quest for deciding (in a Nietzschean manner) who or what we—those of us thrown together in community—shall become.

PART III

SUBJECTIVITY AND DELIBERATIVE DEMOCRACY

Children, she feels, are already far advanced, by the age of three or four, along a path that she, as an autistic person, has never advanced far on. Little children, she feels, already "understand" other human beings in a way she can never hope to.

What is it, then, I pressed her further, that goes on between normal people, from which she feels herself excluded? It has to do, she has inferred, with an implicit knowledge of social conventions and codes, of cultural presuppositions of every sort. . . .

. . . Something was going on between the other kids, something swift, subtle, constantly changing—an exchange of meanings, a negotiation, a swiftness of understanding so remarkable that sometimes she wondered if they were all telepathic.

—Oliver Sacks, *An Anthropologist on Mars*

The disclosure of the "who" through speech, and the setting of a new beginning through action, always fall into an already existing web where their immediate consequences can be felt. . . . Although everybody started his life by inserting himself into the human world through action and speech, nobody is the author or producer of his own life story. In other words, the stories, the results of action and speech, reveal an agent, but this agent is not an author or producer . . . nobody is its author.

—Hannah Arendt, *The Human Condition*

5 Relational Subjectivity

The idea of the subject as an open system, a subject-in-process, is a central aspect of what I'll call a model of relational subjectivity. By this I do not just mean Nancy Chodorow's notion that we have the capacity to relate to and nurture others. I mean something much deeper: our very subjectivity is *constituted* relationally, in the relation between conscious and unconscious, semiotic and symbolic, self and other; also in the various political identities that we hold simultaneously. All these relations involve tension, yet at the same time they are productive. As relational subjectivities we are always "under construction," always producing ourselves and each other. Relational subjects are always deeply indebted to each other.

Yet at first glance this debt seems to come in the form of a threat—of a negation of, and from, the other. A tenet of both poststructuralism and psychoanalytic theory is that our own self-identity is founded on our difference from others. Simply put, I realize myself only when I differentiate myself from others. Yet, though alterity occurs at the interpersonal level, certainly, more fundamentally it occurs intrapersonally. From a psychoanalytic point of view, someone's identity is formed by the repression or rejection of many desires and drives. As these drives are driven underground, so to speak, into the unconscious, a conscious identity is born. Thus, alterity—differentiation of oneself from another—is the very basis for subjectivity.

So it is difficult at first to see how relationships could occur between subjects who at some level are always separating themselves from others. This is difficult enough for someone whose subjectivity is relatively stable, but it is all the more problematic for "borderline" persons, those who have difficulty maintaining the borders between themselves and others, between sanity and psychosis. Borderline patients provide cases that interest Kristeva: the melancholic subject of *Black Sun* shows what goes wrong when one cannot bear either the excess presence of the maternal body or her necessary loss. What goes wrong here is speechlessness, asymbolia. Another borderline case is the self of *Powers of Horror* in a state of abjection. As Alice Jardine writes of Kristeva's notion of abjection: "Much stronger in French, this word designates the psychic state of the borderline subject who is no longer a subject and is no longer sure of an object (or can't find one): the subject who is fascinated with the boundaries between subject and object, with the ambiguous, the mixed, *l'entre-deux*" (Oliver 1993a, 28). While these cases make it difficult to see how a relational subject could emerge, their "cure," though a Lacanian would never call it that, is a relationship—a relationship of love between lovers or between analyst and analysand. The subject needs to come to terms with her own inner alterity and can do this through a transference relation with another. Marilyn Edelstein writes, quoting Kristeva, "For Kristeva, psychoanalysis is perhaps the best way to 'think about the question of the other'. This is so 'because the Freudian message, to simplify things, consists in saying that the other is in me. It is my unconscious. And instead of searching for a scapegoat in the foreigner, I must try to tame the demons which are in me'" (Oliver 1993a, 205).

Short of us all going into analysis, we can find other ways to experience transference love. Though psychoanalysis might be the exemplary situation, Edelstein writes, "human relations with others, with ourselves, with language, and with sociality can all become sites for ethical engagement and for embracing of alterity" (Oliver 1993a, 206). The ontology of subjectivity makes social relationships necessary. This may be an empirical point (subject to empirical investigation) but, if it holds true, it also becomes a prescriptive, even normative, one. To the extent that stable subjectivity requires ethical engagements with others, relationality is something we must attend to.

Perhaps the many cases of social pathologies, of kids shooting kids on school playgrounds, of "ethnic cleansing" and indiscriminate bombing, of urban unrest and social malaise, are symptoms of people's relationality gone untended. Perhaps we need to tend to the "formative project," to borrow a phrase from Michael Sandel, of creating more spaces in which social relationships can occur.[1]

Other aspects of subjectivity raise other problems for relationality. For one, a poststructuralist analysis of subjectivity suggests that we are not transparent to ourselves. As Iris Young notes:

> Because the subject is not a unity, it cannot be present to itself, know itself. I do not always know what I mean, need, want, desire, because meanings, needs, and desires do not arise from an origin in some transparent ego. Often I express my desire in gesture or tone of voice, without meaning to do so. Consciousness, speech, expressiveness, are possible only if the subject always surpasses itself, and is thus necessarily unable to comprehend itself. Subjects all have multiple desires that do not cohere; they attach layers of meanings to objects without always being aware of each layer or the connections between them. Consequently, any individual subject is a play of difference that cannot be completely comprehended. (Young 1990, 231–32)

Young takes this state of affairs to show what is at fault in the political ideal of community: a reliance upon what Foucault called the Rousseauist dream of a transparent society and what Derrida calls the metaphysics of presence. Young uses these poststructuralist critiques of modernity to show what she thinks is amiss with views such as Benjamin Barber's, Michael Sandel's, and Seyla Benhabib's, which call for, respectively, strong democracy, community, and complementary reciprocity. All rely on a notion of the "copresence of subjects" (Young 1990, 231). But, as Young notes, we are not transparent to ourselves, so we could hardly be transparent to others. Moreover, others' understandings of us will hardly match up with our own self-(mis)understandings. "I cannot understand others as they understand themselves. Indeed, because the meanings and desires they express may outrun their own awareness or intention, I

---

[1] In defending a civic republican model of politics, Michael Sandel notes that in order to motivate people to take part well in public life we need to attend to how society cultivates citizens' character. One way or another, and for better or worse, society does shape people's values and character, so we might as well see that it is done well. I am making a parallel claim here: the quality of people's relationships with others—and the attendant opportunities for positive transference—does determine somewhat how stable their subjectivity is. So we should attend to the quality of these relationships.

may understand their words or actions more fully than they" (232). In the next section I address Young's concerns.

Another problem for relationality is that any notion of fixed, unified identity is a fiction—however necessary—that we fabricate in order to get along in the world. This "identity" is fragile, provisional, constantly being remade. It is always bound up with our own internal alterity and with those others among us. We are always at the mercy of relations in ourselves and with others. But this does not mean that we abdicate our responsibilities to act. By accepting relational subjectivity, we must recognize how indebted we are to others even as we attempt to be effective individual agents in the world.

Dilemmas of Modernity

So I am always already divided within, between my "conscious self" and my "unconscious self." How at odds this is with the hopes of modernity. How can I act in my own interest autonomously when I neither know my own interest nor necessarily "rule myself"? It seems that heteronomy, Kant's nemesis, cannot be avoided. In Kant's view, the will has to struggle to guard its autonomy from the threat of heteronomy. The moral disposition is always in conflict with the subject's inclinations. The relational view, conversely, holds that we will always be influenced by passions, fellows, and other interests, no matter how hard we try. If there were no alterity, there would be no possibility for our subjectivity.

This is the dilemma that poststructuralist theory brings to modernity: if we are not each sovereign over our own will, how can we be free? While this question may seem forbidding, I find within it a promise of a new conception of subjectivity that can give rise to a new ethics of community. A split subject is not destined to be at odds with her own alterity. As Kristeva argues, she can come to terms with her strangeness, and thus reconfigure her relationship with others. This entails becoming cognizant of her own alterity. Doing so makes it possible, as Kelly Oliver observes, to conceive a relation between subject and other as a relation of difference. Beyond that, a subject-in-process can embrace alterity as a precondition for subjectivity. Insofar as the unconscious and the strangers around us are constitutive of our own identity (identity being a product of difference), we each need others. Our attitudes toward relationships shift from "putting up" with others to desiring others.

This shift in relationship with alterity results in a new ethics. Kristeva's theory, as Oliver writes,

> does not require a sympathy for others that is founded on their similarity, even identity, to the subject. The subject does not have to imagine that the other is the same as himself. He does not have to impose a Kantian imperative or golden rule in order to insure that he will be treated justly or kindly by others. Rather than love the other as himself, the ethical subject-in-process will love the other *in* herself. She will love alterity because it is within but not because it is homogeneous. (Oliver 1993b, 186)

Here we see how split subjectivity suggests a new ethics, what Kristeva calls *heréthique* (evoking a heretical ethics), an ethics founded upon difference rather than upon the logic of the self-same and, as Marilyn Edelstein writes, "exemplified by a mother who deals with the other through love" (Oliver 1993a, 196).[2] Heterogeneity is a part of the structure of this ethics and opens it up to political application. The subject-in-process makes choices not just about how she will act in her *personal* relationships but also how she will act in her *social* and hence *political* relationships. She will also see that acting is no longer a purely individual enterprise.

The promise of a new ethics also emerges strongly (if cryptically) in the work of Emmanuel Levinas. Rather than take Heidegger's path toward fundamental ontology—in which Being is most fundamental—he argues that ethics always precedes ontology. Our very being is created in the moment of facing another person, perhaps because we sense infinity in the face of the other. When I face someone else, I feel myself absolutely responsible for this other's well-being. In that responsibility I am created. "Responsibility in fact is not a simple attribute of subjectivity, as if the latter already existed in itself, before the ethical relationship," Levinas said in an interview. "Subjectivity

---

[2] Marilyn Edelstein notes that this term *heréthique* was in the original title of the essay later translated as "Stabat Mater," which is collected in *Tales of Love* (Kristeva 1987b). Kristeva's essay "Heréthique de l'amour" was first published in *Tel Quel* in 1977. For a postmodern reading of Kristeva's ethics, see Edelstein's "Toward a Feminist Postmodern Poléthique: Kristeva on Ethics and Politics" in Oliver 1993a.

is not for itself; it is, once again, initially for another" (Levinas 1985, 96). The sense of responsibility to the other originates my subjectivity, though here "my" always comes after the other. Moreover, not only does responsibility to others create my subjectivity, my responsibility is immense. Levinas quotes Dostoyevsky in *The Brothers Karamazov*: "*We are all guilty of all and for all men before all, and I more than the others*" (Levinas 1985, 98). As Levinas says, "I am responsible for a total responsibility, which answers for all the others and for all in the others, even for their responsibility. The I always has one responsibility *more* than all the others" (99).

For anyone interested in social change and political agency, such notions of relational subjectivity may seem to be unfortunate, for they seem to open the door to heteronomy, to manipulation and coercion from others, and to close the door to autonomy. Moreover, some see danger in any poststructuralist theory of subjectivity, for in poststructuralism there seems to be a defeatism and relativism that make political agency impossible.

Yet in the individualistic model of subjectivity, it is a challenge to conceive of why people would choose to come together to build public relationships. The notion of autonomous, unified subjectivity leads to the problem of how people get along in the world; they're bound to just "put up" with others. With this traditional view, it is hard to fathom why individuals need bother to talk together about public matters. In principle (if not in fact), each individual can know and understand public concerns without anyone else's input. When people do talk together about matters of public concern, according to this model, each holds fast to her own position and tries her best to discredit the others' positions. Their self-interests are usually construed as exclusive. Alternatively, a theory of relational subjectivity suggests another model of group action, what we might call complementary agency.[3] By this I mean people coming together in order to create new, broader understandings of what is in their interests. They

---

[3] David Mathews coined the term "complementary action" and he and I developed it (in a somewhat different fashion from what is presented here) in works we co-authored, including *Community Politics* (1990) and *Alternatives for Community Development and Educational Reform* (1990). Complementary action differs from Seyla Benhabib's concept of complementary reciprocity (Benhabib 1986, 341). In my view, complementarity does not entail reciprocity, at least not in the symmetrical sense. See the discussion in Chapter 6 on Young's concept of asymmetrical reciprocity.

help each other flesh out a more comprehensive picture of the whole. Though Young sees the lack of transparency as an obstacle to community, we could regard it as a reason to take community or any intersubjective arena more seriously. To the extent that subjects' wishes, needs, and intentions are opaque to themselves they may need others' perspectives and interpretations all the more. The less transparent we are, the more we need others' understandings. In fact, quite often we develop relations with others in order to get insight into our own identity. For example, friendship is not a sharing of two transparent subjectivities; most people take intimate friendship as a way of expanding their self-understandings, as well as their appreciation of the world around them. Alone, relational subjects' understandings will always be partial and fragmented. Together, they can fill in the blind spots, however provisionally.

To supplement Kristeva's and Levinas's theories of relational subjectivity and ethics, I now turn to two other theoretical approaches: social formation theory and narrative constructions.

Social Formation Theory

Agency can be complementary in part because subjectivity is formed relationally and socially. Michel Foucault and Pierre Bourdieu offer approaches to what could be called "social formation theory." While their views are varied, both take their cue from Marx, insofar as they propose that subjectivity is socially and historically constituted. This seemingly banal observation is really quite radical, at least in terms of traditional theories of subjectivity and political agency. It posits that the subject is who she is by virtue of her situation—that is, how and where and when she is situated. A person's self is always *drawn* (written) from a collectivity. This does not mean that her subjectivity is one with the collectivity, but that she is never truly by herself (neither by *herself* nor *by* herself). Thus, she does not come into the world fully formed and able to make moral rules autonomously. She develops heteronomously.

Does this wreak havoc with the notion that a subject can be a political agent? Not when one looks closely at how Foucault, Bourdieu, and other social formation theorists describe power. If we consider "power" as the ability to act, *podere*, then we would hope that social formation theory would show that people within a given culture still have room to initiate acts, if not by themselves then at least in relation with others. In other words, if social formation theory can grant that people have power, at least in concert with others, then agency in the political sphere is still possible. It will differ, though, from the way agency is traditionally conceived: as the power of a single individual to affect his or her surroundings. It will be more akin to power with others rather than power over others, more like the power Hannah Arendt describes in *The Human Condition*:

> Power is what keeps the public realm, the potential space of appearance between acting and speaking men, in existence. . . . Only where men live so close together that the potentialities of action are always present can power remain with them, and the foundation of cities, which as city-states have remained paradigmatic for all Western political organization, is therefore indeed the most important material prerequisite for power. What keeps people together after the fleeting moment of action has passed (what we today call "organization") and what, at the same time, they keep alive through remaining together is power. And whoever, for whatever reasons, isolates himself and does not partake in such being together, forfeits power and becomes impotent, no matter how great his strength and how valid his reasons. (Arendt 1958, 200–201)

Arendt's work draws heavily on Aristotle's *Politics*, perhaps the first articulation of how society shapes the individual. As social animals, we need to be active in the city—active in a web of public relationships—in order to live well and, Arendt adds, to have power. These ideas inform grassroots organizing efforts from the Industrial Areas Foundations in the United States to Participa in Colombia, as well as in labor organizations and neighborhood associations.

On the whole, social formation theorists offer a useful understanding of the development of institutions and the wielding of power. Unlike traditional Marxist theories which tend to see power moving in one, at most two, directions, social formation theorists see multiple sites of power. For Foucault, even disciplinary power, certainly the most monolithic, is multidirectional. "Discipline makes possible the operation of a relational power," Foucault writes, "that sustains itself by its own mechanism and which, for the spectacle of public events, substitutes the uninterrupted play of calculated gazes." Insofar as power is relational, "its functioning is that of a network of relations from top to bottom, but also to a certain extent from bottom to top and laterally" (Foucault 1979, 176–77). Even in the most monolithic attempt at power, no monopoly can be had. Everyone still has the power to be an agent. For Foucault, agency is best understood through an analysis of the formation of social institutions and practices, that is, genealogically.

Bourdieu, for his part, looks at another side of discipline: the academic discipline of linguistics. As he argues, an asocial theory of linguistics—as in the work of Saussure—also has a way of dominating. To break free from this dominating discipline, Bourdieu seeks to study linguistic practices in terms of real social practices. He moves from the ivory tower to the street corner, noticing how and where and when speech is used. That is, he is looking at how speech is situated. With a Bourdieuian point of departure, various disciplines (e.g., anthropology, political history, even philosophy) can look at how language operates microscopically as well as macroscopically. We can understand the parts in terms of the social and cultural whole.

Where Habermas sees language as a tool that can be used by agents transparently, Bourdieu understands language as a terrain of struggle and polysemy. It is through language, through giving names and by appropriating meanings, that social reality is constructed: "Like 'being' according to Aristotle, the social world can be uttered and constructed in different ways: it can be practically perceived, uttered, constructed, in accordance with different principles of vision and division (for instance, ethnic divisions)" (Bourdieu 1991, 232). By saying that the social world is constructed, Bourdieu does away with the difference between the empirical self and the transcendental self. In other words, there is no identity there in advance to be realized self-consciously, nothing essential there to be recuperated. One's own individual or collective identity is constructed or appropriated. Even if one doesn't want to go so far in doing away with the "in-itself," some accounting should occur:

> The most resolutely objectivist theory must take account of agents' representation of the social world and, more precisely, of the contribution they make to the construction of the vision of this world, and, thereby to the very construction of this world, via the *labour of representation* (in all senses of the term) that they continually perform in order to impose their own vision of the world or the vision of their own position in this world, that is, their social identity. (234)

Bourdieu is not claiming that everything is fabricated *ex nihilo*. "Objectively" speaking, the social world presents to agents a variety of properties to be interpreted. Yet these properties can be interpreted and evaluated in many different ways. Our interpretations are, in a sense, influenced by previous interpretations and symbolic structures; yet the uncertainty of the future offers numerous possibilities and thus schemes of interpretation: "the objects of the social world can be perceived and expressed in different ways" (234). Our interpretations have political implications, especially with regard to how we position ourselves and how much we take as "a given." When interpretations are experienced as "objective" assessments of situations, then the subjective capacity to reconstruct the world diminishes. The laborer who takes it as "a fact" that the owner has all the economic and political power thereby consolidates this interpretation, making this "fact" harder to shake—and a labor strike ever more unlikely. Yet transformation through reinterpretation remains a powerful option:

> The capacity for bringing into existence in an explicit state, of publishing, of making public (i.e. objectified, visible, sayable, and even official) that which, not yet having attained objective and collective existence, remained in a state of individual or serial existence—people's disquiet, anxiety, expectation, worry—represents a formidable social power, that of bringing into existence groups by establishing the *common sense,* the explicit consensus, of the whole group. In fact, this labour of categorization, of making things explicit and classifying them, is continually being performed, at every moment of ordinary existence, in the struggles in which agents clash over the meaning of the social world and their position in it, the meaning of their social identity, through all the forms of speaking well or badly of someone or something, of blessing or cursing and of malicious gossip, eulogy, congratulations, praise, compliments, or insults, rebukes, criticism, accusations, slanders, etc. (236)

It matters not whether something is objectively the case; unless such things are subjectively grasped and articulated, their "reality" is meaningless.

Social formation theory supplements psychoanalytic and poststructuralist understandings of how subjectivity is developed. All these approaches point to the condition of subjectivity forming relationally at every level: from the level of an infant's emergence into language through its position in history and society. Moreover, social formation theory shows that the meaning of events and practices is always socially and culturally shaped. There is no objective standpoint from which subjects can interpret the world. Our history and relationships always position us in some way. This condition is reinforced further in the way we talk with each other everyday, as I show in the next section.

Narrative Constructions

Narrative theory provides another way of thinking about how we are constructed relationally. Of those who think about what we might call the "ontology of the self," I like to imagine that there are two camps: the constructivists and the anticonstructivists. The anticonstructivists argue that there is some essential core self residing in every body. For this camp, there is a self there to be known, obscured perhaps by a lot of nonsense and misapprehensions, but a self that can be uncovered, whether by meditation, exercise, the great books, the right drugs, or a good shrink.

But a good shrink might get one into trouble, because he or she might belong to the constructivist camp, which, despite all its diversity, holds to the notion that the self is not discovered but *created*. While this camp is a more recent phenomenon, it's not terribly new. Hegel inaugurated the idea with his writing on how consciousness comes into being, how spirit comes to know itself, how history—whether personal or world—develops. Marx picked it up with the concept that consciousness is a product of material conditions. And of course the other masters of suspicion, Nietzsche, with his transvaluation of values, and Freud, with his development of a topology of tripartite consciousness, truly undermined any remaining complacency on the matter. Although there is certainly discord between the constructivists and the anticonstructivists, there is even more debate among the constructivists themselves—for example, between those coming out of a Marxist tradition and those coming out of a Freudian one. The heirs of Marxism want a subjectivity, however constructed, that can act as a deliberate, self-knowing agent in the world, whereas the psychoanalysts hold that the self is always split and at odds with its self.

Of the two camps, I find myself with the constructivists, holding the sympathies of various warring factions. With the socialists, I want a subjectivity that allows for agency. With the psychoanalysts, I lack faith in a unified, transparent subjectivity. With the hermeneuts, I believe that meaning is always constructed by interpretation. I don't know how to respond to the anticonstructivists, because at bottom their position seems to be a matter of faith. There's no way to prove or disprove an essential or core self. If I were to show that a particular subjectivity has changed from one point in time to another and on this basis argue that this subjectivity must be under construction, an anticonstructivist could respond with the claim that the essential subject might have been obscured at one point in time and more present at another. He'd say, "See, only now has this person 'come into her own'"—as if there were some essential "own-ness" to come into.

Rather than conduct a pointless argument with my imagined anticonstructivists, I'd like to take up the question of *how* subjectivity comes into being.

We are forever telling stories about who we are and what our purpose in this life is. These stories or narratives do more than provide accounts of our lives; they help constitute our own sense of self or subjectivity. This topic has been amply explored. From a hermeneutic point of view, Paul Ricoeur has written three volumes on it. Hayden White, Alasdair MacIntyre, Frank Kermode, and even Ursula K. Le Guinn have taken up the topic. In the main they favor the notion that subjects create their own narratives. In this section, I offer a different account, namely that our respective narratives are constructed by others, that we "see" ourselves in the stories others tell, so that our individual identities are never constructed individually but rather intersubjectively. Not only do we live in a dense world of interconnected relationships; we come to be ourselves by virtue of that world.

Let me begin with a modest proposition: Narratives construct self-identity and the meaning of a life; our selves are always constructed or at least molded through our stories. If the proposition is right, then how far can we take it? Many have agreed that narratives construct identity and meaning, but they take the proposition in a mild form—arguing roughly that there is some identity "prior" to narrative, that narrative may help give a form or a meaning to a life but does not construct that life out of whole cloth. An extreme form of the proposition would be that there is *nothing* in advance of a narrative, that narrative creates identity. Both views have problems. The mild form begs the question of how something arose in advance of narrative. The extreme form begs another question: if there is no "self" in advance of narration, then *who* narrates? It seems there needs to be something in advance of the narrative. Without a storyteller, how could there ever be a story?

Even as I have hinted that both poles have problems, I do not want to suggest that there is some correct, middle, moderate path. I am not interested in splitting the difference. Both ends are appealing, so much so that I want to entertain them both. Let me begin with a mild form, articulated by Alasdair MacIntyre.

In *After Virtue*, MacIntyre argues that we must heed how narrative gives unity to a life. Narratives make lives intelligible. At the same time, though, he avoids the notion that a narrative singularly constructs a life. He writes that at most we can be "co-authors" of our own lives, with life itself retaining part authorship:

> we are never more (and sometimes less) than the co-authors of our own narratives. Only in fantasy do we live what story we please. In life, as both Aristotle and Engels noted, we are always under certain constraints. We enter upon a stage which we did not design and we find ourselves part of an action that was not of our making. Each of us being a main character in his own drama plays subordinate parts in the dramas of others, and each drama constrains the others. (MacIntyre 1984, 213)

MacIntyre takes issue with those like Louis Mink who maintain that there is no truth outside the narrative. Mink says that all "truths," "meanings," and "lives" are constructed by narratives, just as Sartre through his character Roquentin suggests in *La Nausée*. MacIntyre thinks that Sartre is especially wrong, because for Sartre "there are not and there cannot be any true stories. Human life is composed of discrete actions which lead nowhere, which have no order; the storyteller imposes on human events retrospectively an order which they did not have while they were lived" (MacIntyre 1984, 214). MacIntyre thinks Sartre is wrong on this point because there must be "an order" in the events of a life. MacIntyre is in trouble here, though, because he does agree with Sartre on a related point— that the order of a life is unintelligible without a narrative. So what does MacIntyre mean by "order"? How can there be an order that precedes a narrative when "order" is something that we impose upon a series of events? (I rely on Kant's argument, that we impose cause, effect, relation, et cetera on the phenomenological world; the world itself—whatever that might be—may well lack these qualities.)

There is a strain of Karl Popper in MacIntyre. He thinks a narrative ought to be falsifiable. That is, the stories we tell ourselves ought to be susceptible of being proved false. This would mean that there is some truth or reality against which a narrative can be measured. Here MacIntyre relies upon a distinction between truth and falsity that I think isn't congruent with narrative meaning. How can we measure the veracity of a narrative against "the bare facts" when "the bare facts" are *unintelligible* without narrative? I do not mean to suggest that there are no "bare facts," but rather that we have no way of assessing them independent of the stories we tell.

But, one could reasonably hold, certainly some stories are more valid than others. Why is that? How do we know?

I recall a film made several years ago, *Don Juan de Marco*, in which the main character (played by Johnny Depp) is ostensibly a troubled boy named John from New York who claims to be Don Juan, the greatest lover who ever lived.[4] His psychiatrist, played by Marlon Brando, is trying to decide whether or not to commit John by assessing whether John is delusional or whether he really is Don Juan de Marco, the greatest lover who ever lived. The psychiatrist is faced with conflicting data, the narrative of John's life, as recounted by the character, and facts that seem to counter John's story. In the end, the psychiatrist decides two things: (1) the facts of Don Juan's life *can* be congruent with the story Don Juan tells, even though they might be interpreted otherwise, and (2) one's own narrative truth is far more powerful and compelling than any other interpretation, even if another interpretation might seem more plausible.

Only in the narrowest sense is Don Juan's story falsifiable. After a certain point the audience realizes that narratives can survive countless facts that seem to contradict them. A narrative is not just another testable truth claim. Narratives create truth. It would be simpleminded to ask whether a life narrative corresponds truly to a life meaning, when that life meaning is indebted to its narrative.

---

[4] I'm tempted to put the word *ostensibly* in quotation marks, because I'm using it as a somewhat satirical nod to analytic linguistic philosophy, which tends to hold a neat distinction between signs and referents. Referents are supposedly ostensible, that is, you can point to them, just as we could supposedly point to the real John / Don Juan to decide whether his narrative is true or false. The "fact" is, as I see it, that there is no pointing to the facts of John / Don Juan's life apart from the narrative structure that is constructed about his life. A major question I address in this chapter is how and by whom are meaning-constructive narratives told and accepted.

But Who Is the I Prior to Narrating?

My argument so far has pushed to the extreme version, that there is nothing intelligible outside narratives. I've been rejecting a sort of "correspondence" theory of narrative truth. But this leads to another problem: who narrates? If the meaning of one's own life is only derived from narrative—if even one's own identity comes from narrative—then how does the narrative arise in the first place? We have the proverbial chicken-or-egg puzzle: if meaning and identity are created by self-narration, then there must be some self there in advance of narration.

In trying to solve this puzzle many theorists, MacIntyre included, suggest that there must be some kind of reality that prefigures narration. In this vein, Anthony Paul Kerby describes what he calls "prenarrative experience":

> Our explicit narratives may indeed extend, even change, the meaning of our lived time, but this time is already structured according to our style of being-in-the-world, our habitus. As such, our narrative interpretations do not function ex nihilo but follow naturally upon the structure of experience.
>
> If the temporality of human affairs is indeed experienced at its basic level within a teleological setting, then it is perhaps only narrative understanding that can do it justice. To narrate oneself is to make explicit this prenarrative or "prefigured" (Ricoeur) quality of our unexamined life, to draw out a story it embodies. This is to say that our unexamined life is already a quasi-narrative, and that lived time is already a drama of sorts. Also, and this is quite important, this quasi-narrative can and does serve as a corrective or guide for the act of narration. One cannot tell just any old story without committing some form of injustice to the content of one's experience—what Sartre called "bad faith." (Kerby 1991, 42)

While I disagree with some of it, I am intrigued by what Kerby has to say. I think it is interesting that he sees narrations as *interpretations* of some preverbal experience or lived time.[5] With this notion, we'd see that narratives are hermeneutic activities, ways of giving

---

[5] Let me hold off the question of whether we can make sense of something like "preverbal experience" in order to see whether Kerby can even make sense of what would make for a plausible *interpretation*.

meaning and making sense of something otherwise speechless. Through narration, we give meaning. This suggests, as he writes later in the book, that narratives do not merely correspond to experience but make sense of experience, and that a good narrative is one that makes the best sense of experience. But at the same time, "One cannot tell just any old story . . . ." When someone tells a "wrong" story, that someone is lying or delusional, bound for prison or a psychiatric ward, like Don Juan de Marco.

Kerby's way of speaking calls up notions of fidelity. A good narrative is faithful to experience. One shouldn't tell just any story; one should tell a story that keeps faith with lived experience.

But as Marlon Brando's character found, sometimes a more meaningful narrative takes precedence over a more plausible one. Though it may seem plausible for someone to think that John is just a troubled boy from New York, Don Juan's alternate narrative is more faithful to his self-conception: that he is the greatest lover that ever lived. And as the movie suggests, the women he has known would attest to the faithfulness of the more creative narrative. My point is that even "prenarrative experience" cannot account for narrative truth.[6] We have to keep looking.

So where do we look? I want to look outside the circle of self-narration, beyond the first person to the second and third person. In the remainder of this chapter I explore the possibility that our self-conception derives from the conceptions others have of us. In overhearing others speak about us, we discover or perhaps create a unity of our own self. Our always tenuous, evolving narratives are indebted to the stories others tell about us. Even MacIntyre points to something along these lines. When he talks about personal identity over time, he says that we see ourselves as the "same person" we were five years earlier by virtue of being a character in a story. But MacIntyre never really says who tells this story. I have to supply what is there only implicitly: that the unity of my self comes from the unity that others grant me. Without that, I would never consider myself the same person. Everything would always be new, my thoughts never fixed, my experience always changing. I say *I* to another, as another says *you* to me, as others say *she* to themselves.

---

[6] Thus I sidestep the question of whether "prenarrative experience" is a valid notion.

Lacan's Mirror Stage

To help make my case, I want to draw an analogy with psychoanalytic theory, namely with Lacan's theory of the mirror stage of development. Lacan sought to explain how an infant, whose experience of reality is disorganized and fragmented, comes to see itself as a discrete being. Lacan describes the process by which the child comes to separate itself from its mother's embrace (not just physical but psychical) in order to enter "the symbolic," that is, the realm of language, law, and taboo, the realm of the father. Somehow this infant needs to get an inkling of an idea that it is a discrete being, not one with the universe and its mother's body. There needs to occur, as Lacan puts it, a "primary repression" of this oneness. This occurs, Lacan tells us, at anywhere between six and eighteen months of age when the infant happens to look into a mirror and suddenly recognizes the alien image staring back as its *own* reflection. Aha, the infant muses prelinguistically, *c'est moi.* It is in seeing its reflection that the child develops an idea—a fiction really—of a unified self. Interestingly, this all happens as a result of seeing an *alien* image, something that in fact *is not* the infant.

Lacan suggests that the mirror stage is completed after eighteen months. While the alienation it fosters always continues, he does not discuss the phenomenon itself recurring thereafter. After the mirror stage, the child soon enters into the symbolic. I want to suggest that something like the mirror stage is *repeated in* the symbolic realm of language, notably in the case of recognizing a linguistic image of oneself in the discourse of others. Put simply, this is when one overhears others talking about oneself. Or, when you are speaking with someone, the other person talks about you to yourself. I think this phenomenon, which occurs in the symbolic, is analogous to the mirror stage and performs similar functions. Just as in the mirror stage where the infant fabricates a fictive self-unity from the alien mirror image, in language we derive a sense of self-unity through the way others characterize us.

I use *characterize* purposely, in order to recall MacIntyre's notion that our own unitary self-identity is a function of being a character in a story—implicitly a character in stories others tell. Now, I may well be attributing to MacIntyre something he did not intend, but it is interesting that in order to found self-unity he took advantage of the concept of being a character in stories.[7] "There is no way of *founding* my identity—or lack of it—on the psychological continuity or discontinuity of the self. The self inhabits a character whose unity is given as the unity of a character" (MacIntyre 1984, 217). Notice that MacIntyre uses the passive voice: "unity is given." In order to put this thought in the active voice, we have to ask: who gives this unity? From the way MacIntyre describes it, it is not given by oneself but by another (or at least by the overall tradition and conventions one inhabits). Someone else tells a story, and I find myself in it. I may be called to account for something I did ten years ago. Though I may feel like a different person now, I recognize in this other person's discourse that I am accountable for whatever my former self did.

This is what is so mesmerizing about tales in which the protagonist suffers amnesia. A character tries to recall his own identity either by remembering or by finding others who do. Tell me who I am, says the protagonist in Hal Hartley's film *Amateur*, when he finally encounters someone who knew him before he lost his memory. Even though the character is now a genuinely nice person, the woman who knows his past knows him as an evil, violent man. She refuses to tell him who he is, not to protect him from the truth but to spite him for all he had done to her. As an amnesiac, he lacks knowledge of himself. He's still called to account, even though he's not the "same person." In her eyes, he is the same; and interestingly she takes revenge by denying him self-knowledge, knowledge that only she, an other, has. She can deny him self-knowledge because his identity is initially constructed through the stories others tell, and if they won't tell the game is up. We nonamnesiacs (so far as we know . . .) have within us a store of such stories, a sedimentation, that we may use to gauge new ones offered to us. The amnesiac loses this sedimentation, this (precarious) ground of self-understanding. He has to start from scratch, by calling on others to tell him his story.

Using Lacan's theory of the mirror stage as an analogy can help map out how overhearing others' characterizations of ourselves may forge our own self-identity. Think of such characterizations as linguistic mirror images. As with the mirror stage, they help a person recognize the distinction between self and other even as the person begins to identify with the alien characterizations. The linguistic im-

---

[7] Paul Ricoeur makes the same move with his notions of character and emplotment. See Ricoeur 1992.

age is, to borrow a phrase from Elizabeth Grosz, a totalized, complete, external image—a *gestalt*—of the subject, the subject as seen from outside (Grosz 1990, 48). While this gestalt conflicts with a person's fragmentary experience, it provides the ground for the *ego ideal*, the image of the ego, derived from others, which the ego strives to achieve or live up to. The linguistic mirror image positions a person within a (linguistically organized) discursive field. As these discursive images accumulate, the ego develops. The ego can be seen as a sedimentation of such images. I overhear characterizations of myself and narcissisticly internalize them, and as others are laid over these characterizations, a sediment builds. This sedimentation begins very early in development, and by the time I've acquired a conscious sense of self, it has taken form. In fact, the sedimentation leads to my sense of self.

This sedimentation is powerful, and may be what makes us more resistant to alien characterizations as we grow older. We build up several layers, accruing an ego, which allow us to "answer back" to new characterizations. Yet still new characterizations present a new gestalt and carry their own uncanny quality. Still, when we overhear others speak of us, we stop and listen, morbidly curious, for after all our own sense of self is always on the line.

Lyotard and Thébaud on "Being Narrated"

As I develop this theory that identity is constructed, at least in part, by our overhearing others, I realize that I am to some extent making an empirical claim. If in fact people develop self-identity and meaning *apart* from the stories others tell, then I would be mistaken. The argument here is descriptive, not prescriptive or normative. But it would hardly do for me to select a sample and conduct surveys, asking people whether they develop a sense of self as a result of others' stories, for our self-understanding is largely a matter of our beliefs, not brute facts. So I do not rely on data, but I ask the reader to reflect on whether this description rings true for his or her own self-understanding.

I also rely on philosophical literature, in that I look for texts in which others have developed coherent cases for what seems to be the same phenomenon. One such text is *Just Gaming*, a dialogue between Jean-François Lyotard and Jean-Loup Thébaud. Let me begin with a statement attributed to Lyotard: "I would say that people get into language not by speaking it but by hearing it. And what they hear as children is stories, and first of all their own story, because they are named in it" (Lyotard and Thébaud 1985, 35).

The authors come to this conclusion by way of studies of the Cashinahua Indians of the upper Amazon. Citing André Marcel d'Ans, the authors describe how these Indians tell stories. A storyteller will begin by saying that he will "tell the story of X" (inserting the name of the hero) as he has always heard it. When finishing the story, the storyteller will say: "Here ends the story of X; it was told to you by Y," and here he gives his own name (Lyotard and Thébaud 1985, 32). So in telling stories, the Cashinahua present themselves as narratees (telling stories that had been told to them), as relays, and only in the end do they say their own names. The authors find it striking that "when one of the listeners takes up the story some other time, he 'forgets' the name of the previous narrator, since he does not give the name of the narrator who came before" (32)."It should be added that the proper name, the Cashinahua one, is an esoteric one that allows the localization of the speaker in an extremely exact, and far more formal than real, network of kinship relations. So that, *when he gives his proper name, the teller designates himself as someone who has been narrated by the social body*" (32; emphasis added). This phenomenon of being narrated is even more pronounced in the stories the Cashinahua tell about the marriage moieties. In these, the teller sees himself at once "as the addressee of these narratives and as the subject matter of some others that define the social bonds in the form of kinship relations":

> In saying at the beginning, "I am going to tell you what I have always heard," and at the end, "My name is so-and-so," he situates himself in the two forgotten poles—actively forgotten, repressed—of Western thought and of the tradition of autonomy. These are the poles where one is the recipient of a narrative in which one is narrated, and where one receives a narrative that has been narrated to one. (32–33)

In such storytelling, the speaker gives up any claims to autonomy. He becomes enmeshed in the tradition of the community. He is indebted to the culture's discourse and tradition for his name and identity. The speaker is a relay in a network of stories. Moreover, having heard a story, one is obligated to retell it. This obligation forecloses any independent will (autonomy) not to retell a story. Lyotard and

Thébaud take the case of the Cashinahua to exemplify how "pagan" all our cultures are: we always are able to speak only by virtue of having been spoken; we are both the teller and the told; we cannot extricate ourselves from our traditions. We do not author our own stories. We *are* told.

The Dialectic of Identity: Narrating and Being Narrated

I began with the supposition that we are created through narrative. This is a notion already familiar. I added another idea: our situation as characters is constructed by the stories that others tell. Now, I do not want to leave the reader with the impression that we are always at the mercy of others, mere clay for their images. As we grow up in communities in which our own characterization is told, we become characters who, in turn, tell stories. We come to repeat and embellish the stories that make other identities possible. I see this as going on in overlapping turns, through intricate networks and relationships.

One might argue that the alternative I pose to the constructivist / anticonstructivist debate merely pushes the problem back to infinity. If we are always already "told," where did the telling begin? How would I respond to this question? Well, the telling began, I would say, when language began. This is an inescapable problem. We are born into a language; we learn it by virtue of its having been there before us, entire. But where did it begin? Could it have begun in patches? It must have. If the history of human beings' own "being told" is part of the history of language, then our own identities began with our ancestors in patches as well. There was no first man.

This notion that we are creations of social bodies—narratively constructed—may seem untenable to some, but it strikes me as the most ethical position. It makes me all the more cognizant of how indebted I am to others. It makes me think, with Levinas, that my being can never precede my ethical obligation to others. To the contrary, as Levinas writes, my obligation to others creates my own identity. In finding myself having to respond to others, I find myself.

Theories of social formation and narrative construction point to how our self-identity is fabricated from our situatedness in a web of relations. By making us see how we are all situated within a web of power relations, practices, and material events, these theories show that none of us makes laws for ourselves by ourselves. That is, we can never be fully autonomous, in the strict sense of the term. The lack of autonomy seems problematic until it is coupled with an understanding of the subject-in-process / on-trial. Being a split subject who is socially constituted offers an opening. Instead of trying to live up to the supposed ideal of unity and autonomy, we might try to make use of our intersubjectivity and see ourselves as relational subjects. That we are socially constituted means that we are with others; it also means that we know with others. That we are split internally means that we are bound to be in search of complementarity. We can, as Kristeva suggests, develop a new community of strangers. If we can accept the fact that we are each at odds with ourselves, we might forge a new kind of community.

6 Complementary Agency

How do relational subjects act? That is, can a dispersed "who" originate action? This question first arose with Nietzsche who, as Alan Schrift points out, self-deconstructs his own literary authority. Nietzsche writes in *Ecce Homo*: "I am one thing, my writings are another," phrases that Schrift takes as an interrogation of "the privileged position of the author within the space of interpretation" (Schrift 1995, 27).

Foucault and Derrida have also taken up this question of authorship. Derrida, along with Nietzsche, thinks the tendency to fix subjectivity as something static interrupts the fluidity and relationships that can occur between people and their works. To counter this tendency, Derrida decenters the subject from the position of author of a text to one who becomes part of a web of writing. As Derrida writes, "The 'subject' of writing does not exist if we mean by that some sovereign solitude of the author. The subject of writing is a *system* of relations between strata: the Mystic Pad, the psyche, society, the world" (Derrida 1978, 226–27). So, as Schrift notes, Derrida does not try to do away with the subject; rather, he situates and decenters it (Schrift 1995, 27).

In *Beyond Good and Evil*, Nietzsche raises the matter of how our grammar leads us to think that there is an author, an ego, behind our thoughts. Criticizing Descartes's *cogito*, Nietzsche writes,

> With regard to the superstitions of logicians, I shall never tire of em-
> phasizing a small terse fact, which these superstitious minds hate to
> concede—namely, that a thought comes when "it" wishes, and not
> when "I" wish, so that it is a falsification of the facts of the case to say
> that the subject "I" is the condition of the predicate "think." *It* thinks;
> but that this "it" is precisely the famous old "ego" is, to put it mildly,
> only a supposition, an assertion, and assuredly not an "immediate cer-
> tainty." . . . One infers here according to the grammatical habit:
> "Thinking is an activity; every activity requires an agent." (Nietzsche
> 1966b, section 17)

So if the self or ego is not the agent, the cause of actions, who or
what is? In his project of transvaluing values, Nietzsche seeks ways
not merely to invert our values but to unmask the force that was creating binaries in the first place. As Foucault notes: "For Nietzsche, it
was not a matter of knowing what good and evil were in themselves,
but of who was being designated, or rather *who was speaking* when
one said *Agathos* to designate oneself or *Deilos* to designate others.
For it is there, in the *holder* of the discourse and, more profoundly
still, in the possessor of the word, that language is gathered together
in its entirety" (Foucault 1973, 305). Foucault takes this Nietzschean
understanding of subjectivity and uses it to develop a theory of the
subject as an "author function," a task not only to create works but
to make oneself (Foucault 1982, 138–48). The will to create subjectivity occurs within a network of relations, institutions, and contexts.
Yet while bound by social constraints, it can still creatively construct
itself.

In a community of relational subjects, we might say, the "author
function" is shared. No text or practice can be understood adequately
without seeing how it derives from and moves in a complex social
fabric. I use the term "author function" as a metaphor for agency in a
polis. In contemporary literary theory, the notion that there is one
self-sufficient author of a text is being replaced by the understanding
that texts are "written" in a culture with a history. The author is not
dead; the author is, rather, dispersed, inseparable from a social and
historical realm. Like authors, political agents are always comple-
mented by others. The lack of individual autonomy does not spell the
end of creations in literature or in politics. Texts and politics are always created complementarily, out of a multitude of inner and social
drives.

A theory of relational subjectivity could be the beginning of a new understanding of political agency, what I am calling complementary agency—complementary in the sense that agency need not be the ability of atomic individuals but could be the activity of heterogeneous subjects-in-process helping each other along. A central way in which they help each other is by improving their collective knowledge and understanding. In this conception, no citizen is all-knowing and purely self-legislating. Our heterogeneous subjectivities call on us to call on others whose partial knowledge can complement our own partial knowledge. This is what occurs in public deliberations, whether a New England town meeting or any of the thousands of citizen deliberations that are held annually in the United States and abroad.[1] Public deliberation offers a way for complementary agents to increase and improve knowledge about matters affecting the public as a whole.

Complementary agency is also about choice and action. Having gotten a better picture of the whole through their deliberations with others, relational subjects are better able to make sound choices about issues that affect them in common. They are also then in a better situation to implement those choices, whether by holding their governments accountable to the public will or by direct grassroots activities. The natural arena for complementary agency—in its tasks of improving knowledge, making choices, and action—is civil society, the nongovernmental public sphere of society.

This chapter and the next focus primarily on how through complementary agency relational subjects are able to provide better means of political knowing. The last part of this chapter also discusses how complementary agency can fulfill other functions of citizenship that Habermas's work suggests are necessary. The final chapter more broadly examines the way relational subjectivity and complementary agency can offer an alternative to liberal and communitarian politics.

As I discuss below, Seyla Benhabib and Iris Young show how public deliberations that bring together many different perspectives provide new knowledge. Theories such as these are indebted to Hans-Georg

---

[1] This would include the work of the National Issues Forums in the United States, a network of citizen organizations that regularly hold deliberative forums to discuss issues facing the nation. For information contact the National Issues Forums office at 200 Commons Road, Dayton, Ohio 45459. It also includes Deliberative Polling, the work of James Fishkin at the University of Texas. See Fishkin 1995, chapter 5.

Gadamer's hermeneutic theory, which appreciates the particular perspectives that interpreters bring with them as they seek understanding (Gadamer 1990). According to Gadamer, we do not achieve understanding by trying to be purely disinterested, "objective," and
unbiased interpreters; we achieve understanding when we fuse our
own partial and particular views with those of others. Gadamer's primary concern is with how an interpreter in one historical period can
understand the meaning of a text written in an earlier historical period. As he sees it, the meaning of a text always includes the meaning
it has for the reader in the reader's own period / horizon. "What I described as the fusion of horizons was the form in which this unity ac-
tualizes itself, which does not allow the interpreter to speak of an
original meaning of the work without acknowledging that, in understanding it, the interpreter's own meaning enters in as well"
(Gadamer 1990, 576). Gadamer also considers the hermeneutic practice involved in actual conversations; the structure is the same.
"What is to be grasped is the substantive rightness of [the other person's] opinion, so that we can be at one with each other on the subject. Thus we do not relate the other's opinion to him but to our own
opinions and views" (385). We might add that even in real-time conversations there is always a difference, in the Derridean sense, between and within each participant's discourse (cf. Young 1990, 231).
Accordingly, even everyday conversations require interpretation.

In a model of complementary agency, public deliberation is a
hermeneutic activity; people come together in order to create new,
broader understandings of what is in their interests. They help each
other flesh out a more comprehensive picture of the whole. Alone,
their understanding will always be partial and fragmented; together,
they can fill in the blind spots, however provisionally. In a relational
model of subjectivity, the key is for people to recognize their relationality and use it to address common political concerns.

Drawing upon both Gadamer's hermeneutics and Levinas's ethics,
I accept that the subject is fragmented and "on trial" but take this as
an opportunity. Everyone's insights and knowledge are always partial
and provisional. By understanding that one's own knowledge is incomplete, people can come to welcome the insights that others bring.
Moreover, as Levinas writes, the others in our midst call forth in us a
need to respond, and in this sense of responsibility we come to have a
sense of self. To put it another way, we are indebted to others for our
subjectivity. These new self-understandings suggest a new under-

standing of political community: instead of a group of individuals who are struggling to overcome their differences, community could mean a group that welcomes and uses difference.

I want to focus now on two feminist democratic theorists and how they attend to these issues: Seyla Benhabib and Iris Young. Both consider the question of whether difference is a problem or an opportunity for democratic deliberative politics. They agree that different, particular perspectives can and should contribute to public deliberation.

Benhabib on Practical Rationality and Symmetrical Reciprocity

Benhabib shows how difference is an opportunity for deliberative democracy in a discussion of practical rationality (Benhabib 1996, 67–94). Here she departs from the more modest claims of other deliberative theorists who claim that deliberation among free and equal citizens is important primarily because it provides legitimacy and respects the democratic norms of fairness and equality. It helps bring out what a democratic public will is, but doesn't necessarily produce better judgments. A few, among them David Estlund, argue that deliberation is important because it produces better information (Bohman and Rehg 1997, 173–204). Estlund's arguments for the epistemic value of deliberation are weak, claiming basically that the more people involved in deciding something, the more likely they are to "get it right" (i.e., a weak Condorcet jury theorem). Moreover, these weak arguments don't say why deliberation is crucial, only that the numeric strength of public conversations increases their epistemic value.

Adopting a different approach, Benhabib points out three ways in which public deliberation produces more rational outcomes. First, deliberation imparts information (Benhabib 1996, 71). The more people involved in deliberation, the more perspectives and information are available for making a sound decision. Benhabib welcomes differences and particularities into deliberation, maintaining that Rawls's wish to leave these out of deliberations as part of the nonpublic "background culture" of society is mistaken. She criticizes the sharp distinction that Rawls makes between public and nonpublic realms by pointing out that the affinities people display in their associations in civil society have a very public character (75–76). In civil

society, there is an ongoing "anonymous conversation" about matters of the commonweal, and these are important components of a
deliberative democracy (74).

A second sense in which the deliberative process provides practical
rationality is by offering a way for participants to develop, articulate,
and order their preferences (71). Contrary to the economic model of
political preferences, which supposes that people's interests are pre-
political (that is, prior to the give and take of discourse in the public
sphere), Benhabib's deliberative model specifies that participants decide what is in their own interests in the course of their deliberations.
Recognizing that interests and preferences are political, not prepoliti-
cal, deliberation gets a better gauge of what public will is on an issue.

And third, the process of public deliberation calls on participants to
reflect upon their own views, especially insofar as they are trying to
"woo" others to adopt their views (71–72). Participants have to imagine how all others would respond to the views offered. "Nobody,"
Benhabib writes, "can convince others in public of her point of view
without being able to state why what appears good, plausible, just,
and expedient to her can also be considered so from the standpoint of
all involved" (72). While the deliberative process is never perfect, we
can safely presume that a majority decision flowing from it has some
"presumptive claim to being rational until shown to be otherwise."
In a parliamentary democracy, the outcomes can always be reexam-
ined another day; no outcome is ever final.

I think Benhabib's account of how deliberation provides practical
rationality is an important contribution to deliberative theory. All
three points are good ones, though the third has some presuppositions that I, following Iris Young, believe are unwarranted and unpro-
ductive. I refer to the notion that participants in deliberation adopt
the "standpoint of all" in reflexively considering their own views. In
her book Situating the Self, Benhabib argues that we can do this by
reversing perspectives with others, by striving for symmetry and reciprocity. Here Benhabib is developing Habermas's point in his discourse ethics that, in communicative situations, participants appeal
to a "generalized other." Benhabib wants to make the generalized
other more concrete, that is, to appreciate the perspectives of actual
others in our many daily encounters. We do so by putting ourselves
in their position in order to understand fully how things appear to
them.

Iris Young takes issue with Benhabib on this point. Drawing on Irigaray, she contends that "the idea of symmetry in our relations obscures the difference and particularity of the other position" (Young 1997a, 44). In our deliberations with others we should have the moral respect and humility to recognize that we may not understand others' perspectives. Instead of trying to adopt the standpoint of all others, we should listen carefully to them. Rather than presume that we can know how the world seems to them, we need to ask, we need their voice in the deliberations, and we need to listen. In Iris Young's corrective to Benhabib, difference calls for more deliberation with others, and difference can make deliberations more productive. For as Benhabib herself notes, the more perspectives, the more information the deliberation produces.

Young on Difference and Communicative Democracy

For her own part, Iris Young is very supportive of a discussion-based democratic model. While it is not her favorite model, she characterizes deliberative democratic theory as an alternative to the interest-based model of politics. Whereas interest-based politics takes participants as guardians of their own private, individualistic concerns, deliberative politics sees citizens as involved in "coming together to talk about collective problems, goals, ideals, and actions" (Young 1997a, 61). As the theorists of deliberative democracy put it, this kind of politics helps create a public interested in the common good of all. Young describes what deliberative theorists take to be the positive features of their model. In their deliberations, citizens

> sort out good reasons from bad reasons, valid argument from invalid. The interlocutors properly discount bad reasons and speeches that are not well argued, and they ignore or discount rhetorical flourishes and emotional outbursts. Putting forward and criticizing claims and arguments, participants in deliberation do not rest until the "force of the better argument" compels them all to accept a conclusion. (Young 1997a, 61)

Although she favors the general outlines of this alternative to interest-based politics, Young disagrees with the thinking behind the Habermasian notion that in a deliberative setting the "force of the

better argument" will prevail. By limiting deliberation to argumentation, deliberative theorists favor the Enlightenment version of reason, which has been shaped by its male-dominated, classist, and
racist origins. Moreover, such reason is generally combative and
exclusionary:

> Instead of defining discussion as the open reciprocal recognition of the
> point of view of everyone, these institutions style deliberation as ago-
> nistic. Deliberation is competition. Parties to dispute aim to win the
> argument, not to achieve mutual understanding. Consenting because of
> the "force of the better argument" means being unable to think of fur-
> ther counterargument, that is, to concede defeat. (63)

Young points out that this argumentative procedure excludes voices
and cultures that traditionally communicate in other ways. As an alternative to the argumentative deliberative model, she offers a model
of what she calls "communicative democracy." This kind of democracy would also be discussion based, but it would welcome other
kinds of communication, including greeting, rhetoric, and storytelling (69–74).

Deliberative theorists claim that discourse should be guided by reason and free from any other cultural, rhetorical, or power influences.
But because of the agonistic norms, "power reenters the arena" (64).
By excluding "rhetorical flourishes," forms of greeting, bodily and
emotional expressions, and other not strictly rational forms of discourse, deliberative democracy would empower those who have been
trained to argue in more linear and logical ways. "In many formal situations the better-educated white middle-class people, moreover, often act as though they have a right to speak and that their words carry
authority, whereas those of other groups often feel intimidated by the
argument requirements and the formality and rules of parliamentary
procedure, so they do not speak, or speak only in a way that those in
charge find 'disruptive'" (64).

Young also notes that the deliberative model presumes unity is either a starting point or the goal of democratic communication. She
points out that Walzer and sometimes Habermas write as if there
were some antecedent communal or consensual unity from which
participants deliberate. She disagrees, saying that it is unwarranted to
presume that there are "sufficient shared understandings to appeal to
in many situations of conflict"; moreover, often the point of political

discussion is to move beyond one's present views. Beginning with the presumption of unity would keep participants from transcending their current ideas.

A larger problem with the presumption of unity is the notion that the goal of deliberation is to reach consensus. Reaching consensus often means deciding what is in the common good. But here what is "common" may exclude what is particular, and this might come through denigrating the "particular" perspectives of less privileged participants. Consensus might be reached at the expense of those whose cultural styles and values are different from those of the more privileged members of society.

Young wants to preserve the plurality of concerns, orientations, and goals that arise in public forums. For these reasons, she urges us to adopt a broad "communicative" model rather than a deliberative one.

While I share Young's general concerns, I think we should not abandon the term *deliberation*. Rather than drop the term, I would like us to expand our theoretical ideas about what it means. In my work with the Kettering Foundation, the National Issues Forums, and Deliberative Polling, I have observed scores of deliberative forums. When citizens deliberate, they use their own vernacular; they tell stories about what happened to them that led them to hold their views; they listen to other people's stories and get a glimpse of how things appear to people different from themselves; they weigh the costs and consequences of various courses of action in terms of what they find valuable. They regularly use greeting, rhetoric, and storytelling. And they definitely do not obey the limits that philosophers of deliberative democracy set. Are they not deliberating? Or are the philosophers missing something? Greeting, rhetoric, and storytelling are central aspects of deliberation, not separate ventures.

Multiple Political Identities

Another aspect of complementary agency is recognizing that we may hold a multiplicity of political identities within us as well as among us. Each of us is an ensemble or an intersection of relations. I am half Greek and half Texan, a woman, southerner, intellectual, wife, union activist, mother, and breadwinner. These identities intersect to form my own identity, but it is an identity that as a result of these various identities is in tension. I was raised in an environment in which the roles of wife and breadwinner were at odds, as were woman and intellectual, southerner and union activist, foreigner and American. Such are the tensions that give rise to political turmoil. To the extent that we internalize these conflicts, the political becomes personal. Likewise, the project of trying to make sense of one's own political identity is politically transformative. I've seen this phenomenon cause much strife for one of my former students who is half Anglo-American and half African-American. In every paper he wrote for me he struggled with this mixed identity, with feeling that he had no place in society. He was angry, confused, and hurt, with the political clash between blacks and whites in American society being felt in his own person. You might even say that his attempt to work through his internal difference and tension was political in the sense that his own identity was part and parcel of an American identity struggle. To the extent that he was able to work through this difference, the polity works through its struggle as well.

Antonio Gramsci, the leader of the Italian Communist Party who was imprisoned by Mussolini, was aware of this phenomenon. As quoted in James Joll's study, Gramsci wrote:

> Man does not enter into relations with the natural world just by being himself part of it but actively by means of work and technique. Further: these relations are not mechanical. They are active and conscious. . . . Each of us changes himself, modifies himself to the extent that he changes and modifies the complex relations of which he is the heart. In this sense, the real philosopher is, and cannot be, other than the politician, the active man who modifies his environment, understanding by environment the ensemble of relations which each of us enters to take part in. If one's individuality is the ensemble of these relations, to create one's personality means to acquire consciousness of them and to modify one's own personality means to modify the ensemble of these relations. (Joll 1977, 117–18)

As Gramsci argues, to modify or form one's own identity is to modify the ensemble of political relations.

I wonder whether the pain my former student felt would have been transformed if he had thought of it as a political pain and not just a personal one. As a multiracial young person in a racist society, he tended to take slights personally, feeling ever the victim. (Isn't this the complaint of so many critics of "identity politics"—that it leads to a culture of victimization?) Perhaps, by seeing his own struggles as ways of transforming the larger political world, such a person could gain a greater sense of place and purpose.

In many respects, his struggles are those of us all. To become a more open society, we ought to find ways to help him—and all of us like him—along. Instead of taking relational subjectivity as the end of politics, we should see it as the very possibility of politics. In recognizing and living with our own internal alterity, we can come to welcome those others in our midst. Recognizing our relational subjectivity leads us to look for others to supplement our own partial self-understanding. Instead of putting up with others, we can welcome others' understandings.

Functions of Citizenship

Recall that in *Strangers to Ourselves* Kristeva says that the goal of psychoanalysis is not to eradicate our own radical strangeness but to welcome it so that we might also welcome others. Psychoanalytic theory, then, can move us from the personal to the social. It points to a theory of complementarity, which can become a bridge to a new kind of community. Ending the myth of unitary subjectivity makes it possible for us to overcome many barriers to community.

But can this complementary agency carry out the functions of citizenship that Habermas's theory suggests? As I discussed in Chapter 3, Habermas's political theory suggests the following outline of the functions of citizenship:

(1) citizenship should be seen as an intersubjective enterprise; it cannot be carried out by isolated individuals;

(2) citizens have to create the space in which citizenship can occur; that is, they have to move beyond their purely private networks and into more public ones, in the process creating and maintaining civil society;

(3) from within this civil society, citizens need to create discursive spaces in which they address matters of common concern—that is, they need to create the political public sphere;

(4)   effective citizenship calls for the ability to "ferret out, identify, and effectively thematize latent problems of social integration" (Habermas 1996, 358);

(5)   citizens will need to engage in this opinion- and will-formation process *spontaneously*, without the prompting of formal systems; otherwise the channels of communication would flow from center to periphery rather than the deliberative-democrat way, from periphery to center;

(6)   citizens should be able to bring these issues to the attention of formal legislative bodies "in a way that *disrupts* the latter's routines." (Habermas 1996, 358)

There is no reason that subjects-in-process cannot become public agents and carry out these functions. They can do so by acting with others complementarily. Already we see that they are predisposed to being able to meet the first criterion, acting intersubjectively. These functions do not require that each individual person carry them out atomistically and discretely. Habermas recognizes that this work is performed intersubjectively. Moreover, I believe that these functions are actually and ideally best carried out when people act (and know and constitute themselves) relationally. In fact, it is our relational subjectivities that make it possible for us to be citizens in the world.

Points 2 and 3 concern whether subjects-in-process are able to move beyond their purely private networks and into more public ones. For speaking beings who operate as "open systems," this would be a natural occurrence, since such subjectivities would not be inclined to remain within a private arena. As we've seen, their "own" subjectivity is always already intersubjective. And their "identity" is always already imbued with the political identities in the public sphere. There is a close, indeed inseparable, relation between their working out their "own" issues and working out public ones. In this respect, speaking beings are always constituting a civil society and inclined to create political public spheres.

The ability to "ferret out, identify, and effectively thematize latent problems of social integration" does not come quite so naturally. Kristeva would say it calls for psychoanalysis, the one-to-one relation between analysand and analyst in which language becomes the means for interpretation and integration (though full integration or "healing" will never be the goal of a Lacanian approach). But though psychoanalysis for all is not feasible, we can see the discursive space of the political public sphere as an opportunity for relational subjects to work through and thematize the issues that affect their interrelations. If anything, much more is at stake for relational subjects than is at stake for discretely autonomous subjects—and so the subject-in-process may be more motivated to carry out this function. Habermas faces the question of why the public will engage in public deliberation, but relational subjects will not share such problems of motivation. Likewise, point 5, the matter of spontaneity, is not a difficulty, for the subject as an open system, as a being thrust into the symbolic and propelled by the semiotic, will seek to transgress his or her appointed place. He or she will push from margin to center, will thematize issues that bear on the common life that speaking beings share. And further, to address point 6, he or she will do so in a way that transgresses the law. To the extent that the semiotic aspect of signification comes to the fore in public deliberations, the community of "strangers" in common will articulate political issues in a way that *disrupts* the status quo. This is not just a matter of speculation. Look around at the new social movements, the very ones Habermas points to, and the ways that they articulate issues. Whether by "acting up," by putting "earth first," by proclaiming themselves a "queer nation," or calling for "grrrl" power, new social movements signify semiotically, transgressing the order of the symbolic and the laws of the fathers.

When they are functioning well, relational subjects carry out these functions through language, through public discourse. Through public deliberation, they work to develop a kind of "public knowledge" of the political terrain; and they use this commonly created knowledge to make choices, that is, to decide how their communities should act. Relational subjects construct knowledge of their common world with others—producing an understanding richer than what is constructed individually. In other words, they deliberate together to form a public will on matters of common concern. In the following chapter, I further explore how such knowledge is created.

7 Ways of Knowing

In the most general sense, politics is the art of deciding what ought to be done about matters of common concern.[1] When we engage in politics, no matter how partisan, the ultimate question is always, "What should we do?" This is a prescriptive question, asking what a future course of action should be. It is tempting to call this area of inquiry *political epistemology*, because epistemology is the study of knowledge. But the term comes from the Greek word *episteme*, which means understanding or measuring something that is. In politics, however, what has to be known is *what should be or what we should do*, not what is. In this chapter I want to investigate the ways of knowing needed for politics, how relational subjects can develop this knowledge, and what it encompasses. Borrowing from Richard Rorty, I'll say that there have been two approaches to political ways of knowing: objectivity and solidarity.

Objectivity is the view that the best way to decide on a course of action is to step outside our context and culture so that we can dispassionately examine what course of action to take. The idea here is that we cannot grasp "the truth" so long as our particular situation colors our thinking. We need to think clearly, without bias, in order for our knowledge to be valid. To do so, we must imagine ourselves divested of our actual circumstances, culture, history, and material

[1] This chapter is adapted from an essay published in *Standing with the Public: The Humanities and Democratic Practice*, Kettering Foundation Press, 1997.

concerns. Usually those who are taken with the ideal of objectivity hold a companion ideal: that the standards we are looking for are universal. That is, they are unchanging and good for everyone in all contexts.[2] The desire for objectivity doesn't necessitate a notion of universal truths. But the two make sense only together. The only reason you would need to try to know free from any particular interests would be if the truth were the truth no matter what your particular concerns were. In other words, only in a universe that has universal truths would particular concerns be irrelevant. In such a universe, particular concerns just get in the way of knowledge.

Alternatively, there is the view that we are able to know *because* of our experience; we know what course of action is best through our active involvement in the world, from our "situatedness," our context and history. In this view, we know the world as we help make it. We know it by virtue of our relationship to it. This view often gets called, disparagingly, *relativism*, because in it truth (whatever that might mean) is relative to a particular point of view. A more charitable, even accurate, term is the one that Richard Rorty uses: *solidarity*. It describes the view that "there is nothing to be said about either truth or rationality apart from descriptions of the familiar procedures of justification which a given society—*ours*—uses in one or another area of inquiry" (Rorty 1991, 23). In other words, matters are judged according to criteria held by the group, not according to any external, supposedly universal criteria. Truth is right here, in our midst.

When it comes to political matters, according to solidarity, choice and purpose are internally derived. That is, the community decides what is best according to its own history, customs, and values. From the standpoint of solidarity, there are no external standards to appeal to in making choices about purpose and direction. Rather than try to "measure up" to some external standard, the community creates its own standards, which it may well refine over time.

Of the two points of view about political knowledge, the objectivist one has reigned for well over two thousand years. Its first ardent spokesman was Plato, and its most recent eloquent defender is

---

[2] One such standard often appealed to is that of equality: all persons are equally deserving of respect and dignity. By appealing to this standard, many groups of people have been able to fight for better living standards and for the ability to take part in political decision making. I don't want to lose sight of the issue, though. The question is not whether standards like equality are worthwhile; the question is whether those standards are universal and best found objectively.

Walter Lippmann. Both argue directly against "solidarity" or the contextualist point of view. In this chapter, I come to solidarity's defense.
I argue that the bias toward objectivity is a bias against knowledge
that the public holds, and thus a bias against democracy. To mount a
strong defense, I look at knowledge in its many forms, from the (supposedly) objective approach of the natural sciences to the contextual
approach of the humanities and of the public.

In the Ancient World

The lines of the objectivity-solidarity debate were first fully drawn
in Athens in the fifth century B.C. The philosophers took the objectivist position, and the Sophists worked out of solidarity. The
Sophists were, on the whole, itinerant teachers who earned their living by educating.[3] They taught by rhetoric: telling stories, questioning old myths (like the Eleatic myth of another reality greater than
the phenomenal one), unraveling inconsistencies, and looking for explanations. Their mission was to prepare men for success in the city,
since the Athenian conception of a realized human being was that of
a citizen—just as Aristotle (very much an anti-Sophist) claimed that
man was a political being. The Sophists believed that young men
could learn the virtues or excellences (arete) needed for citizenship
by learning how to persuade and speak publicly, by learning as much
as possible about their own culture and history—the literature and
grammar of Greece past and present. In many respects, the Sophists
broke with the old traditions and saw religion as a human invention.
They examined the difference between nature and convention, arguing that it was important to know how to use the conventions of
whatever city one visited. They believed that there was no truth
apart from what was true in a given city, which helps explain Pro-
tagoras's dictum: "Man is the measure of all things; of the things
which are, that they are, and of the things which are not, that they
are not." Many of their critics (at the time and through the ages)
blamed them for corrupting young men, for teaching someone how to
make something bad appear good and something false appear true.

Into the midst of this way of knowing and educating came Socrates

---

[3] My description is an amalgam—very much a generalization of the Sophists' various views and methods.

and Plato, who asked whether virtue could really be taught (no, they said) and, even if it could, whether the Sophists' way of teaching would provide an answer (no, again). Both Plato and after him Aristotle argued against the Sophists' contextualist approach to knowledge, saying that rational inquiry was superior to contextual accounts.

Plato indicted the Sophists most vigorously. He did so by arguing for an objectivist view of truth. In his view, there were two worlds: the everyday, visible world of material objects, which are apprehended through the senses, and the invisible world of the Forms (the immaterial models for all the particular things in the visible world), which is known only through pure reason. For Plato, this second world of the Forms was the real world—because in it were the unchanging, eternal, universal Forms. This world *caused* the everyday, visible world. The visible world just reflected the unchanging world of the Forms. One couldn't really know anything about the visible world, because that world is always in flux. True knowledge is of the invisible world. True knowledge requires the intelligible grasp of the universal Forms.

According to Plato, everyone already has knowledge of this world of Forms. The knowledge is innate, but unfortunately forgotten. Most people live their lives thinking that the everyday world of material objects is all there is, but they are mistaken, Plato maintains. The everyday world is a mere reflection of the real, and so these unfortunate people see only images, images always liable to change. Instead of knowledge, these people have only opinions. Instead of knowing what's best and true, they know only what *seems* to be best and true. They are caught up in the world of seeming and becoming, and have no inkling of the real world of being.

To awaken the knowledge we were born with requires having the right nature (that of a philosopher) and decades of education. In Plato's ideal state, those with the philosopher's nature would be trained to recognize the most supreme of the Forms: the Form of the Good. Once able to know the Form of the Good, the philosopher would be a just ruler, able to make just political decisions because he or she was properly enlightened.

The Good is known objectively, by those who have risen above the flux and fray of the everyday world. It is outside of human experience, so knowing it requires looking beyond the phenomenal world of appearances. Those who have this knowledge are able to decide what courses of action are in the true interests of the polis. Others are not. Therefore only these philosopher-rulers, possessing objective knowledge of the Good, can and should make political decisions.

As I understand him, Plato argues for this view because he thinks there must be—and is—a standard by which to know which actions are just. The Form of the Good is this standard. Only with this standard could a philosopher-ruler make sound decisions. Without a standard, a ruler would decide arbitrarily and irrationally. All sorts of injustices would prevail: some might rule out of a lust for power, others for vanity, others by whim.

For such reasons Plato criticizes democracy. The democratic man, Plato claims in the *Republic*, is always at the mercy of his desires. He thinks that whatever he desires at the moment is the highest good and lets these desires rule him:

And so he lives on, yielding day by day to the desire at hand. Sometimes he drinks heavily while listening to the flute; at other times, he drinks only water and is on a diet; sometimes he goes in for physical training; at other times, he's idle and neglects everything; and sometimes he even occupies himself with what he takes to be philosophy. He often engages in politics, leaping up from his seat and saying and doing whatever comes into his mind. If he happens to admire soldiers, he's carried in that direction, if money-makers, in that one. There's neither order nor necessity in his life, but he calls it pleasant, free, and blessedly happy, and he follows it for as long as he lives. (561c–e)

The democratic man, as Plato calls him, values the freedom to do whatever he feels like doing at any given time. In this, he values freedom above all else, namely the freedom to change his mind about what is good. But for Plato, this is folly. There is only one Form of the Good. While many actual things might partake of this Form, they don't do so willy-nilly. Whether something is good or not is an objective fact. When the mass of people rule, as in a democracy, they are usually mistaken about what's good, including what's good for them. The only way to ascertain what is good is to step outside human experience and desire and to look instead to what is unchanging.

With these epistemological views, Plato naturally took issue with the Sophists, who used human experience in the phenomenal world as their guide. Like the democrats, the Sophists favored experience over philosophic abstraction; they relied on history, literature, and culture for their accounts, not on external notions of the Good. For the Sophists, it did not make sense to look outside the culture to educate those within it. The culture already had a repository of educative material.

Plato worried that this sort of training would leave people vulnerable to manipulation and demagoguery. These orators and itinerant teachers gave the public mere images and spurious narratives. Instead of by such teachers, the public should be guided by a specially trained class of experts. At bottom, Plato's theory of knowledge underlay his criticism of democracy. For their own good, the people should not rule. This view did not die with the ancient world. It is as alive today as ever.

Seduced by the Sciences

There is a curious similarity between Plato's era and ours. Just as Plato thought that guardians rather than the people should rule, the American progressive movement around the turn of the twentieth century contended that a select group of trained professionals should help run the country, whether by advising leaders or by helping lead and manage directly. We could call these eras "postdemocratic" because both were backlashes against democracy.[4] "Who knows what's good for the public?" The postdemocratic answer to this question is "the disinterested judge"—someone who stands outside particularities and contexts and is able to judge dispassionately.

In the modern era, the model for this approach is the natural sciences, which seem to epitomize the value of objective research, with the scientist-subject looking dispassionately at the objective world. Some argue that research in the natural sciences is not really so objective (e.g., Thomas Kuhn and Paul Feyerabend), but for the sake of argument let's grant that the natural sciences may call for objectivity. The important question for us is this: should the objective standpoint

---

[4] Plato was reacting both to democracy associated with Pericles and to the regime that followed, "the thirty." In the early decades of the twentieth century, the progressives were responding to supposedly scientific studies that showed that 60–70 percent of the men enlisted in the armed services were "mentally deficient." If so many average Americans were incapable of reasoning, then how could they be able to govern themselves? For a summary of this history, see Westbrook 1991, 182–90.

of the natural sciences be the model for political knowledge? For better or worse, many twentieth-century thinkers have answered affirmatively.

In the name of science, progress, and professionalism, the progressive movement in the early part of the century called for careful managing of society. As Oscar Handlin writes, "From the progressives of the first two decades of the century Americans had learned that government was a science and, like any other, was best left in the hands of trained experts." Just as with Plato's model, the modern notion of leadership was tied to education and expertise: "Only men educated to understand the intricate machinery could administer either industry or government" (Handlin 1968, 834).

Moreover, the expert needed to be able to rise above the partisan interests that tended to drag down government. "The expert had the additional virtue of disinterestedness," Handlin writes. Ideally, the expert would excel in nonpartisan efficiency (834–35).

This movement became entrenched in America's understanding of ideal governance. As Robert Westbrook writes, the neoprogressives of the 1930s "argued for the identification of the good society with the rationalized society, which to them meant a society managed by an elite of far-sighted planners. They called for the creation of a new social order guided by 'experts who are not representatives of the capitalists but of the public interest'" (Westbrook 1991, 455).[5] The ideals of expertise, disinterestedness, objectivity and efficiency pervaded other areas as well: engineering, the clergy, social work, and the other emerging professions. With the rise of professionalism came a growing gap between the people and its leaders.

Influenced by the progressive movement—though departing from it considerably—was one of the most influential critics of participatory democracy, Walter Lippmann. During the First World War he helped develop propaganda for the army, and afterward he became a journalist and a nonacademic political theorist. Lippmann is famous (or infamous, depending upon your point of view) for his book *The Phantom Public*: "The accepted theory of popular government," he wrote, "rests upon the belief that there is a public which directs the course of events. I hold that this public is a mere phantom. It is an abstraction" (Lippmann 1965, 89). In part he meant that there is no

[5] In this passage Westbrook is quoting from "What We Hope For," *New Republic*, 10 February 1932, 337.

fixed public; it shifts all the time, depending upon what issue is on the table. In a later book, *The Public Philosophy*, he gave another reason to be wary of phrases like "The People." Such phrases are ambiguous: On the one hand they connote a unitary, historic community that encompasses the living, as well as their predecessors and successors. On the other hand "The People" is also equated with the numerous actual living members of a society, its voters.

> It is often assumed, but without warrant, that the opinions of The People as voters can be treated as the expression of the interests of *The People* as an historic community. The crucial problem of modern democracy arises from the fact that this assumption is false. The voters cannot be relied upon to represent *The People*. The opinions of voters in elections are not to be accepted unquestioningly as true judgments of the vital interests of the community. (Lippmann 1965, 86)

The People as voters, as those actual citizens of a political community, are incapable of knowing what is in their own interests as a political community. They might individually know what seems to be good for themselves or their neighborhood, but they cannot know what is in the greater good. They are unable to look beyond their self-interests to the public interest. After all, the two interests may clash. Moreover, most people are too busy, Lippmann says, and the environment is too vast for people to make sound judgments. When their imperfect, self-interested views are aggregated, as they are in an election or in a public opinion poll, the result is no better. And it's certainly not, according to Lippmann, the same thing as the true public interest.

The true public interest is what is good for everyone, despite what everyone thinks. Citizens are often mistaken about their true interests, especially given that their knowledge about the environment is imperfect and that they may desire harmful things. Various individuals will hold different notions about what would be in the public interest, but the true public interest is the same for everyone: "Living adults share, we must believe, the same public interest." And this interest "is often at odds with . . . their private and special interests. . . . Put this way, we can say, I suggest, that the public interest may be presumed to be what men would choose if they saw clearly, thought rationally, acted disinterestedly and benevolently" (Lippmann 1965, 88–89).

Here we have one statement of Lippmann's epistemological criteria for how to ascertain what is in the public interest. As he makes plain, the people lack these criteria: they are irrational; they have entirely too many interests at stake; and they are too concerned for their own well-being to look after someone else's. Rather than rely on the people, who are too much in the thick of things, we should rely on those who have risen above the fray. These are the statesmen of the world—not mere politicians, who are still beholden to particular interests, but those men whose minds are "elevated sufficiently above the conflict of contending parties" that they are able to "adopt a course of action which takes into account a greater number of interests in the perspective of a longer period of time" (Lippmann 1965, 455).

The true statesman, according to Lippmann, is able to do single-handedly what a whole public is unable to do—objectively discern what is in the public interest. To accomplish this, Lippmann advises that the statesman make a point of *not* consulting the public. He makes this astounding recommendation so bluntly that I must quote at length:

> It is not deference to democracy for public men to evade their responsi-
> bilities and ask the mass of the people to do the work that public men
> are supposed to do. Once they refuse to lead opinion and prefer to be led
> by public opinion, they make impossible the formation of a sound pub-
> lic opinion. For obviously the President and the Administration offi-
> cials and the congressmen in touch with them have the means for in-
> forming themselves on the realities of the labor situation and of the
> defense program and of the war that no one else, not even the most con-
> scientious newspaper reporters, can possess. If with their responsibili-
> ties and their means of knowing what is what, they sit around waiting
> for the Gallup poll and the fan mail, they will get a Gallup poll and a
> fan mail from a people that have not been able to know what men must
> know in order to judge wisely. (Lippmann 1965, 99)

So what should a statesman know, according to Lippmann, in order to judge wisely? He needs to know the "hidden interests" of the public "which are permanent because they fit the facts and can be harmonized with the interests of their neighbors" (456). To be able to have this amazing knowledge without ever consulting the public, the statesman should have "the insight which comes only from an objective and discerning knowledge of the facts, and a high and imperturbable disinterestedness" (457).

There we have it: the paradigmatic case for objectivity. In case the reader is not as appalled by this as I am, let me make a few comments. Note that the model of objectivity calls for the virtue of disinterestedness. This is an interesting word, *disinterested*. As Ernesto Cortés, Jr., says, *interested* comes from *inter-esse*, to be between. So to be disinterested is to have nothing at stake, to be completely uninvolved, to be elsewhere. The twentieth-century ideal of disinterestedness really means being removed from society. Those we look to for guidance, then, have—or at least pretend to have—nothing at stake here. Why should the disinterested statesman bother at all with the good of the public? It seems all too likely that those who claim to have nothing at stake in public matters may well believe that the public does not matter much after all.

Apart from being offended by Lippmann's sentiments, I also think that he is simply wrong. The model of objective knowledge that he holds so dear doesn't work in politics. No one but an omniscient god could know without consulting the public what the public will value over the long run, how citizens' different interests can be harmonized, and what is really "good" for them. These "public facts," if you will, do not reside in some platonic heaven; they are contingent, provisional facts, produced by the public.

In the mid-1980s I attended graduate school in public policy and quickly learned that *public policy* did not refer to policy made by the public but rather policy made for the public by an elite cadre of experts.

Though policy schools have been around for only thirty years, they draw from a long history. For centuries there have been those trained and destined to serve in some public capacity. These intellectuals have tended to see themselves as easily transplantable—able to move from one country to the next, serving one leader or another. Before this past century they were trained in the humanities, though they were still prototypes of "disinterested" experts for they lacked any sustained relationship to the communities that they served.

They were what we might call "traditional" intellectuals, to follow Gramsci's phrasing.[6] The term *traditional intellectual* refers to certain intellectual workers who came to see themselves as independent

---

[6] Imprisoned by Mussolini during the Second World War, Gramsci spent his days writing his notebooks, now widely read commentaries on the prospects of transforming Western capitalist societies. To avoid the prison censors, Gramsci steered clear of the jargon of communism, and in the process he developed a set of terms and concepts that have remarkable applications.

of any particular groupings or strata, as free inquirers into truth. Gramsci noted that, though these intellectuals claim to be independent, they in fact act to preserve the status quo, wittingly or not. A traditional intellectual is bent on preserving the norms. Even as he or she dabbles in a particular area of scholarship, nothing will really change. This intellectual's masquerade as independent is dependent upon there being a certain organization of society—one that remains untouched. So in the long run he or she is completely indebted to this social order.

Today's traditional intellectuals, let me venture, are equally dependent on society's being constructed in a particular form. (So we might wonder just how objective they truly are.) For one thing, they need a society in which expert knowledge is valued and lay knowledge is disdained. In other words, for the expert's knowledge to have any value, we must ensure that the everyday knowledge of regular people—call it common sense—is disparaged. What this means is that practical knowledge always trails far behind scientific knowledge, that expert knowledge is always the ideal. Moreover, we come to equate knowledge with expertise and public opinion with error.

The Rise and Fall of the Public Sphere

With the devaluation of public knowledge, the public's role in deciding matters of common concern has diminished even as the franchise has expanded. Once upon a time—whether in theory or in fact—private citizens were able to join with others through associations and through public conversations to make choices about public matters. In doing so, they created a sphere or realm sometimes called the public sphere or civil society. This realm exerted a force upon government, a force that called the government to account in some way to this public.

In many political and theoretical circles, the term "public sphere" has gained new currency. As I noted earlier, an important contribution here was the 1992 publication of *The Structural Transformation of the Public Sphere*, the English translation of the 1962 book in which Habermas traced the rise and fall of a political arena which is neither private nor governmental. The public sphere is that place where public opinion is formed. "A portion of the public sphere is constituted in every conversation in which private persons come together to form a public," writes Habermas. "Citizens act as a public when they deal with matters of general interest."

Habermas concluded that the public sphere has withered away. Robert Holub sums up Habermas's argument nicely:

> The public sphere, at least its bourgeois prototype, began to decline during the course of the past century. . . . The collapse occurs because of the intervention of the state into private affairs and the penetration of society into the state. Since the rise of the public sphere depended on a clear separation between the private realm and public power, their mutual interpenetration destroys it. . . . As we progress into the twentieth century, the free exchange of ideas among equals becomes transformed into less democratic communicative forms, for example public relations. (Holub 1991, 6)

Habermas analyzed the public sphere as both a historical development, which failed, and a normative ideal, which still holds sway. As I see it, the public sphere is still alive today, though extremely malnourished. The public realm between the state and private spheres survives in community organizations, churches, labor unions, study circles, the National Issues Forums, and many other nongovernmental organizations in the United States and in countries abroad. The rise of civil associations in Eastern Europe helped bring down the Berlin Wall, and the few that exist in China exert a force for accountability upon the Chinese government. Yet none of these public spheres fulfills its potential, in large part because they are maligned for being realms of solidarity, not objectivity. Vibrant public spheres will value public knowledge, the force of public opinion, and the importance of the public's being the source of legitimacy for government. Yet, as we've seen, solidarity is hardly ever nurtured or valued in contemporary society.

Many today think invigorating this realm is vitally important. But many forces work against this end, namely the same forces that favor disinterestedness, objectivity, and expert knowledge. The public sphere has little or no value in a model of politics that takes elite knowledge as its ideal. Just as my colleagues in policy school would never look to the public for guidance in making policy, those who value expert knowledge would just as soon there not be a public with which to contend.

In many respects, the plight of the public sphere is one with the plight of the arts and humanities. Neither is seen to have anything worthy to contribute to public policy making. Their knowledge is suspect for being supposedly subjective, baseless, relative, arbitrary, and standardless. Yet to the contrary, as I discuss below, the public and the humanities offer ways of knowing that our society greatly needs. We need them in all those situations in which "expertise" seems to miss the point, as when we are deciding matters of value, meaning, and purpose—in other words, for all the truly hard questions.

Knowing What We Ought to Do

There are many ways of knowing, with different ways suitable for different purposes. This is an ancient distinction. In fact, one of the clearest—and still useful—expositions of the differences was made by Aristotle. He divided knowledge into three sorts: theoretical, productive, and practical. Only one of these is suitable for politics, for deciding what we as a community or polis ought to do on matters of public concern.

The Limits of Theoretical Reason

The theoretical sciences aim at describing the world as it is. For Aristotle, this was the highest form of knowledge, since one engaged in it as an end in itself: knowledge for knowledge's sake. The theoretical scientist, according to this definition, wants to know how things work. The subjects of theoretical knowledge, for Aristotle, include metaphysics, physics, and mathematics.

Theoretical knowledge isn't concerned with action. It doesn't seek to change anything. In its proper scope, it has no ulterior motives and so has no moral or political concerns. This ancient definition is still apt today. Those interested in research for its own sake are aiming for understanding—not for putting this understanding to any particular use. In the theoretical sciences, whether in microbiology or in fractal geometry, researchers investigate how a system or entity operates. If the research produces knowledge that can be used, then the theoretician turns the results over to the technician. *Using* this knowledge takes us out of the realm of theory and into the realm of action.

The Limits of Instrumental Reason

While theoretical knowledge shuns action, other forms of knowledge embrace it.[7] Aristotle called his second designation *productive knowledge*. This is the knowledge used to produce a given product. The physician uses her own knowledge to produce health, the chef to produce a delightful meal, the cobbler to produce shoes. Productive knowledge helps a practitioner produce some end, but it doesn't designate what the end ought to be. The end is given in advance, whether by an earlier choice of careers or the predetermined designations within a more traditional society.

Yet we have to be careful that production doesn't become an end in itself. As I noted above, the more theoretical knowledge produced, the more tempting it is to put this knowledge to use. In his critique of what he called technological society, Erich Fromm described the principle that seems to privilege means over ends: "the maxim that something *ought* to be done because it is technically *possible* to do it" (Fromm 1968, 32). This violates the tradition that said "that something should be done because it is needed for man, for his growth, joy, and reason, because it is beautiful, good, or true. Once the principle is accepted that something ought to be done because it is technically possible to do it, all other values are dethroned, and technological development becomes the foundation of ethics" (Fromm 1968, 32–33). In this century, productive reason has been put to such ill use. In fact, the logic of production—of instrumentality and technology—seems to have overridden the sort of reason needed in deciding ends.

Under this heading of productive reason, I'd like to include a more modern designation, that of instrumental reason. This is the term used by some twentieth-century philosophers to criticize the rationale that guides bureaucracies and other large systems. Wherever instrumental reason reigns, ends are generally predetermined and unquestioned. Reason works here to fulfill these often unacknowledged

---

[7] Although I'm classifying knowledge into three types, I do not mean to endorse this classification. I am much more persuaded by the pragmatist notion that knowledge is always tied to action. In his book *Philosophy and the Mirror of Nature*, Richard Rorty tries to show "that the notion of knowledge as the assemblage of accurate representations is optional—that it may be replaced by a pragmatist conception of knowledge which eliminates the Greek contrast between contemplation and action, between representing the world and coping with it" (Rorty 1979, 11). My point in classifying knowledge is to show that, even under traditional conceptions, there are forms of knowledge that are suitable for acting and choosing ends.

ends. It tackles the question of *how* to produce a particular end: whether the end is amassing a fortune or winning a war. Sometimes the means seem to be ends in themselves. For example, efficiency is often idealized, but the most efficient society would not be the most humane one. As my former economics professor Malcolm Gillis, said, the question of when and how to increase efficiency should never be decided by economists; it's a political matter that should be answered by the political process.

Max Weber was one of the first to critique instrumental reason, saying that it was like an iron cage—not the liberating force that the Enlightenment promised. In response to his critique of reason, other philosophers—including Jürgen Habermas—have tried to show that this reason was just one sort. Habermas argues that there is yet another sort of reason that might fulfill the Enlightenment's promise of freedom and a more progressive society.

The Hermeneutics of Defining Meaning and Purpose

Both theoretical and instrumental reason are compatible with the objectivist approach. Theoretical reason seeks to understand some object or entity. Instrumental reason seeks the most efficient means to reach some predetermined end. But the third way of knowing that Aristotle defined calls on the self-reflective approach of solidarity.

Aristotle calls this third way of knowing *phronesis*. This term is generally translated as *practical wisdom*, but I'd like to broaden the translation to include practical intelligence or reason. *Phronesis* is the sort of wisdom or reason involved when human beings act, especially when they decide what to aim for. It is "the capacity for deciding what is good and advantageous" for oneself (*Nicomachean Ethics*, 1110a25–26). It is reason needed in deciding what one's ends should be: "Production has an end other than itself, but action does not: good action is itself an end. That is why we think that Pericles and men like him have practical wisdom. They have the capacity of seeing what is good for themselves and for mankind, and these are, we believe, the qualities of men capable of managing households and states" (1110b5–10). Practical reason is a kind of legislation: "Practical wisdom issues commands: its end is to tell us what we ought to do and what we ought not to do" (1143a7–9).

In the course of discussing practical wisdom, Aristotle also discusses political wisdom and deliberation. He says that there are two kinds of practical wisdom concerning the state: "the one, which acts as practical wisdom supreme and comprehensive, is the art of legislation; the other, which is practical wisdom as dealing with particular facts, bears the name which [in everyday speech] is common to both kinds, politics, and it is concerned with action and deliberation" (1141b24–27). Here I am going to part company with Aristotle. Elsewhere (1112b11–24) he argues that we deliberate only about means, not ends. His thinking seems to run as follows: The man of practical wisdom has the virtue of being able to know what the proper ends ought to be. He has this wisdom due to his experience and just nature. (A young man is too inexperienced to have this virtue.) There are times, though, when it is necessary to investigate the ways to achieve these ends. This is when deliberation is required.

I disagree with Aristotle's point that the man of practical wisdom just knows what the proper ends are without deliberating. For one thing, Aristotle simply makes this claim; he doesn't (as far as I know) give a reason for it. For another, in politics the proper ends aren't self-evident, even to someone with this wisdom. Rather, practical wisdom is the product of practical intelligence, and this intelligence would entail sorting through all the many proper ends or "legislation" to decide what coheres best with the group's ideals.

I agree with Aristotle that political wisdom requires deliberation, but I'd add that in a democracy political deliberation is not a solitary venture (of "the man" of practical wisdom) but a joint venture of all the citizens who have a stake in the matter. Deliberation entails more than sorting through various options; it entails bringing together multiple points of view and concerns.

How would this sort of practical reasoning work? At present, there are various views. Some think it really isn't a *reasoning* at all, but rather a practice of interpretation. For these thinkers, *reason* implies some universal standards whereas a practice can be contingent and contextually defined. For my purposes, the distinction is not terribly relevant. The important point is that there is a way of thinking about ends that is neither purely theoretical nor instrumental. It is a way of taking into consideration the particulars, the context, the history of a community while making sense of what the community is and what it aspires to. It is a community thinking together about what its meaning is and what its purpose ought to be. One name for this practice is *hermeneutics*, the art of interpretation. Hermeneutics is the practice of making sense of something that might not have any objective meaning. Gadamer argues that interpretations are never the final arbiters of meaning. Rather they are provisional, always subject to

change. The same is true for communities. What we think is important and decisive one day may change the next. As new participants
and points of view enter a community's conversation, new understandings will arise. The more open a community is to change—including this change in interpretations—the less exclusive and rigid it
is, the less likely it is to become a homogeneous, uninviting place,
and the more willing it is to adapt to new developments. The more
hermeneutic a community is, the healthier it is.

Another take on practical reason is that it is, properly speaking, a
form of reason, not just provisional interpretation. This is the position that Habermas takes in his account of moral reasoning. Habermas maintains that there is a form of reasoning that guides our communicative practice. To put it briefly, he thinks that all human
beings hold certain rules about what kind of claims would be valid:
namely, that claims be comprehensible, true, sincere, and appropriate. These are our expectations when taking part in conversation, including conversations about what moral and political ends we ought
to seek.

> Just as an individual can reflect on himself and his life as a whole with
> the goal of clarifying who he is and who he would like to be, so too the
> members of a collectivity can engage in public deliberation in a spirit of
> mutual trust, with the goal of coming to an understanding concerning
> their shared form of life and their identity solely through the unforced
> force of the better argument. In such ethical-political discourses . . .
> participants can clarify who they are and who they want to be, whether
> as members of a family, as inhabitants of a region, or as citizens of a
> state. (Habermas 1993, 23)

This communicative reasoning is internal to our communicative
practice, so it would seem to fit in nicely under the model of solidarity. Unfortunately, it does so only partially. One of the expectations
that Habermas believes everyone shares is that in order for a moral
claim to be justified it has to be justifiable to everyone—within and
outside a community: "moral knowledge that raises a claim to universal validity must in addition detach itself from the contexts in
which ethical knowledge remains embedded" (Habermas 1993, 24).
Habermas uses the term *moral* in a very specific sense: as a universal
claim. For claims that are valid only within a particular community,
he uses the term *ethical*. He argues that these claims can be reflec-
tive, which grants them a rational status. So we might follow Haber-

mas up to this point. We might say (though there isn't room to make this argument here) that we all hold certain presuppositions about what moral or political claims are valid, that we can try to reach understanding and make choices together, but that we need not try to step outside our situatedness to justify these claims. After all, from the perspective of solidarity, there is no need to transcend our context. We need to try to universalize our claims only if we want statements that are universalizable: an unnecessary tautology.

We need not depart from solidarity by going as far as Habermas does to describe a way of knowing in politics. As I discussed in Chapter 6, hermeneutics can fill the bill. As Gadamer argues, others' partial knowledge can complement one's own partial knowledge. For Gadamer, understanding is always a matter of interpretation, which takes place in a hermeneutic "conversation" between the interpreter and the interpreted. For Gadamer, the meaning of a text is never fixed; it is constantly being remade in every interpretive exchange. I want to extend Gadamer's theory of understanding texts to a theory of how people come to understand each other and their world. They do it always, maybe only, by bringing together their various horizons of understanding, supplementing each other.

There is an immense difference between objective knowledge and public knowledge, but it is not that one is worthy and the other not. The difference is that the two have different criteria. Scientific knowledge is based on certain standards of rightness; public knowledge is judged on the basis of soundness. When we dismiss public knowledge, we dismiss the search for sound knowledge, knowledge about what course of action is most sustainable and consistent. Knowing what is a good end or purpose is political wisdom, the very wisdom that communities need in making political choices.

Who Can Know What's in the Public Interest?

I hope that by now I've answered the question with which this chapter began. The kind of knowledge we need in politics, in order to decide what course of action is best, is the kind used in solidarity: practical reason, which involves interpretation and deliberation. So now I turn to a final question: who is best suited to provide this knowledge? Certainly not those who claim to be objective and disinterested. Rather, we should look to those who are actively involved in interpreting, judging, and making their world: the public itself.

Why the public? Because it has the most at stake in political matters and it has the most knowledge about what should be done. Those
who favor objectivity worry that particular, subjective perspectives
are always partial ones, and that particular, special interests will
override the public interest. Yet only insofar as partial perspectives
remain partial will this be the case. The challenge is to bring these
partial perspectives together, to engage the participants to weigh
other points of view, to reconsider their own views in light of others.
This is done when people come together in public conversations, in
deliberation. Through deliberation, partial perspectives can be woven
into a new whole. Each participant can bring to the table an array of
considerations, and once at the table the participants can consider
views they might not have considered before. Through such deliberations, the public can articulate what the public interest is—far better
than Lippmann's statesman ever could.

But because the public sphere and contextual understanding (solidarity) have been denigrated, the public may need an ally in this venture. What other field of inquiry shares so much with the public's
way of knowing but the humanities? The process of creating sound
public knowledge shares a great deal with the knowledge-making
procedures in the arts and the humanities. These procedures include
interpretation, judgment, imagination, and expression. They can be
carried out well or poorly; we know the difference. Intellectuals in
the arts and the humanities don't have the luxury of appealing to
tried-and-true formulas; they must make decisions case by case, taking into consideration contexts and purposes, values and destina-
tions. In short, they must do the very things that the public must do
in deciding what judgment or course of action is best.

In this respect, then, the arts and humanities scholars are natural
allies for the public. They can speak for the value of contextual interpretation, which is much like public ways of knowing. And in doing
so, in strengthening the public sphere, they can shore up their own
place in a society that sees little need for them—that slashes funding
for the arts and humanities, that endows chairs in engineering rather
than the classics, that collapses and disbands whole departments in
the arts and humanities. In short, the relationship between these intellectuals and the public sphere is mutual, a true inter-estedness, in
the best sense.

But for this to happen, humanities scholars will have to modify or
even abandon their aspirations for specialization—which narrows

one's focus—and expertise, which is an attempt to "rise above" the layperson's understanding. For the humanities to ally themselves with the public, they will need to see their work as closely bound up with the public's mission.

Writing from his prison, Antonio Gramsci offered an alternative to traditional, disinterested intellectuals: "organic" intellectuals, intellectuals who are fully cognizant of their social and political roots. He saw a political need for this kind of intellectual, who grows out of a political community, and thus he suggested a way in which intellectuals could be inter-ested in public life: "The mode of being of the new intellectual can no longer consist in eloquence, which is an exterior and momentary mover of feelings and passions, but in active participation in practical life." This active participation meant being a "constructor, organizer, 'permanent persuader' and not just a simple orator" (Gramsci 1971, 10). Gramsci's organic intellectual takes an active role in shaping society, rather than just specializing in some arcane area of scholarship. By seeing themselves as organic intellectuals, humanities scholars could see their public origins as the wellspring, the purpose, and the gauge of their intellectual work.

This notion of organic intellectual may seem odd, for at first glance it seems that the humanities are quite separate spheres from the public. But this is an illusion born of hundreds of years of specialization. What the humanities scholar studies is nothing more than the products of the public lifeworld according to the very vernacular of that lifeworld. The social and natural scientists might try to rise above that vernacular and perspective, but the humanities scholar, by choice of practice, has chosen them. It is only natural, then, for the humanities and the public to join forces: an alliance that will strengthen both the public sphere and democratic practice.

8 Deliberative Communities

In *The Public and Its Problems*, John Dewey writes that democracy is "the idea of community life itself" (Dewey 1980, 148). At first glance, to equate democracy with community seems to skirt the problem of democracy in a pluralist society: how a heterogeneous and diverse society can come to any kind of agreement about matters of common concern. The "idea of community life itself" seems to be an ideal of transcendence, that we transcend our individuality and take part in a unity that is greater than our finite selves. Yet we need not take community to be such an ideal; we can think about community in a way that addresses the democratic problem.

What if, following Kristeva, we conceived of selves as subjects-in-relation, indebted to and open to others? And likewise, if we were to move beyond Kristeva, we thought of communities as spaces of relation, open to change, inclining to the never-assimilated other? In his essay "The Inoperative Community," Jean-Luc Nancy describes community as being-in-common as opposed to common being. Community is not an entity, he argues, warning us away from essentializing community, away from the path toward totalitarianism. Where totalitarianism closes off politics, being-in-common makes politics possible.

Most discourses on community betray a longing for some lost era:

The lost, or broken, community can be exemplified in all kinds of ways, by all kinds of paradigms: the natural family, the Athenian city, the Roman Republic, the first Christian community [etc.]—always it is a matter of a lost age in which community was woven of tight, harmonious, and infrangible bonds and in which above all it played back to itself, through its institutions, its rituals, and its symbols, the representation, indeed the living offering, of its own immanent unity, intimacy, and autonomy. (Nancy 1991, 9)

This is the model of community as immanence, as an entity held together by bonds, a community that "is not only intimate communication between its members, but also its organic communion with its own essence" (9). Though the community is made up of its members, it is something more, something in its own right, something with which its members identify, sometimes to the point of being willing to die for it, as if their deaths for the community will help them transcend their mortality. Through the community, they can become immortal. But such a community eludes us; it seems to have receded into some archaic age, and with its loss we mourn the absence of "familiarity, fraternity and conviviality" (10).

Against this, Nancy makes the startling claim that "community has not taken place" (11). There never was such a community: "It did not take place for the Guayaqui Indians, it did not take place in an age of huts; nor did it take place in the Hegelian 'spirit of a people' or in the Christian agape" (11). Rather, "the thought of community or the desire for it might well be nothing other than a belated invention that tried to respond to the harsh reality of modern experience" (10), namely, the disenchantment of our world, the receding of the divine, the death of God. But though Nancy is suspicious of nostalgia for a long-lost community, he takes this nostalgia to be an indication that we do in fact experience community, or rather that community is already there—so long as we do not succeed in "resurrecting" or bringing about the kind of immanence we imagine to be community.

How is some kind of community already there? In coming to grips with our finitude we experience community. In coming to see, through others' mortality, that we are mortal we come to see ourselves in relation to others; there's no longer a possibility of absolute and separable subjectivity. Death belies subjectivity: Cartesian subjectivity ought to be able to represent its own death, but it cannot. So there is some "I" there that is not "a subject." "That which is not a subject opens up and opens onto a community whose conception, in turn, exceeds the resources of a metaphysics of the subject" (Nancy 1991, 14).

Let me back up a moment in order to try to clarify the difference between the kind of community we sometimes pine for and the kind of community to which Nancy is pointing. Recall that the former kind of community is one for which, supposedly, one is willing to die, the idea being that one's death will do some good, that it will be a work, or project of some kind. But in the second community Nancy is describing, we are all too aware that our deaths will occur and that they will do no good. We are all too finite, an awareness that community exposes us to. As Nancy writes:

> What community reveals to me, in presenting to me my birth and my death, is my existence outside myself. Which does not mean my existence reinvested in or by community, as if community were another subject that would sublate me, in a dialectical or communal mode. *Community does not sublate the finitude it exposes. Community itself, in sum, is nothing but this exposition.* It is the community of finite beings, and as such it is itself a *finite* community. In other words, not a limited community as opposed to an infinite or absolute community, but a community *of* finitude, because finitude "is" communitarian, and because finitude alone is communitarian. (Nancy 1991, 27)

In his inquiry into community and politics, Nancy carves out a guiding principle: "community does not consist in the transcendence (nor in the transcendental) of a being supposedly immanent to community. It consists on the contrary in the immanence of a 'transcendence'—that of finite existence as such, which is to say, of its 'exposition'" (Nancy 1991, xxxix). Were we to invert this principle, that is to say, that community consists in transcendence, we would get totalitarianism. Think of the role of the Führer or the Aryan race in Nazi Germany: these were supposed to be the essence of the Fatherland, by which all else was subsumed, assimilated, or expelled. Were we to ignore the guiding principle we would get management and power (ibid.). In his analysis, Nancy points us toward this question: "how can the community without essence (the community that is neither 'people' nor 'nation', neither 'destiny' nor 'generic humanity', etc.) be presented as such? That is, *what might a politics be that does not stem from the will to realize an essence?*" (xxxix–xl; emphasis added)

We cannot address community without addressing politics or,

rather, as Nancy would have it, the political. Whereas politics is a *practice*, the political is a *space*:

> The political is the place where community as such is brought into play. It is not, in any case, just the locus of power relations, to the extent that these relations set and upset the necessarily unstable and taut equilibrium of collectivity . . . there would be no power relations, nor would there be such a specific unleashing of power (there would merely be a mechanics of force), if the political were not the place of community—in other words, the place of a specific existence, the existence of being-in-common, which gives rise to the existence of being-self. (Nancy 1991, xxxvii)

Nancy distinguishes "being-in-common" from the usual way in which community is construed: as common being. This usual way of thinking of subjectivity and community "presupposes that we are brought into the world, each and everyone of us, according to a dimension of 'in-common' that is in no way 'added onto' the dimension of 'being-self', but that is rather co-originary and coextensive with it" (xxxvii).

To be a self, for Nancy, is to be exposed to the in-common. Not to some substance that underlies community, for there is no such thing; but to an exteriority. What is "proper to existence" is that one's own face is always "exposed to others, always turned toward an other and faced by him or her, never facing myself" (xxxvii–viii). The West has always known this, though of late we seem to have forgotten it: that our subjectivity is an effect of relations within a city. Not something "added on" but something indebted to our situatedness within a city. "Aristotle says that we live in cities," Nancy writes; "this is the *political* way of life—not for reasons of need, but for a higher reason, itself without reason, namely to 'live well' (*eu zein*): here 'well' means neither a comfort, nor a having; it is the ownmost difference of man, which means also, for Aristotle (but for Plato as well), the sharing of a *logos*" as both language and reason (xxxviii).

Here community is not a melting pot that homogenizes all difference but a mode of *clinamen*—leaning toward the other. "One cannot make a world with simple atoms," Nancy writes. "There has to be a *clinamen*. There has to be an inclination or an inclining from one toward the other, of one by the other, or from one to the other"

(3). Instead of being a Hegelian absolute, the community becomes a space of relations, allowing people to be relational selves. My face always faces another, my interiority is always posed to the exterior, to another face. Apart from others, subjectivity is inconceivable. Accordingly, the borders of selves and of communities are always in flux, never fixed, always open.

Dewey, in his writing on associated activity, provides an account that fills in what a *clinamen* might do:

> Human beings combine in behavior as directly and unconsciously as do atoms, stellar masses and cells; as directly and unknowingly as they divide and repel. They do so in virtue of their own structure, as man and woman unite, as the baby seeks the breast and the breast is there to supply its need. They do so from external circumstances, pressure from without, as atoms combine or separate in presence of an electric charge, or as sheep huddle together from the cold. Associated activity needs no explanation; things are made that way. (*Dewey 1980*, 151)

Nancy's discussion of community sounds esoteric, but it has much to add to our understanding of politics. Nancy would take issue with much that underlies most political philosophies. His first target would be the traditional understanding of sovereignty, whether of the individual or the community or both, that manifests itself in three competing strains of political philosophy: liberalism, communitarianism, and deliberative democracy. Liberalism sees the individual as sovereign, as the ultimate atom whose freedom must always be maintained. This is a negative freedom, freedom from the compulsions of a collectivity. In the name of the individual, liberalism arms itself against community, communism, and communitarianism, all terms (usually but not for Nancy) for being with, being one, a one to which the individual would have to sacrifice himself. But in its armament against community, liberalism sets up its own acknowledgment of community. In hailing the individual, liberalism admits, as Nancy writes, that "the individual is merely the residue of the experience of the dissolution of community. By its nature—as its name indicates, it is the atom, the indivisible—the individual reveals that it is the abstract result of a decomposition" (Nancy 1991, 3).

But we are equally mistaken if we turn away from individualism and toward a communism or communitarianism without reconsidering our enchantment with the absolute. Just as liberalism takes the individual to be a world unto itself, communitarianism tends to see the community as a world and an essence unto itself. "The ab-solute can appear in the form of the Idea, History, the Individual, the State, Science, the Work of Art, and so on. Its logic will always be the same inasmuch as it is without relation" (Nancy 1991, 4).

In reaction to the empty, procedural state, communitarians claim that there have to be some conceptions of the good around which citizens can rally. This is the glue that binds together the mosaic of individuals into a unity. Rather than just abiding by a set of common procedures, citizens will share the same conceptions of the good life. The identity of the individual partakes in the identity of the state: another unity. In this sense, this kind of communitarianism violates Nancy's principle against essentializing community. It closes its eyes to our finitude, in favor of a transcendental unity.

Communitarianism hopes to bring community together around a shared set of values, but where would these values come from? Who decides what they should be? Offering a version of deliberative democracy, Habermas argues that individuals can reason together through discourse, universalizing their claims, reaching some accord on what the good ought to be. The outcome will be a set of goods that ought to hold in any rational community.

Nancy criticizes attempts like Habermas's as misguided. He writes, "how do we communicate? But this question can be asked seriously only if we dismiss all 'theories of communication', which begin by positing the necessity or the desire for a consensus, a continuity and a transfer of messages" (Nancy 1991, xi). Nancy argues that the yearning for unity is the longing for immanence always shadowed by death. In order to find community, we need to look instead for what is different—namely, I would say, the voice of the others we encounter in public deliberations.

With Kristeva's theory of the subject as an open system and Nancy's conception of community as *clinamen*, we can supplement and open up deliberative democracy. I want to offer a way of practicing deliberative democracy that sees individuals as always in relation with each other (as well as "internally"). Instead of universalizing their claims from the standpoint of the sovereign subject, subjects see themselves as indebted to others and as necessarily open to difference.

"It is not a question of establishing rules for communication,"

Nancy writes, "it is a question of understanding before all else that in 'communication' what takes place is an *exposition*: finite existence exposed to finite existence, co-appearing before it and with it" (Nancy 1991, xi). Nancy's concern is with writing, following Derrida's inversion of the priority of speech over writing. But we may invert this inversion once again to heed the importance of speech, especially deliberative speech. For the most part, theoreticians of deliberative democracy seem to pay scant attention to the *experience* or *inclination* of those involved in deliberation. The word *deliberation* comes from the Latin word for pound, as on a scale. It means to weigh carefully all the possible understandings and courses of action. Deliberation is not concerned solely with "the force of the better argument" or even with regulative ideals of equity and noncoercion (though of course these are important). Unlike debating, which calls for a clinging to one's own position against those of all interlocutors, deliberation means being willing to release one's own view and adopt another.

The very postures we adopt are in keeping with the way we are talking: In debating, the interlocutors appear to dig in their heels and lean backward, as if to hold their own preconceptions safe from any other views and as if to say, "I am not about to change my mind." Alternatively, in deliberating, interlocutors appear to lean forward and to open themselves up to other views. Their posture seems to say, "I care deeply about all this, yet I am willing to change my mind because a great deal is at stake." Deliberators literally seem to be inclining to the other. Deliberation is an openness to what is other. In deliberation, even the term "one's own" loses meaning in the sense that being-open-to-otherness becomes one's attitude. The discourse involved in deliberation is a discourse of leaning to others; it is *clinamen*. In deliberating, participants are aware of their own finitude, that their understandings are partial, and so seek the views of others. Deliberation as such is a natural outgrowth of the community of finitude that Nancy describes.

Such a deliberative practice can avoid the totalizing tendency of communitarianism while, unlike liberalism, providing some positive content of what the good might be. But this content is always provisional, always subject to change. It is produced through conversations, open to voices from the margins. In fact, the margins are vital to the life of this being-in-common for if the margins are excluded then the core becomes fixed, exclusive, rigid, and petrified.

When subjects are relational, when agency is complementary, and when discourse is deliberative, we can create new possibilities, meanings, and purpose. In such a setting politics can take place; in being-in-common people can decide anew who they are and what their purpose should be.

Bibliography

Adams, Hazard, and Leroy Searle, eds. 1986. *Critical Theory since 1965*. Tallahassee: Florida State University Press.

Adorno, Theodor W. 1973. *Negative Dialectics*. London: Routledge.

Agacinski, Sylviane. 1991. "Another Experience of the Question, or Experiencing the Question Other-Wise." In Eduardo Cadava, Peter Connor, and Jean-Luc Nancy, eds. Who *Comes after the Subject?* New York: Routledge.

Arendt, Hannah. 1958. *The Human Condition*. Chicago: University of Chicago Press.

Aristotle. 1941. *The Basic Works of Aristotle*. Edited by Richard McKeon. New York: Random House.

———. 1962. *Nicomachean Ethics*. Translated by Martin Ostwald. Englewood Cliffs, N.J.: Prentice Hall.

———. 1998. *Politics*. Translated by C. D. C. Reeve. Indianapolis: Hackett.

Balibar, Etienne. 1991. "Citizen Subject." In Eduardo Cadava, Peter Connor, and Jean-Luc Nancy, eds. Who *Comes after the Subject?* New York: Routledge.

———. 1994. "Subjection and Subjectivation." In Joan Copjec, ed. *Supposing the Subject*. London: Verso.

Barthes, Roland. 1977. "The Death of the Author." In Barthes, *Image-Music-Text*. New York: Hill and Wang.

Benhabib, Seyla. 1984. "Epistemologies of Postmodernism: A Rejoinder to Jean-François Lyotard." *New German Critique* 33 (Fall): 103–27.

———. 1986. *Critique, Norm, and Utopia*. New York: Columbia University Press.

———. 1992. *Situating the Self: Gender, Community, and Postmodernism in Contemporary Ethics*. New York: Routledge.

————, ed. 1996. *Democracy and Difference: Contesting the Boundaries of the Political.* Princeton: Princeton University Press.

Bernasconi, Robert, and Simon Critchley, eds. 1991. *Re-Reading Levinas.* Bloomington: Indiana University Press.

Bernstein, Richard J., ed. 1985. *Habermas and Modernity.* Cambridge: MIT Press.

Best, Steven, and Douglas Kellner. 1991. *Postmodern Theory: Critical Interrogations.* New York: Guilford Press.

Blanchot, Maurice. 1988. *The Unavowable Community.* Translated by Pierre Joris. Barrytown, N.Y.: Station Hill Press.

Blanck, Rubin, and Gertrude Blanck. 1986. *Beyond Ego Psychology: Developmental Object Relations Theory.* New York: Columbia University Press.

Bleicher, Joseph. 1980. *Contemporary Hermeneutics: Hermeneutics as Method, Philosophy as Critique.* London: Routledge & Kegan Paul.

Bohman, James. 1996. *Public Deliberation: Pluralism, Complexity, and Democracy.* Cambridge: MIT Press.

Bohman, James, and William Rehg, eds. 1997. *Deliberative Democracy: Essays on Reason and Politics.* Cambridge: MIT Press.

Bourdieu, Pierre. 1977. *Outline of a Theory of Practice.* Translated by Richard Nice. Cambridge: Cambridge University Press.

————. 1991. *Language & Symbolic Power.* Translated by Richard Nice. Cambridge: Harvard University Press.

Bourdieu, Pierre, and J. C. Passeron. 1983. "Sociology and Philosophy in France since 1945: Death and Resurrection of a Philosophy without a Subject." *Social Research* 34: 166–212.

Brennan, Teresa. 1992. *The Interpretation of the Flesh: Freud and Femininity.* London: Routledge.

————, ed. 1989. *Between Feminism and Psychoanalysis.* London: Routledge.

Burke, Kenneth. 1969. *A Grammar of Motives.* Berkeley : University of California Press.

Butler, Judith. 1990. *Gender Trouble: Feminism and the Subversion of Identity.* New York: Routledge.

————. 1993. *Bodies That Matter.* New York: Routledge.

Butler, Judith, and Joan W. Scott, eds. 1992. *Feminists Theorize the Political.* New York: Routledge.

Cadava, Eduardo, Peter Connor, and Jean-Luc Nancy, eds. 1991. *Who Comes after the Subject?* New York: Routledge.

Calhoun, Craig, ed. 1992. *Habermas and the Public Sphere.* Cambridge: MIT Press.

Caputo, John D. 1987. *Radical Hermeneutics: Repetition, Deconstruction, and the Hermeneutic Project.* Bloomington: Indiana University Press.

Cohen, J. L., and A. Arato. 1992. *Civil Society and Political Theory.* Cambridge: MIT Press.

Conway, Daniel W. 1997. *Nietzsche & the Political.* London: Routledge.

Copjec, Joan. 1994a. *Read My Desire: Lacan against the Historicists*. Cambridge: MIT Press.

———, ed. 1994b. *Supposing the Subject*. London : Verso.

Cornell, Drucilla. 1992. *The Philosophy of the Limit*. New York: Routledge.

———. 1995. *The Imaginary Domain: Abortion, Pornography, & Sexual Harassment*. New York: Routledge.

Critchley, Simon. 1992. *The Ethics of Deconstruction: Derrida and Levinas*. Oxford: Blackwell.

Critchley, Simon, and Peter Dews, eds. 1996. *Deconstructive Subjectivities*. Albany: State University of New York Press.

Daly, Markate, ed. 1994. *Communitarianism: A New Public Ethics*. Belmont, Calif.: Wadsworth.

Derrida, Jacques. 1978. *Writing and Difference*. Translated by Alan Bass. Chicago: University of Chicago Press.

———. 1982. *Margins of Philosophy*. Translated by Alan Bass. Chicago: University of Chicago Press.

———. 1985. *The Ear of the Other*. Edited by Christie McDonald. Lincoln: University of Nebraska Press.

———. 1988. *Limited Inc*. Translated by Samuel Weber. Evanston: Northwestern University Press.

———. 1992. *The Other Heading: Reflections on Today's Europe*. Translated by Pascale-Anne Brault and Michael B. Naas. Bloomington: Indiana University Press.

———. 1996. "Adieu." Translated by Pascale-Anne Brault and Michael B. Naas. *Critical Inquiry* 1 (Autumn): 1–10.

Descartes, René. 1967a. *The Philosophical Works of Descartes. Volume I*. Translated by Elizabeth S. Haldane and G. R. T. Ross. Cambridge: Cambridge University Press.

———. 1967b. *The Philosophical Works of Descartes. Volume II*. Translated by Elizabeth S. Haldane and G. R. T. Ross. Cambridge: Cambridge University Press.

———. 1993. *Meditations on First Philosophy*. Edited by Stanley Tweyman. London: Routledge.

Dewey, John. 1980. *The Public and Its Problems*. Athens, Ohio: Swallow Press.

Dews, Peter. 1986. "Adorno, Post-Structuralism, and the Critique of Identity." *New Left Review*, no. 157: 28–44.

———. 1987. *Logics of Disintegration*. London: Verso.

Doane, Janice, and Devon Hodges. 1992. *From Klein to Kristeva: Psychoanalytic Feminism and the Search for the "Good Enough" Mother*. Ann Arbor: University of Michigan Press.

Dreyfus, Hubert L., and Paul Rabinow. 1982. *Michel Foucault: Beyond Structuralism and Hermeneutics*. Chicago: University of Chicago Press.

Eco, Umberto. 1989. *The Open Work*. Translated by Anna Cancogni. Cambridge: Harvard University Press.

———. 1990. *The Limits of Interpretation*. Bloomington: Indiana University Press.

Farrell, Frank B. 1996. *Subjectivity, Realism, and Postmodernism: The Recovery of the World in Recent Philosophy*. Cambridge: Cambridge University Press.

Feyerabend, Paul. 1975. *Against Method: Outline of an Anarchistic Theory of Knowledge*. London: Verso.

Fine, Reuben. 1990. *The History of Psychoanalysis*. New expanded ed. New York: Continuum.

Fishkin, James S. 1995. *The Voice of the People: Public Opinion and Democracy*. New Haven: Yale University Press.

Fletcher, John, and Andrew Benjamin, eds. 1990. *Abjection, Melancholia, and Love: The Work of Julia Kristeva*. London: Routledge.

Foucault, Michel. 1972. *The Archaeology of Knowledge and the Discourse on Language*. Translated by A. M. Sheridan. New York: Pantheon Books.

———. 1973. *The Order of Things*. New York: Random House.

———. 1979. *Discipline and Punish: The Birth of the Prison*. Translated by Alan Sheridan. New York: Vintage Books.

———. 1982. "The Subject and Power." In Hubert L. Dreyfus and Paul Rabinow. *Michel Foucault: Beyond Structuralism and Hermeneutics*. Chicago: University of Chicago Press.

———. 1986. "What Is an Author?" In Hazard Adams and Leroy Searle, eds. *Critical Theory since 1965*. Tallahassee: Florida State University Press.

Fraser, Nancy. 1992a. "Rethinking the Public Sphere: A Contribution to the Critique of Actually Existing Democracy." In Craig Calhoun, ed. *Habermas and the Public Sphere*. Cambridge: MIT Press.

———. 1992b. "The Uses and Abuses of French Discourse Theories for Feminist Politics." In Fraser and Bartky.

Fraser, Nancy, and Sandra Lee Bartky, eds. 1992. *Revaluing French Feminism: Critical Essays on Difference, Agency, and Culture*. Bloomington: Indiana University Press.

Freud, Sigmund. 1914a. "On Narcissism. An Introduction." *The Standard Edition of the Complete Psychological Works of Sigmund Freud* (SE), vol. 14. London: Hogarth Press.

———. 1914b. "The Unconscious." *SE* 14.

Fromm, Erich. 1968. *The Revolution of Hope: Toward a Humanized Technology*. New York: Harper & Row.

Gadamer, Hans-Georg. 1981. "Hermeneutics as a Theoretical and Practical Task." In Gadamer, *Reason in the Age of Science*. Cambridge: MIT Press.

———. 1990. *Truth and Method*. 2d rev. ed. New York: Crossroad.

Gallop, Jane. 1982. *The Daughter's Seduction: Feminism and Psychoanalysis*. Ithaca: Cornell University Press.

Gilligan, Carol. 1982. *In a Different Voice*. Cambridge: Harvard University Press.

Gramsci, Antonio. 1971. *Selections from the Prison Notebooks*. Edited and translated by Quintin Hoare and Geoffrey Nowell Smith. New York: International Publishers.

Grosz, Elizabeth. 1989. *Sexual Subversion: Three French Feminists*. Sydney: Allen & Unwin.

————. 1990. *Jacques Lacan: A Feminist Introduction*. London: Routledge.

Guberman, Ross Mitchell, ed. 1996. *Julia Kristeva Interviews*. New York: Columbia University Press.

Guess, Raymond. 1981. *The Idea of Critical Theory: Habermas and the Frankfurt School*. Cambridge: Cambridge University Press.

Habermas, Jürgen. 1970. *Toward a Rational Society: Student Protest, Science, and Politics*. Translated by Jeremy L. Shapiro. Boston: Beacon Press.

————. 1971. *Knowledge and Human Interests*. Translated by Jeremy L. Shapiro. Boston: Beacon Press.

————. 1975. *Legitimation Crisis*. Translated by Thomas McCarthy. Boston: Beacon Press.

————. 1979. *Communication and the Evolution of Society*. Translated by Thomas McCarthy. Boston: Beacon Press.

————. 1984. *The Theory of Communicative Action. Volume 1. Reason and the Rationalization of Society*. Translated by Thomas McCarthy. Boston: Beacon Press.

————. 1986. *Autonomy & Solidarity: Interviews with Jürgen Habermas*. Edited by Peter Dews. London: Verso.

————. 1987. *The Theory of Communicative Action. Volume 2. Lifeworld and System: A Critique of Functionlist Reason*. Translated by Thomas McCarthy. Boston: Beacon Press.

————. 1989. *Jürgen Habermas on Society and Politics: A Reader*. Edited by Steven Seidman. Boston: Beacon Press.

————. 1990a. *Moral Consciousness and Communicative Action*. Translated by Christian Lenhardt and Shierry Weber Nicholsen. Cambridge: MIT Press.

————. 1990b. *The Philosophical Discourse of Modernity*. Translated by Frederick G. Lawrence. Cambridge: MIT Press.

————. 1992a. *Postmetaphysical Thinking: Philosophical Essays*. Translated by William Mark Hohengarten. Cambridge: MIT Press.

————. 1992b. *The Structural Transformation of the Public Sphere: An Inquiry into a Category of Bourgeois Society*. Translated by Thomas Burger with the assistance of Frederick Lawrence. Cambridge: MIT Press.

————. 1993. *Justification and Application: Remarks on Discourse Ethics*. Translated by Ciaran P. Cronin. Cambridge: MIT Press.

————. 1994. *The Past as Future*. Translated and edited by Max Pensky. Lincoln: University of Nebraska Press.

————. 1996. *Between Facts and Norms: Contributions to a Discourse Theory of Law and Democracy*. Translated by William Rehg. Cambridge: MIT Press.

Handlin, Oscar. 1968. *America: A History*. Chicago: Holt, Rinehart, and Winston.

Hartmann, Heinz. 1964. *Essays on Ego Psychology: Selected Problems in Psychoanalytic Theory*. New York: International Universities Press.

Hegel, G. W. F. 1942. *The Philosophy of Right*. Translated by T. M. Knox. Oxford: Oxford University Press.

———. 1977. *Phenomenology of Spirit*. Translated by A. V. Miller. Oxford: Oxford University Press.

Heidegger, Martin. 1977. *The Question Concerning Technology and Other Essays*. New York: Harper & Row.

Heller, Thomas C., Morton Sosna, and David E. Wellbery, eds. *Reconstructing Individualism: Autonomy, Individuality, and the Self in Western Thought*. Stanford: Stanford University Press.

Holub, Robert C. 1991. *Jürgen Habermas: Critic in the Public Sphere*. London: Routledge.

hooks, bell. 1984. *Feminist Theory from Margin to Center*. Boston: South End Press.

Horster, Detlef. 1992. *Habermas: An Introduction*. Philadelphia: Pennbridge Books.

Ingram, David. 1987. *Habermas and the Dialectic of Reason*. New Haven: Yale University Press.

———. 1995. *Reason, History, and Politics: The Communitarian Grounds of Legitimation in the Modern Age*. Albany: State University of New York Press.

Irigaray, Luce. 1984. *An Ethics of Sexual Difference*. Translated by Carolyn Burke and Gillian C. Gill. Ithaca: Cornell University Press.

———. 1994. *Thinking the Difference: For a Peaceful Revolution*. Translated by Karin Montin. New York: Routledge.

Jameson, Fredric. 1971. *Marxism and Form*. Princeton: Princeton University Press.

———. 1981. *The Political Unconscious: Narrative as a Socially Symbolic Act*. Ithaca: Cornell University Press.

———. 1988. *The Ideologies of Theory: Essays 1971 / 1986. Volume 2. Syntax of History*. Minneapolis: University of Minnesota Press.

Johnson, Barbara, ed. 1993. *Freedom and Interpretation: The Oxford Amnesty Lectures 1992*. New York: Basic Books.

Joll, James. 1977. *Antonio Gramsci*. New York: Viking Penguin.

Kant, Immanuel. 1965. *Critique of Pure Reason*. Translated by Norman Kemp Smith. New York: St Martin's Press.

———. 1970. *Kant's Political Writings*. Cambridge: Cambridge University Press.

Keane, John, ed. 1988. *Civil Society and the State: New European Perspectives*. London: Verso.

Kellner, Douglas. 1988. "Postmodernism as Social Theory: Some Problems and Challenges." *Theory, Culture, and Society* 5, nos. 2–3: 239–70.

Kerby, Anthony Paul. 1991. *Narrative and the Self*. Bloomington: Indiana University Press.

Kohlberg, Lawrence. 1971. "From Is to Ought: How to Commit the Naturalistic Fallacy and Get Away with It in the Study of Moral Development." In T. Mischel, ed. *Cognitive Development and Epistemology*. New York: Academic Press.

———. 1981. *The Philosophy of Moral Development*. San Francisco: Harper and Row.

———, et al. 1987. *Child Psychology and Childhood Education: A Cognitive-Developmental View*. New York: Longman.

Kretzmann, John P., John L. McKnight, and Nicol Turner. 1996. *Voluntary Associations in Low-Income Neighborhoods: An Unexplored Community Resource*. Evanston, Ill: Institute for Policy Research, Northwestern University.

Kristeva, Julia. 1980. *Desire in Language*. Translated by Thomas Gora, Alice Jardine, and Leon S. Roudiez. New York: Columbia University Press.

———. 1982. *Powers of Horror: An Essay on Abjection*. Translated by Leon S. Roudiez. New York: Columbia University Press.

———. 1984a. *Revolution in Poetic Language*. Translated by Leon S. Roudiez. New York: Columbia University Press.

———. 1984b. "My Memory's Hyperbole." Translated by Athena Viscusi. *New York Literary Forum* 12–13: 261–76.

———. 1986. *The Kristeva Reader*. Edited by Toril Moi. New York: Columbia University Press.

———. 1987a. *In the Beginning Was Love: Psychoanalysis and Faith*. Translated by Arthur Goldhammer. New York: Columbia University Press.

———. 1987b. *Tales of Love*. Translated by Leon S. Roudiez. New York: Columbia University Press.

———. 1989a. *Language the Unknown: An Initiation into Linguistics*. Translated by Anne M. Menke. New York: Columbia University Press.

———. 1989b. *Black Sun*. Translated by Leon S. Roudiez. New York: Columbia University Press.

———. 1991. *Strangers to Ourselves*. Translated by Leon S. Roudiez. New York: Columbia University Press.

———. 1993a. *Nations without Nationalism*. Translated by Leon S. Roudiez. New York: Columbia University Press.

———. 1993b. "The Speaking Subject Is Not Innocent." In Barbara Johnson, ed. *Freedom and Interpretation: The Oxford Amnesty Lectures 1992*. New York: Basic Books, 1993, , 147–74.

———. 1995. *New Maladies of the Soul*. Translated by Ross Guberman. New York: Columbia University Press.

———. 1996. *Sens et non-sens de la révolte: Pouvoirs et limites de la psychanalyse I*. Paris: Librairie Arthème Fayard.

———. 1997. *The Portable Kristeva*. Edited by Kelly Oliver. New York: Columbia University Press.

Kurzweil, Edith. 1995. *Freudians and Feminists*. Boulder, Colo.: Westview Press.

Lacan, Jacques. 1977. *Écrits. A Selection*. London: Tavistock.

———. 1978. *The Four Fundamental Concepts of Psycho-Analysis*. Translated by Jacques-Alain Miller. New York: W. W. Norton.

———. 1982. *Feminine Sexuality: Jacques Lacan and the école freudienne*. Edited by Juliet Mitchell and Jacqueline Rose. Translated by Jacqueline Rose. New York: W. W. Norton.

Leland, Dorothy. 1992. "Lacanian Psychoanalysis and French Feminism: Toward an Adequate Political Psychology." In Nancy Fraser and Sandra Lee Bartky, eds. *Revaluing French Feminism: Critical Essays on Difference, Agency, and Culture*. Bloomington: Indiana University Press.

Levinas, Emmanuel. 1969. *Totality and Infinity: An Essay on Exteriority*. Translated by Alphonso Lingis. Pittsburgh: Duquesne University Press.

———. 1981. *Otherwise than Being or Beyond Essence*. The Hague: Martinus Nijhoff.

———. 1985. *Ethics and Infinity: Conversations with Philippe Nemo*. Translated by Richard A. Cohen. Pittsburgh: Duquesne University Press.

———. 1989. *The Levinas Reader*. Edited by Sean Hand. Oxford: Blackwell.

———. 1991. *La mort et le temps*. Paris: Editions de l'Herne.

———. 1994. *Outside the Subject*. Translated by Michael B. Smith. Stanford: Stanford University Press.

Lipnack, Jessica, and Jeffrey Stamps. 1982. *Networking: The First Report and Directory*. Garden City, N.Y.: Dolphin Books.

Lippmann, Walter. 1965. eds. *The Essential Lippmann*. Edited by Clinton Rossiter and James Lare. New York: Vintage Books.

Lyotard, Jean-François. 1984. *The Postmodern Condition: A Report on Knowledge*. Translated by Geoff Bennington and Brian Massumi. Minneapolis: University of Minnesota Press.

———. 1988. *The Differend: Phrases in Dispute*. Translated by Georges Van Den Abbeele. Minneapolis: University of Minnesota Press.

Lyotard, Jean-François, and Jean-Loup Thébaud. 1985. *Just Gaming*. Translated by Wlad Godzich. Minneapolis: University of Minnesota Press.

MacIntyre, Alasdair. 1984. *After Virtue*. 2d ed. Notre Dame, Ind: University of Notre Dame Press.

Mackey, Louis. 1983. "Slouching toward Bethlehem: Deconstructive Strategies in Theology." *Anglican Theological Review* 65: 255–72.

Marks, Elaine, and Isabelle de Courtivron, eds. 1980. *New French Feminisms: An Anthology*. New York: Schocken Books.

Mathews, David, and Noëlle McAfee. 1990a. *Community Politics*. Dayton, Ohio: Kettering Foundation.

———. 1990b. *Alternatives for Community Development and Educational Reform*. Dayton, Ohio: Kettering Foundation.

McAfee, Noëlle. 1989. "Deconstructo-Speak: Jacques Derrida Duels the

Worldly Philosophers." In the *Washington City Paper*, January 6, 1989. Washington, D.C.

——. 1993. "Abject Strangers: Toward an Ethics of Respect." In Kelly Oliver, ed. *Ethics, Politics, and Difference in Julia Kristeva's Writing*. New York: Routledge.

——. 1997. "Ways of Knowing: The Humanities and the Public Sphere" In James F. Veninga and Noëlle McAfee, eds. *Standing with the Public: The Humanities and Democratic Practice*. Dayton, Ohio: Kettering Foundation Press.

Meehan, Johanna, ed. 1995. *Feminists Read Habermas: Gendering the Subject of Discourse*. New York: Routledge.

Meier, Christian. 1990. *The Greek Discovery of Politics*. Cambridge: Harvard University Press.

Meltzer, Françoise, ed. 1987. *The Trial(s) of Psychoanalysis*. Chicago: University of Chicago Press.

Mitchell, W. J. T., ed. 1981. *On Narrative*. Chicago: University of Chicago Press.

——, ed. 1983. *The Politics of Interpretation*. Chicago: University of Chicago Press.

Moi, Toril. 1988. *Sexual/Textual Politics*. London: Routledge.

Mouffe, Chantal. 1988. "Radical Democracy: Modern or Postmodern?" In Andrew Ross, ed. *Universal Abandon? The Politics of Postmodernism*. Minneapolis: University of Minnesota Press.

——. 1992. "Feminism, Citizenship, and Radical Democratic Politics." In Judith Butler and Joan W. Scott, eds. *Feminists Theorize the Political*. New York: Routledge.

Moulier, Yann. 1989. Introduction. In Antonio Negri. *The Politics of Subversion*. Cambridge, U.K.: Polity Press.

Nancy, Jean-Luc. 1991. *The Inoperative Community*. Translated by Peter Connor, Lisa Garbus, Michael Holland, and Simona Sawhney. Minneapolis: University of Minnesota Press.

Nancy, Jean-Luc, and Philippe Lacoue-Labarthe. 1992. *The Title of the Letter: A Reading of Lacan*. Translated by François Raffoul and David Pettigrew. Albany: State University of New York Press.

Negri, Antonio. 1989. *The Politics of Subversion*. Translated by James Newell. Cambridge, U.K.: Polity Press.

Negt, Oskar, and Alexander Kluge. 1993. *Public Sphere and Experience: Toward an Analysis of the Bourgeois and Proletarian Public Sphere*. Translated by Peter Labanyi, Jamie Owen Daniel, and Assenka Oksiloff. Minneapolis: University of Minnesota Press.

Nietzsche, Friedrich. 1966a. *Gay Science*. Translated by Walter Kaufmann. New York: Random House.

——. 1966b. *Beyond Good & Evil: Prelude to a Philosophy of the Future*. Translated by Walter Kaufmann. New York: Random House / Vintage Books.

——. 1989. *On the Genealogy of Morals*. Translated by Walter Kaufmann and R. J. Hollingdale. New York: Random House / Vintage Books.

Nohria, Nitin, and Robert Eccles. 1992. "Face-to-Face: Making Network Organizations Work." In N. Nohria and R. Eccles, eds. *Networks and Organizations*. Boston: Harvard Business School Press.

Oliver, Kelly, ed. 1993a. *Ethics, Politics, and Difference in Julia Kristeva's Writing*. New York: Routledge.

Oliver, Kelly. 1993b. *Reading Kristeva: Unraveling the Double-bind*. Bloomington: Indiana University Press.

——. 1995. *Womanizing Nietzsche: Philosophy's Relation to the "Feminine."* New York: Routledge.

Onians, Richard Broxton. 1954. *The Origins of European Thought: About the Body, the Mind, the Soul, the World, Time, and Fate*. Cambridge: Cambridge University Press.

Passerin d'Entrèves, Maurizio, and Seyla Benhabib, eds. 1997. *Habermas and the Unfinished Project of Modernity: Critical Essays on The Philosophical Discourse of Modernity*. Cambridge: MIT Press.

Plato. 1992. *Republic*. Translated by G. M. A. Grube, revised by C. D. C. Reeve. Indianapolis: Hackett.

Perez-Diaz, Victor M. 1993. *The Return of Civil Society*. Cambridge: Harvard University Press.

Putnam, Robert. 1993. *Making Democracy Work*. Princeton: Princeton University Press.

Rehg, William. 1997. *Insight and Solidarity: The Discourse Ethics of Jürgen Habermas*. Berkeley: University of California Press.

Rescher, Nicholas. 1996. *Process Metaphysics: An Introduction to Process Philosophy*. Albany.: State University of New York Press.

Ricoeur, Paul. 1974. *The Conflict of Interpretations*. Evanston: Northwestern University Press.

——. 1992. *Oneself as Another*. Chicago: University of Chicago Press.

Robbins, Bruce, ed. 1993. *The Phantom Public Sphere*. Minneapolis: University of Minnesota Press.

Roderick, Rick. 1986. *Habermas and the Foundations of Critical Theory*. London: Macmillan.

Rorty, Richard. 1979. *Philosophy and the Mirror of Nature*. Princeton: Princeton University Press.

——. 1985. "Habermas and Lyotard on Postmodernity." In Richard J. Bernstein, ed. *Habermas and Modernity*. Cambridge: MIT Press.

——. 1991. *Objectivity, Relativism, and Truth: Philosophical Papers, Volume One*. Cambridge: Cambridge University Press.

Ross, Andrew, ed. 1988. *Universal Abandon? The Politics of Postmodernism*. Minneapolis: University of Minnesota Press.

Rousseau, Jean-Jacques. 1987. *The Basic Political Writings*. Translated and edited by Donald A. Cress. Indianapolis: Hackett.

Sacks, Oliver. 1995. *An Anthropologist on Mars: Seven Paradoxical Tales.* New York: Alfred Knopf.

Sandel, Michael. 1996. *Democracy's Discontent: America in Search of a Public Philosophy.* Cambridge: The Belknap Press of Harvard University Press.

Schrift, Alan. 1995. *Nietzsche's French Legacy: A Genealogy of Poststructuralism.* New York: Routledge.

Seibt, Johanna. 1997. "Existence in Time: From Substance to Process." In J. Faye (et al.) *Perspectives on Time. Boston Studies in Philosophy of Science.* Dordrecht: Kluwer.

Seligman, Adam. 1992. *The Idea of Civil Society.* New York: Free Press.

Smith, Adam. 1937. *The Wealth of Nations.* New York: Random House.

Solomon, Robert C. 1988. *Continental Philosophy since 1750: The Rise and Fall of the Self.* Oxford: Oxford University Press.

Spivak, Gayatri Chakravorty. 1987. *In Other Worlds: Essays in Cultural Politics.* New York: Methuen.

Stephens, Mitchell. 1994. "The Theologian of Talk." *Los Angeles Times,* Magazine, October 23, 1994, p. 26.

Taylor, Charles. 1985. "Alternative Futures: Legitimacy, Identity, and Alienation in Late Twentieth Century Canada," In Alan Cairns and Cynthia Williams, eds. *Constitutionalism, Citizenship, and Society in Canada.* Toronto: University of Toronto Press.

———. 1989. *Sources of the Self: The Making of the Modern Identity.* Cambridge: Harvard University Press.

Turkle, Sherry. 1981. *Psychoanalytic Politics: Freud's French Revolution.* Cambridge: MIT Press.

Veninga, James F., and Noëlle McAfee, eds. 1997. *Standing with the Public: The Humanities and Democratic Practice.* Dayton, Ohio: Kettering Foundation Press.

Walzer, Michael. 1991. "The Idea of Civil Society: A Path to Social Reconstruction." *Dissent* 38 (Spring): 293–304.

———. 1992."The Civil Society Argument." In Chantal Mouffe, ed. *Dimensions of Radical Democracy.* London: Verso.

Warnke, Georgia. 1994. *Justice and Interpretation.* Cambridge: MIT Press.

Warren, Mark E. 1995. "The Self in Discursive Democracy." In Stephen K. White, ed. *The Cambridge Companion to Habermas.* Cambridge: Cambridge University Press.

Weir, Allison. 1995. "Toward a Model of Self-Identity: Habermas and Kristeva." In Johanna Meehan, ed. *Feminists Read Habermas: Gendering the Subject of Discourse.* New York: Routledge, 1995, 263–82.

Westbrook, Robert. 1991. *John Dewey and American Democracy.* Ithaca: Cornell University Press.

White, Stephen K. 1988. *The Recent Work of Jürgen Habermas.* Cambridge: Cambridge University Press.

———, ed. 1995. *The Cambridge Companion to Habermas*. Cambridge: Cambridge University Press.

Whitebook, Joel. 1985. "Reason and Happiness: Some Psychoanalytic Themes in Critical Theory." In Richard J. Bernstein, ed. *Habermas and Modernity*. Cambridge: MIT Press.

Williams, Raymond. 1985. *Keywords: A Vocabulary of Culture and Society*. New York: Oxford University Press.

Young, Iris Marion. 1990. *Justice and the Politics of Difference*. Princeton: Princeton University Press.

———. 1997a. *Intersecting Voices: Dilemmas of Gender, Political Philosophy, and Policy*. Princeton: Princeton University Press.

———. 1997b. "Difference as a Resource for Democratic Communication." In James Bohman and William Rehg, eds. *Deliberative Democracy: Essays on Reason and Politics*. Cambridge: MIT Press.

Ziarek, Ewa. 1993. "Kristeva and Levinas: Mourning, Ethics, and the Feminine." In Kelly Oliver, ed. *Ethics, Politics, and Difference in Julia Kristeva's Writing*. New York: Routledge.

Index

abjection, 18; borderline patients and, 130; Kristeva and, 74–77; Kristeva on, 115

abortion, 100

absolute, the, 27, 188, 189

act (doing), 54; as power, 135

action, 177n. 7, 181; Arendt on, 127; lifeworld and, 85, 86; norms and, 90; reconstructive sciences and, 44

activity: associated, 188; Nietzsche on, 152; spontaneous, 55

administration, the administrative, 11; Habermas and, 89, 90; Habermas on, 88, 91

Adorno, Theodor, 23, 24

After Virtue (MacIntyre), 141

Agacinski, Sylviane, 53

agency, 15, 39, 139; "author function" and, 152; Foucault and, 137; subjectivity and, 134. *See also* complementary agency; political agency; social agent

alterity, 73, 76, 77, 161; versus autonomy, 9; identity and, 129; subjectivity and, 132

Amateur (film), 146

amnesiac, the, 146

analysand, the, 18, 163; Kristeva and, 70; Lacan and, 61, 65, 66; love and, 130

analyst, the, 18, 163; Kristeva and, 70; Lacan and, 61, 65; love and, 130

Ans, André Marcel d', 148

Anthropologist on Mars, An (Sacks), 127

Arendt, Hannah, 5, 98, 127, 136; on power, 136

argument, 2, 101, 157–58

Aristotle, 5n. 2, 51, 136; on the city-state, 3; knowledge and, 176–77; on politics, 178; practical wisdom and, 178–79; reason and, 5; on substance, 53

arts, the, 176, 182

associations, 174, 175; civic, 84; legitimacy of government and, 98

asymbolia, 75, 130

Athens, Greece, 2, 166

atomism, 14

author, authorship, 141; Arendt on, 127; Cashinahua Indians and, 149; Nietzsche and, 151–52

authority, 14, 87; reason and, 24; speaking and, 40–41

autoeroticism v. narcissism, 62

autonomy, the autonomous, 17, 27, 135, 150; antagonism and, 7; in the communication community, 33; communicative reason and, 11; community and, 36; Habermas and, 37, 38–43; versus heteronomy, 8; heteronomy and, 132; identity and, 77; internalizing of conflicts and, 31; Kant and, 38, 39;